JOB
ECCLESIASTES

Dianne Bergant, C.S.A.

A Michael Glazier Book
THE LITURGICAL PRESS
Collegeville, Minnesota

A Michael Glazier Book
published by
THE LITURGICAL PRESS

The Bible text in this publication is from the Revised Standard Version of the Bible, copyrighted 1946, 1952, © 1971, 1973 by the Division of Christian Education of the National Council of the Churches of Christ in the U.S.A., and used by permission.

Cover design by Lillian Brulc.
Typography by Peg McComick.

Distributed outside U.S., Canada, and the Philippines by Gill & Macmillan, Ltd., Goldenbridge, Inchicore, Dublin 8 Ireland.

2	3	4	5	6	7	8	9

Library of Congress Cataloging-in-Publication Data
Bergant, Dianne.
    Job, Ecclesiastes / Dianne Bergant.
        p.   cm. — (Old Testament message ; v. 18)
    Reprint. Originally published: Wilmington, Del. : M. Glazier, 1982.
    "A Michael Glazier book."
    "The Bible text in this publication is from the Revised Standard version"—T.p. verso.
    Includes bibliographical references.
    ISBN 0-8146-5252-2
    1. Bible. O.T. Job—Commentaries. 2. Bible. O.T. Ecclesiastes—Commentaries. I. Bible. O.T. Job. English. Revised Standard. 1990. II.Bible. O.T. Ecclesiastes. English. Revised Standard. 1990. III. Title. IV. Series.
BS1415.3.B47   1990
223'.1077—dc20
                                                90-42838
                                                  CIP

CONTENTS

The Book Of Ecclesiastes

Editors' Preface

Old Testament Message brings into our life and religion today the ancient word of God to Israel. This word, according to the book of the prophet Isaiah, had soaked the earth like "rain and snow coming gently down from heaven" and had returned to God fruitfully in all forms of human life (Isa 55:10). The authors of this series remain true to this ancient Israelite heritage and draw us into the home, the temple and the marketplace of God's chosen people. Although they rely upon the tools of modern scholarship to uncover the distant places and culture of the biblical world, yet they also refocus these insights in a language clear and understandable for any interested reader today. They enable us, even if this be our first acquaintance with the Old Testament, to become sister and brother, or at least good neighbor, to our religious ancestors. In this way we begin to hear God's word ever more forcefully in our own times and across our world, within our prayer and worship, in our secular needs and perplexing problems.

Because life is complex and our world includes, at times in a single large city, vastly different styles of living, we have much to learn from the Israelite Scriptures. The Old Testament spans forty-six biblical books and almost nineteen hundred years of life. It extends through desert, agricultural and urban ways of human existence. The literary style embraces a world of literature and human emotions. Its history began with Moses and the birth-pangs of a new people, it came of age politically and economically under David and Solomon, it reeled under the fiery threats of prophets like Amos and Jeremiah. The people despaired and yet were re-created with new hope during the Babylonian exile. Later reconstruction in the homeland and then the trauma of apocalyptic movements prepared for the revelation of "the mystery hidden for ages in God who created all things" (Eph 3:9).

While the Old Testament telescopes twelve to nineteen hundred years of human existence within the small country of Israel, any single moment of time today witnesses to the reenactment of this entire history across the wide expanse of planet earth. Each verse of the Old Testament is being relived somewhere in our world today. We need, therefore, the *entire* Old Testament and all twenty-three volumes of this new set, in order to be totally a "Bible person" within today's widely diverse society.

The subtitle of this series—"A Biblical-Theological Commentary"—clarifies what these twenty-three volumes intend to do.

Their *purpose* is theological: to feel the pulse of God's word for its *religious* impact and direction.

Their *method* is biblical: to establish the scriptural word firmly within the life and culture of ancient Israel.

Their *style* is commentary: not to explain verse by verse but to follow a presentation of the message that is easily understandable to any serious reader, even if this person is untrained in ancient history and biblical languages.

Old Testament Message—like its predecessor, *New Testament Message*—is aimed at the entire English-speaking world and so is a collaborative effort of an international team. The twenty-one contributors are women and men drawn from North America, Ireland, Britain and Australia. They are scholars who have published in scientific journals, but they have been chosen equally as well for their proven ability to communicate on a popular level. This twenty-three book set comes from Roman Catholic writers, yet, like the Bible itself, it reaches beyond interpretations restricted to an individual church and so enables men and women rooted in biblical faith to unite and so to appreciate their own traditions more fully and more adequately.

Most of all, through the word of God, we seek the blessedness and joy of those

who walk in the law of the Lord!...

who seek God with their whole heart (Ps. 119:1-2).

Carroll Stuhlmueller, C.P.   Martin McNamara, M.S.C.

THE BOOK OF JOB

INTRODUCTION

"Order is heaven's first rule." Who has not heard this proverb? Who has not been urged to utilize it as a norm of conduct? This short but concise maxim might well serve as a condensation of the content, form, and theology of the wisdom of Ancient Israel. First, what has come to be known as the wisdom movement was, in reality, a humanistic outlook on life. It encouraged a systematic reflection on daily living in order to discover the underlying principles of causality. Order is the basic concern of this world view. As regards form, the above introductory statement of wisdom is expressed in a proverb, the primary literary form of this literature. Finally, even though the leaders within the movement did not mandate the following of rules, their teaching embodied directions for mastering life by conforming to its governing principles. This teaching is the essence of wisdom theology.

WISDOM IN GENERAL

Looking more closely at the phenomenon of wisdom in the Ancient Near Eastern world ones sees that its scope is both extensive and profound. It is very generous in bestowing the designation 'wise' on a vast variety of occupations and abilities. The acquisition of such practical skills as sailing and writing is afforded the same applause as the refinement of the various crafts of the artisans or the expertise of the diplomats. An ability of every kind is the fruit of much discipline and faithfulness to some governing principles and enables the possessor to achieve a kind of harmony with life. In addition to this broad inclusion of skills, wisdom's range encompasses the most basic and soul-searching questions that confront every woman and man. "What is the origin of the universe and what holds it together?" "What is the meaning of suffering?" "What role does God play in life as humans experience it?"

Certain matters that are addressed in the proverbial literature themselves throw some light on the likely provenance of the sayings. The bulk of the instruction seems directed toward the achievement of general successful living. Such instruction probably took place in the most fundamental social group — the family. There the collected wisdom of the society was handed down to the next generation in the hope that it would be recognized and valued for what is was — the tested truths of experience, and that it would equip the youth with the skills necessary for coping with reality and succeeding in life. The home was the first school; the parents, the first sages. Directions in the management of the affairs of state as well as diplomatic courtesies suggest a political setting as origin of other teachings. Explicit mention of royal protocol indicates that the court was yet a third source of instruction and transmission of a heritage of experience. This does not exhaust the probable sites of training in wisdom but suggests its broad scope of influence and the variety of its applicability.

The primary interest of the wisdom writings is in the development of the appropriate attitudes toward life. The pupils were trained in the virtues of diligence, discipline, prudence, moderation, i.e., all of the qualities deemed indispensable for achieving success. The ancients believed that there was order and regularity in the universe. This order flowed from laws inherent in the world. Harmony in life could be realized only when one discerned this order and was reconciled with it. Wisdom is the ability to perceive this reality and live accordingly. All training had such wisdom as its goal. Ethical norms did not really enter the picture. Repeated experience, not law, taught which avenue of behaviour would result in the desired end. Both nature and society were stable and the individual had but to respond appropriately. Even though it was held that a design or pattern did exist, each experience called for a unique response. There was no pattern for the proper behavior itself. Therefore, attitudes toward life, oneself, others, the world had to be fostered to insure 'wise' conduct.

The sages were humanists. They were attentive to human welfare, values, and dignity. Whatever benefited humankind was a good to be pursued. What was in any way injurious was to be avoided and condemned. Success or happiness as defined by the respective society was the criterion for judging the value of any endeavor. It was also a recognizable outcome, leaving no doubt as to the degree of attainment of the goal. There is a great deal of pragmatism in this view of life. If the desired end could not be accomplished by one approach, this was to be discarded for a more effective one. This outlook should not be viewed as an example of the end justifying the means. The ancients believed that goodness was a force that determined life. It evidenced itself in whatever built up or sustained or enriched life. Therefore, the end gave evidence of the goodness of the means. Once again, repeated experience, not law, taught what was good. Being students of human experience taught the sages to be realists. They were slow to expect heroism. Daily living seldom called for such feats. It was in the constant, persistent, familiar ebb and flow of normal life that the patterns of existence surfaced. Wisdom was content to deal with this ever-present challenge.

By focusing primarily on human welfare, the wisdom movement underscored the significance of human values, human concerns and human pursuits. These had intrinsic worth and did not need some other external force to confirm them. Such attitudes proceeded from a conviction regarding the dignity of humankind. Although many of these impressions are not openly stated in the literature, they are implicit in what is said.

WISDOM IN ISRAEL

This overview has addressed the topic of wisdom in the Ancient Near East in general. Was there anything unique about Israel's perspective? Even a superficial look at the early religious traditions shows that the predominant conviction of the people was their belief that God was active in their history. Yahweh had chosen them, guided them, revealed the divine will to them, rewarded and punished them. Yahweh was the principal in the drama of life. The later historical material suggests that a process of secularization began to take place in the earlier period of the monarchy. This shift in outlook is reflected in those narratives which highlight human enterprise. The move toward secularization was not a denial of the presence and action of God. It was, rather, a different way of understanding it and articulating it. Israel encountered God *through* human experience, not *in addition to* it. Every aspect of human life, not merely the formal religious or cultic behavior, was under the control of Yahweh. If there was an order in the universe, it had been established by Yahweh. Conformity to this order was conformity to the will of God. The wise person was, in this respect, a religious person as well.

In later sapiential literature there is explicit mention of the law and its place of honor in the lives of those who sought wisdom and its rewards. Believing that the divine order is the governing principle of the world, Israel gloried in her privileged status of being the possessor of the explicit will of God. Her sages taught that obedience to the law presumed knowledge of Yahweh and subsequent commitment to the divine will. This is what was meant by 'fear of the Lord'. Only beginning with this knowledge and commitment could the Israelite hope to be skilled in the craft of a good living. "The fear of the Lord is the beginning of wisdom" (Prov 1:7; 9:10; 15:33; Job 28:28; Ps 111:10).

A second reason for some of the distinctive features of Israel's wisdom flows from the anthropological understandings of the people. A view of humanity that precluded success except as bestowed from an outside agent will insist on unwavering adherence to imposed prescriptions. A contrary view that denies any external influence and holds the individual as absolute will recommend a far different approach to coping with life. Another anthropological distinction lies in the attitude toward the innate goodness of the person or the lack thereof. If a human being is intrinsically evil, any hope of happiness in a world of order is futile. Only goodness promises success.

Finally, the concept of God to which Israel was committed outstripped that of any of her contemporaries as to the degree of governance of the world attributed to the deity. No other God had universal and exclusive dominion in the world. No other God had entered into so total a relationship with a people. No other God had invited such complete and intimate devotion in return. This theological point of view influenced every dimension of Israel's life and, therefore, her perspective on wisdom.

THE DILEMMA AND JOB

A rule of order or inherent governing principles constituted the undergirding of the ancient view of the universe. Compliance with these principles gave rise to a gently flowing life replete with the blessings of peace and prosperity. A disruption in the enjoyment of such an existence was attributed to failure in observing the authoritative conventions. On occasion, the ancient traditions do acknowledge the limitations of this world view. A few literary compositions challenge the universal applicability of this theory. Inexplicable manifestations of human suffering are thrust to the forefront in the hope of discovering some yet unknown meaning. The tightly constructed world view was incapable of offering an explanation. This dilemma threatened the entire structure of order and had to be resolved or neutralized if the system was to survive. It was within this challenging struggle that fundamental questions were probed. "What is the origin of the universe and what holds it together?" "What is the meaning of suffering?" "What role does God play in life as humans experience it?"

Israel was but one among several ancient peoples who wrestled with these problems and left evidence of this struggle in literary form. There is an Akkadian poem *Ludlul bel nemeqi,* translated "I will praise the lord of wisdom," that is often compared to the biblical book of Job. A nobleman is plagued with misfortune and cries out for an explanation. Marduk, his "lord of wisdom," intervenes and resolves the predicament. The poem is primarily a hymn in thanksgiving for deliverance from adversity.

The book of Job is the classic example of a challenge thrown in the face of the claim of an ordered world. Every aspect of this masterpiece flows from, or points to, the notion of inherent laws or appropriate modes of behavior. The argument of the book presupposes the theory of underlying order, for therein lies the ground for the challenge. Job has been faithful in compliance with the directions given him by his tradition and his station in life. In spite of this, he is not only deprived of his rightful dues, but suffering and ignominy are heaped onto him besides.

The book has a rather simple literary structure. It consists of a prose prologue and epilogue which probably originated as an ancient folktale of a wise man who was tested, found faithful, and subsequently rewarded for his faithfulness. The major part of the book, the poetic dialogue section, consists of three dialogue cycles of accusation by his companions and rejoinders by Job, additional instruction and exhortation by a fourth character, and ending with Yahweh's speeches. It is in this major section that the drama unfolds, the anthropological and theological positions are revealed, and are challenged or defended.

The literary style is consistent with the major themes of the work. The assertion of the book is both challenge and defense of a world view. The overall form of the work resembles a legal disputation with an initial accusation by Job, defense and counter accusation by his companions, defense and repeated accusation by Job and so on throughout the dialogues. In addition to this general approach, explicit legal forms are employed as part of the argument, as are the more traditional proverbial forms.

INTERPRETATION

Certain aspects of the book of Job have as many interpretations as there are interpreters. There is disagreement about the date of the book, the place of origin, the authenticity of various parts of the work. Even agreement on the principal theme is not universal. While these questions are not the primary concern of this commentary, it is important to state the position of the author on these matters.

Evidence from the book itself is given in order to substantiate a pre-exilic dating. Some of Job's lamentation is reminiscent of Jeremiah and the imminence of the exile may have been the historical reality which precipitated the struggle out which the book emerged. However, similarities with the theology and style of Deutero-Isaiah seem to outweigh this data, tipping the scale in favor of a post-exilic dating. More specifically, it would be prior to the third century B.C.E. (Before the Common Era) when Satan appears to be a proper name in Chronicles (1 Chron 21:1) rather than a title as it is found in Job.

While the struggle that is dramatized is with a universal and perennial problem and there is much in the book that has international flavor and appeal, Job is definitely an Israelite composition. Several characteristics suggest foreign influence and even borrowing, but the focus is Israelite and whatever may have originated elsewhere has been employed for the ends of Israelite theology.

Like most pieces of ancient literature, Job is a composite rather than the exclusive product of an individual. The present commentary is not primarily concerned with the different stages of the composition and development of the book, but rather with the final form. This cannot be adequately achieved, however, without addressing some of the major textual difficulties as well as the question of literary integrity.

The Hebrew of the Book of Job contains some of the most obscure vocabulary in the entire scriptures. This in itself has lead to a variety of translations and interpretations. In addition to this, the text has survived in such a state of corruption and disarray that scholars have often felt the necessity of rearranging passages in order to make better sense of it. This has often been done after painstaking comparison with early translations of the Greek, Latin and Syriac versions.

The compositional relationship between the Prologue/Epilogue and the Dialogue has been a perennial subject of debate among Joban scholars. Nor is there agreement regarding the authenticity of several units within the Dialogue itself, e.g., the Wisdom Poem (Chapter 28), the Elihu Speeches (chapters 32-37), the second Yahweh Speech (Chapter 40). While attention will be given to these questions when they appear throughout the commentary, the major concern there is with the final form of the book. This is what has come down to us and it is through this form that the message is conveyed. Therefore, the book will be treated as a final product and each section will be examined in its role of contributing to the total picture. From this standpoint, each section is authentic regardless of when it was incorporated into the whole.

Finally, the universal appeal of the book of Job stems from the nature of the questions asked and the perception of the answers given. As stated above, various interpretations are put forward as the principal message of the work: human integrity, innocent suffering, the incomprehensibility of God, trust in God. In reality, these interpretations are not mutually exclusive, but interrelated. They all express different emphasis and nuances of the all-encompassing mystery of the presence of God in the world.

All of the issues of Job cannot be treated within the scope of this book. The writer has decided to favor those themes, images and literary forms that cluster around the broad concept of order which seems to be the basic concern of the wisdom perspective.

CHAPTER ONE
PROLOGUE

Most people have heard of the patience of Job, but few realize that such a characterization is only found in the early chapters of the book. In fact, one might say that there are really two distinct portraits of the man. The first is limited to the prose prologue and epilogue, while a second and totally different picture dominates the major portion of the book. Although they are independent of each other, both sketches are necessary for an appreciation of the struggles of the character.

The prose prologue (1:1—2:13) and the epilogue (42:7-17) probably originated as a popular folktale told about a righteous man who had been sorely tested by the circumstances of life, remained faithful to his principles, and was rewarded by his god for his faithfulness. Such a narrative pattern appears in the literature of other Ancient Near Eastern cultures as well as in that of Israel. It is used here as the literary framework for the drama but it also provides a significant theological contribution to the work. This will become clear as the commentary unfolds. The prologue consists of a description of Job himself and a series of four scenes which alternate between heaven and earth.

JOB, THE MAN
Job 1:1-5

1 There was man in the land of Uz, whose name was Job; and that man was blameless and upright, one who feared God, and turned away from evil. ²There were born to him seven sons and three daughters. ³He had seven thousand sheep, three thousand camels, five hundred yoke of oxen, and five hundred she-asses, and very many servants; so that this man was the greatest of all the people of the east. ⁴His sons used to go and hold a feast in the house of each on his day; and they would send and invite their three sisters to eat and drink with them. ⁵And when the days of the feast had run their course, Job would send and sanctify them, and he would rise early in the morning and offer burnt offerings according to the number of them all; for Job said, "It may be that my sons have sinned, and cursed God in their hearts." Thus Job did continually.

Job is described at the outset as a perfect Hebrew man. The well chosen words, "blameless and upright, one who feared God and turned away from evil", are technical terms within the wisdom movement which characterize a well rounded, balanced, and righteous man. He is not only a man of integrity, in right relationship with God and with others, but he has the perfect number of children in the right proportion (v. 2), as well as an abundance of flocks and herds. The numbers 'three', 'seven', and 'ten', or multiples of them, had mystical significance in ancient cultures symbolizing completeness, entirety and soundness. Job's personal life, his relationships and his possessions are all in proper balance. He is a man who has been blessed with all of the good things of life.

As was stated earlier, the ancient wisdom teaching claimed that personal virtue was rewarded with happiness. Job is a man of perfect virtue. According to this theory, it is only right that he should be rewarded with perfect happiness. This is a picture of the wise man par excellence. He is further acclaimed "the greatest of all the people of the east" (v. 3b). This is the second of several references to Edom, a land renowned for its wisdom. Uz, the home of Job (v. 1) appears to have been located somewhere in the region of Edom or Aram. The friends who will come to sit with Job are also associated with Edom. In these three short verses the author has drawn a detailed profile of the ideal wise man of the east.

Verses 4-5 complete the characterization. Job is not only concerned with his own righteousness but with that of his children as well. He acts in the manner of the ancient patriarchs, blessing and interceding for others lest they be found unworthy to stand before God. This idealization ends with a statement asserting that such benevolent behavior is typical of Job. His righteousness is not sporadic but is consistent.

SCENE ONE — HEAVEN
Job 1:6-12

> 6Now there was a day when the sons of God came to present themselves before the LORD, and Satan also came among them. 7The LORD said to Satan, "Whence have you come?" Satan answered the LORD, "From going to and fro on the earth, and from walking up and down on it." 8And the LORD said to Satan, "Have you considered my servant Job, that there is none like him on the earth, a blameless and upright man, who fears God and turns away from evil?" 9Then Satan answered the LORD, "Does Job fear God for nought? 10Hast thou not put a hedge about him and his house and all that he has, on every side? Thou hast blessed the work of his hands, and his possessions have increased in the land. 11But put forth thy hand now, and touch all that he has, and he will curse thee to thy face." 12And the LORD said to Satan, "Behold, all that he has is in your power; only upon himself do not put forth your hand." So Satan went forth from the presence of the LORD.

The first scene takes place in heaven. The description reminds one of the council of the gods of Ancient Near Eastern mythology where the principal god is surrounded by the divine court. Monotheistic Israel did not tolerate other gods who might rival Yahweh and so his council was composed of the 'sons of God' who were angels or some other heavenly but not divine beings. Though not explicitly called a 'son of God', the satan is among them. He stands before Yahweh and so should not be considered an enemy of good. The word 'satan' appears with an article indicating that here the word is a title or description and not a proper name. It probably means adversary and, therefore, refers to the role that the satan will play in this drama. In what way is he an adversary? The answer to this question comes to light in the dialogue that takes place between him and the Lord.

When the Lord questions him about his whereabouts, the satan replies that he has been roaming around the earth, acting as a patrol. Nowhere is it even suggested that he is the actual cause of evil. He seems, rather, to be on the watch for it, prepared to make his report back to God. The Lord continues to query, "Have you considered my servant Job . . ." While there are many people throughout the Hebrew traditions who are called servants of God, very few times is this reference 'my servant' placed in the mouth of God himself. This is reserved for only the most prominent figures. Among these few are Abraham, Jacob, Moses, Caleb, David and Job. In fact, throughout the book, whenever the Lord refers to Job, the endearment 'my servent' precedes the name (cf. 2:3; 42:7, 8a, b, c). The Lord continues to speak of Job using the technical description of the wise man that first appeared in v. 1, "a blameless and upright man, who fears God and turns away from evil." In placing this characterization in the mouth of the Lord, the author gives it not only added strength but divine force as well. The author has taken great pains to show that Job's virtue is recognized on earth and in heaven.

In a very real way, the drama and the struggle of the book revolve around the satan's challenge found in verse 9. "Does

Job fear God for nought?" Recalling the theory of order and
the inherent consequences of actions, the satan is suggesting
that Job is righteous because of the rewards that he enjoys
and will continue to enjoy. It is easy to be loyal to God when
things are going right and one is happy with life. The wager
is stated in verse 11. Take away his prosperity, the good
things in his life, and he will not only give up his way of
integrity, but he will actually curse God. The satan is not
really an instigator of evil. He is neither tempting Job to sin
nor tempting the Lord to injustice. He is proposing a test of
the genuineness and the depth of Job's integrity and a
challenge of the limits of the ordered world view. The Lord
accepts the challenge. The satan is given power over Job's
goods but not over Job himself.

It is God who permits the righteous man to suffer. This is
clear to the reader even though it is not clear to Job. The
reader also knows that this is a test proposed by the satan.
But why does God allow it? Is the reason to show that God is
right about Job? Must God's confidence in Job's integrity be
justified? Or is the test directed toward Job himself? Must he
demonstrate, without knowing and without knowing why,
that his loyalty is disinterested? But why should he be asked
to do this since virtue and blessing are inherently associated?
Why should Job be asked to have one and not the other?
Isn't that expecting too much of him? Isn't such expectation
unjust? Or is the ordered world view being challenged?
Perhaps there really is no inherent relationship between
one's actions and the degree of the enjoyment of life. Perhaps both the Lord and the satan know this, but not the
human actors of the drama. Whatever the case may be, the
Lord allows something to occur that is contrary to the
accepted understanding of order, and this at the instigation
of the one who patrols the earth looking for disorder.

SCENE TWO — EARTH
Job 1:13-22

> [13]Now there was a day when his sons and daughters
> were eating and drinking wine in their eldest brother's

house; [14]and there came a messenger to Job, and said, "The oxen were plowing and the asses feeding beside them; [15]and the Sabeans fell upon them and took them, and slew the servants with the edge of the sword; and I alone have escaped to tell you." [16]While he was yet speaking, there came another, and said, "The fire of God fell from heaven and burned up the sheep and the servants, and consumed them; and I alone have escaped to tell you." [17]While he was yet speaking, there came another, and said, "The Chaldeans formed three companies, and made a raid upon the camels and took them, and slew the servants with the edge of the sword; and I alone have escaped to tell you." [18]While he was yet speaking, there came another, and said, "Your sons and daughters were eating and drinking wine in their eldest brother's house; [19]and behold, a great wind came across the wilderness, and struck the four corners of the house, and it fell upon the young people, and they are dead; and I alone have escaped to tell you."

[20]Then Job arose, and rent his robe, and shaved his head, and fell upon the ground, and worshiped. [21]And he said, "Naked I came from my mother's womb, and naked shall I return; the LORD gave, and the LORD has taken away; blessed be the name of the LORD."

[22]In all this Job did not sin or charge God with wrong.

The next seven verses are filled with rapidly moving action. All of Job's possessions are systematically snatched from him. The blessings that were sketched in verses 2-3, sons and daughters, sheep, camels, oxen and she-asses, are all lost. One messenger informs him of the loss of his oxen and asses and the murder of his servants. On his heels comes a second messenger with similar news, then a third and a fourth. Each carries word of death and destruction. This word is conveyed to the reader through a very precise literary pattern. The messenger reports, "and I alone have escaped to tell you." This is followed by the introductory verse, "While he was yet speaking, there came another, and said . . . " This technique underscores the swift action of the story as well as the idea of calamity heaped upon calamity. It is also another literary device that contributes to the underlying structured style of the prologue. Havoc has been unleashed upon Job, but the telling of it is very orderly.

Job's response is not what the satan had predicted. He mourns in the customary fashion. Instead of cursing, he blesses the Lord. His response to all of his misfortune is the response of a sage. Verse 21 consists of three different and completely independent sayings. In proverbial form he acknowledges that possessions belong to human life. He came into life with none and he will leave life with none. This is followed by a saying that is similar to one frequently recited at the time of death in northern Arabi. "His Lord has given him; his Lord has taken him." The third saying is a benediction that is also found in Psalm 113:2. Juxtaposed as they are, the sayings produce a progressive reflection on life. I (Job) am very vulnerable, especially at birth and at death; my birth and my death are in the hands of the Lord; blessed be the name of the Lord.

The chapter ends with a statement of Job's reaction to this adversity. He had not compromised his integrity by altering his virtuous life. He had demonstrated that his righteousness was authentic and not merely for the sake of reward. Nor had he accused God of injustice. All of this suggests that either he was able to alter his world view and admit that virtue was not automatically rewarded with prosperity, or that he did not question the apparent rupture in the presumed order.

SCENE THREE — HEAVEN
Job 2:1-7a

> **2**   Again there was a day when the sons of God came to present themselves before the LORD, and Satan also came among them to present himself before the LORD. ²And the LORD said to Satan, "Whence have you come?" Satan answered the LORD, "From going to and

fro on the earth, and from walking up and down on it. "
[3]And the LORD said to Satan, "Have you considered my
servant Job, that there is none like him on the earth, a
blameless and upright man, who fears God and turns
away from evil? He still holds fast his integrity, although
you moved me against him, to destroy him without
cause." [4]Then Satan answered the LORD, "Skin for skin!
All that a man has he will give for his life. [5]But put forth
thy hand now, and touch his bone and his flesh, and he
will curse thee to thy face." [6]And the LORD said to
Satan, "Behold, he is in your power; only spare his life."
[7]So Satan went forth from the presence of the LORD,

Once again the scene is the heavenly court of the Lord.
The staging and the initial activity are described in the same
manner as it had been earlier. The introductory dialogue
between the Lord and the satan is repeated, as is the characterization of Job by Yahweh. In fact, with a minimal
amount of variation, verses 1-3a are identical with verses 6-8
of the first chapter. This technique is in keeping with the
author's concern for precision, order and uniformity. The
drama moves forward with verse 3b. In the earlier section of
the first chapter, Job is not only described as a righteous
man but the reader has the opportunity of observing him as
one.

The satan challenges the depth of Job's commitment and
the Lord allows Job to be tested. The second time the
characterization is used by the Lord it has a deeper meaning.
Job is indeed virtuous with virtue that has been tried and his
triumphed. "He still holds fast his integrity." The Lord
admits in verse 3b that there is no inherent relationship
between Job's affliction and the manner of life that he is
accustomed to living. The implication of this admission is
that in normal situations there is such a connection. The
reader is left with several serious questions. Has the writer
portrayed Yahweh as an adherent of the theory of strict
retribution thereby authenticating it as the orthodox position? Has Yahweh allowed Job to fall victim to an unknown

testing because Yahweh himself has fallen into the snare of the satan? Is Yahweh so confident of the righteousness of Job that he has consented to the ordeal in order that the instigation of the satan come to light? What is the real motivation of the satan? Given the world view of order, why should Job be faulted if his integrity is for the sake of reward? The reader is faced once again with the enigmatic question of the meaning of the book. Only at its conclusion can some or all of these questions be satisfactorily addressed.

Although his first challenge has proven empty, the satan is undaunted. The proverb he quotes and then interprets is meant to suggest the kind of adversity that will really expose the hitherto unchallenged self-interest of Job. "Skin for skin" most probably refers to a form of barter. One is willing to pay any price for that which is valued as priceless. The most prized possession is one's own life. No cost is too great if life can be safeguarded. Even integrity will be sacrificed. Turning to the literal meaning of 'skin', the satan proposes that Job be smitten in the flesh. He will then be willing to relinguish anything and everything in order to protect his life. The satan assures the Lord that Job will curse him to his face. Once again the Lord yields with one stipulation. Job's life must be spared. This is to be a test of his integrity. Death would prove nothing and would certainly question the integrity of the Lord himself. The satan departs and returns to the earth.

SCENE FOUR — EARTH
Job 2:7b-10

and afflicted Job with loathsome sores from the sole of his foot to the crown of his head. [8]And he took a potsherd with which to scrape himself, and sat among the ashes.
[9]Then his wife said to him, "Do you still hold fast your integrity? Curse God, and die." [10]But he said to her, "You speak as one of the foolish women would speak. Shall we

receive good at the hand of God, and shall we not receive evil?" In all this Job did not sin with his lips.

The final scene of this narrative drama takes place on earth. The account of the sufferings of Job is brief but descriptive. His affliction is not localized but covers his entire body. It is loathsome and, because of it, he becomes an outcast of society.

The advice that Job receives from his wife reflects the traditional view of retribution. Clinging to his integrity has been a worthless venture. Who would blame him if he cried out against God? True, God would probably strike him dead, but at least then he would have relief from his misery. The one point his wife seems to overlook is the unexplained nature of Job's suffering. Why should he relinquish his claim of integrity? He *is* righteous. While this advice may well proceed from her concern for Job, he rejects it as totally inappropriate. He does not chastise his wife, but declares that she has allowed this situation to distort her perception. She is talking like a foolish woman. The verbs in verse 10b are plural, implying that she is included in what he has to say. Previously they both had enjoyed the good things of life. Now they both suffer from this tribulation. Their situation in life comes from God. This is a slightly different view from the one which holds that the good and evil in life are somehow unleashed by good or evil deeds. In the former view, God can dispense with reward or punishment freely. He is not bound to comply to human wishes or behavior. The author completes his account of this the second and more personal ordeal of Job by assuring the reader that even in the face of this adversity, Job holds fast to his virtue. He has, unbeknown to himself, passed the test and shown that his commitment to the Lord is authentic and beyond question. He is not merely motivated by the promise of reward. The satan has been confounded.

At this point, the reader could turn to the epilogue (42:10-17) and there find that Job has been vindicated, is healed, and has had his possessions restored and even doubled. The ordered world view is intact; the theory of retribution holds true; and both the wife and the satan are used by the author to enable the true mettle of Job to emerge. Here is an example of authentic righteousness. His is a commitment to the Lord and not merely to some underlying principle of order.

This may well have been the original form and meaning of the folktale. However, now this bit of prose is only one part of a much larger whole. As stated in the INTRODUCTION, it must be examined in light of its contribution to the entire book. As it stands, it sets the stage for the drama that takes place in the dialogues. The reader knows of the origin of Job's hardships. The prologue has supplied this information. The reader is also aware of Job's ignorance of the exchange that took place between the Lord and the satan. In addition to its original meaning, the prologue now serves a second end. It provides the backdrop that is necessary for an appreciation of the complexity of Job's struggle and his resistance to the counsel given to him by others.

APPENDIX
Job 2:11-13

> [11]Now when Job's three friends heard of all this evil that had come upon him, they came each from his own place, Eliphaz the Temanite, Bildad the Shuhite, and Zophar the Naamathite. They made an appointment together to come to condole with him and comfort him. [12]And when they saw him from afar, they did not recognize him; and they raised their voices and wept; and they rent their robes and sprinkled dust upon their heads toward heaven. [13]And they sat with him on the ground seven days and seven nights, and no one spoke a word to him, for they saw that his suffering was very great.

This short section adds nothing to the movement of the prologue. It is an appendix that joins the folktale with the major portion of the book. In it the friends are introduced.

The name Eliphaz appears in the genealogy of Esau (cf. Gen 36:4, 11) who was associated with Edom (cf. Gen 25:30) a land with a reputation for wisdom. Naamah, the home of Zophar, is in Ammon which is adjacent to Edom. The name Bildad is very similar to yet another descendant of Esau (cf. Gen 36:27). It would seem that the author has taken great pains to show that these men are natives of the land of the wise. They stand within a well established tradition of wisdom. They are not strangers but are called friends of Job, who earlier (1:3) had been called "the greatest of all the people of the east." Job could well have been in his society what each of these men were in theirs, the respected sage. They did not come to advise him but to support and comfort him. They performed the rites of mourning, rending their garments and sprinkling dust on their heads. The official period of sorrow was seven days. Those who came to console the chief mourner were to be silent until the grieving one spoke. The three men show themselves true friends and authentic mourners. So ends the prose prologue.

Having examined the form and the meaning of the prologue in itself, one must give some attention to the additional role that it plays in the overall meaning of the book. One could say that this section is a statement on order. Both in its literary characteristics and in the theology that it conveys it puts forward the traditional and accepted world view. The movement from a well established order to a situation of disruption is evident in the flow of the narrative itself, as well as in the change from a precisely structured form to an apparent labyrinth of circular arguments. In other words, the prologue and the epilogue are more than the prose husk of the more significant poetry. The very literary form serves to underscore the theological movement of the book. This will become clearer with the move from the poetry back to the prose epilogue later in the book.

CHAPTER TWO
FIRST CYCLE OF SPEECHES

As one moves from the prologue to the dialogues, which constitute the major section of the book, it becomes immediately obvious that the structure, the content and the characters have all assumed different perspectives. Unlike the measured and stereotypical quality of the prose, the poetry is a collage of forms and images which follows no pattern. The linear progression of the narrative folktale gives way to circular poetic argumentation. Gone are the patient and accepting Job and his silent compassionate friends. In their places are an angry broken man searching desperately for understanding and three self-righteous critics propounding advice that is empty and accusatory. What has happened? What is the author trying to do? Although the latter question cannot be answered until the entire book has been examined, the former question must be raised repeatedly throughout this commentary in order that its underlying meaning may not escape the careful reader.

The shift that has taken place can best be understood against the backdrop of the basic theme of order. The author employs every possible device to illustrate the collapse of this order. The catastrophic reversal of Job's fortune is an acomplished fact. Its repercussions unfold within the dialogues as Job turns into an unruly intractable resenter refusing to accept unquestioningly the present circumstances of his life. His consoling friends become unflinching supporters of the ordered worldview against which Job rails. They contend that the chaos that has overtaken him is an observable indication of some serious disorder in his life. He insists that it is his misfortune that is the real disorder rather than the result of moral misbehavior of which he is guilty and, therefore, deserving of such punishment. The major literary forms employed all presume this thematic backdrop. Job laments his situation. He disputes the justice of it as well as the justice of God who allows it. The friends defend the order and God's justice in this order. The nature imagery all presupposes intrinsic regularity. Everything about the dialogues speaks of the struggle between order and chaos.

This is the longest section of the book, consisting of about thirty-nine chapters. The arguments are repetitious and, with the exception of the Yahweh Speeches, offer very little variety of thought. Commentary on this material will tend to be monotonous, but this monotony is an essential part of the author's treatment of the problem. By adding layer upon layer of the same accusation and rebuttal, the author brings the reader into the very midst of the impasse. It does not take long to recognize the pointlessness of the controversy. The reader is soon ready for Job's abandonment of human counsel and support and his insistence on divine intervention. The style of presentation contributes to the statement about the inadequacy and, at times, burden of human wisdom.

RETURN TO CHAOS
Job 3:1-10

> **3** After this Job opened his mouth and cursed the day of his birth. ²And Job said:
> ³"Let the day perish wherein I was born,
>   and the night which said,
>   'A man - child is conceived.'

4Let that day be darkness!
  May God above not seek it,
  nor light shine upon it.
5Let gloom and deep darkness claim it.
  Let clouds dwell upon it;
  let the blackness of the day terrify it.
6That night—let thick darkness seize it!
  let it not rejoice among the days of the year,
  let it not come into the number of the months.
7Yea, let that night be barren;
  let no joyful cry be heard in it.
8Let those curse it who curse the day,
  who are skilled to rouse up Leviathan.
9Let the stars of its dawn be dark;
  let it hope for light, but have none,
  nor see the eyelids of the morning;
10because it did not shut the doors of my mother's womb,
  nor hide trouble from my eyes.

The prologue ends with all of the participants of the drama sitting in silence. The friends come to Job, grieve with him, and speak not a word. After seven days and seven nights, the official period of mourning, Job breaks the silence, lamenting that he had ever been born.

Light-darkness imagery is usually intended to contrast day and night. Day/light is preferred over night/darkness. Such is not the case here. Job curses the day of his birth. Both day and night are despised and he grieves that they had not been confined to deep gloom and darkness. The imagery that is used is strongly mythological suggesting that the contrast between light and darkness is really a battle between order and chaos. In the first chapter of Genesis, the earth is described as formless, void, dark and abysmal. Into all of this God calls light. Chaos has been conquered by order. Here Job cries for the disarrangement of this struc-tured cosmos. Actually, it has already been disarranged, for the fabric of his life has been unraveled for no apparent reason. To pretend that order remains anywhere is to deny the facts.

Job pleads that his birth day perish, that darkness and deep gloom come over it rather than light. He is asking for more than a mere reversal in nature, for that would mean that the night would then be light and this is not what he wants. Even night, one particular night, would be consumed by darkness and emptiness if he had his way. It would never again be a time of conception and fertility. Job wants both that particular day and that one night condemned to the absolute darkness of chaos. He calls upon those who, by means of incantation, are able to conjure up Leviathan, the mythical monster of chaos. The ancients believed that an eclipse was a return to the utter darkness of chaos when this monster swallowed up the day.

Why does Job cry out for such total disorder? Why should he blame the day of his birth or the night of his conception? The misery that he experiences seems to be a violation of the basic harmony of life. He is a righteous man and yet he is devoured by agony. He has reached that point in his suffering where he bemoans the fact that he was ever born and he curses that day. If the present day has fallen victim to the terrors of chaos, the first day of his life should know the same fate, for it is responsible for his coming forth from the womb.

Earlier the satan had predicted that Job would curse God. This did not happen. Instead his life and the time of its beginning is the subject of Job's imprecation. Jeremiah expressed the same sentiments in almost identical language (cf. Jer 20:14-18). In addition to this denunciation, the prophet also cursed the man who brought the news of his birth to his father. Suffering has brought both Jeremiah and Job to the point of wishing that their lives had never begun, but Job goes further. He realizes that if one can no longer trust the regularity in life, it makes little sense to trust the rhythms in nature or in the universe. Why trust anything? Is this Job's blasphemy? Does he curse God by denying God's providence and universal power? Is he accusing God of having lost control? Because he is dealing with cosmic matters, is he suggesting that the all-powerful God has been defeated by the monster of chaos? This would imply cataclysmic upheaval and, possible, ultimate utter destruction.

DEATH AT BIRTH
Job 3:11-19

> [11]"Why did I not die at birth,
>   come forth from the womb and expire?
> [12]Why did the knees receive me?
>   Or why the breasts, that I should suck?
> [13]For then I should have lain down and been quiet;
>   I should have slept; then I should have been at rest,
> [14]with kings and counselors of the earth
>   who rebuilt ruins for themselves,
> [15]or with princes who had gold,
>   who filled their houses with silver.
> [16]Or why was I not as a hidden untimely birth,
>   as infants that never see the light?
> [17]There the wicked cease from troubling,
>   and there the weary are at rest.
> [18]There the prisoners are at ease together;
>   they hear not the voice of the taskmaster.
> [19]The small and the great are there,
>   and the slave is free from his master.

Job has regretted his conception and his birth. Now he bemoans having survived after birth. He wonders why he was cherished, received on the knees or at the breast in his first days of life. To be treated in this way at the beginning of life instills false hopes for continued security. His present life belies that hope. Had he met with an early death he would have been spared the trouble and weariness that he now knows. Evan a stillbirth would have been better than his present lot. There is no thought here of a life of peace after death. The focus is on death as a termination of the affliction and suffering. This entire section speaks of rest and relief. Death would put an end to trouble and weariness, to imprisonment and hard labor, and to enslavement. Each of these images symbolizes life as Job encounters it. Being born into a life like this is certainly not a blessing. It is a calamity, a tragedy. Death is the relief. One can only curse the day of such a birth and look to death for rest from life.

WHY BIRTH?
Job 3:20-26

> 20Why is light given to him that is in misery,
>   and life to the bitter in soul,
> 21who long for death, but it comes not,
>   and dig for it more than for hid treasures;
> 22who rejoice exceedingly,
>   and are glad, when they find the grave?
> 23Why is light given to a man whose way is hid,
>   whom God has hedged in?
> 24For my sighing comes as my bread,
>   and my groanings are poured out like water.
> 25For the thing that I fear comes upon me,
>   and what I dread befalls me.
> 26I am not at ease, nor am I quiet;
>   I have no rest; but trouble comes."

One of the most significant themes in the wisdom tradition is 'the way'. The way, or the path, or the road to wisdom is the manner of living that will insure harmony and happiness. Men and women must search for this way. A life of true wisdom is, in fact, a life of searching for and finding this way. Verse 25 highlights the struggle of Job. The way that he must travel is hidden from him. He is expected to live a life in accord with the underlying principles of order but the way to these principles and their comprehension is kept from him. Once again Job challenges the value of enduring such an existence. No wonder he tastes bitterness and questions why he should have ever seen the light of the day of birth. The inviting search for wisdom has turned into a frantic seeking after death as if it were a treasure beyond value. The satan had accused the Lord of hedging Job in, protecting him. Now Job accuses God of hedging him in, confining him, imprisoning him.

The scope and intensity of Job's outburst seems to diminish as his complaint progresses. In the beginning he attacks the cosmic order itself. Then he challenges the purpose of his own birth. Finally he wonders about the sufferings of anyone. Each of the three sections consists of a challenge from Job and a reason for this challenge. He curses the day of his birth for it did not shut his mother's womb. He demands to know why he did not die at birth for then he would be at rest from struggle. He wants to know why he continues to live for his agony and torment are life, food and drink that sustain his miserable life and he is overwhelmed by what he most fears, the possibility that it will never end. He is trapped, hedged in with no end in sight and no comprehension as to the meaning of this suffering and 'the way' through it.

The poetic dialogues have begun with Job's own reflection on his plight. He is taken up with what appears to him to be the hopelessness of the situation. His lament is not about the reasons for his sufferings, but about the life of suffering itself. At this point he blames no one, neither himself nor another. Nor does he ask for an explanation. His plea is for deliverance.

THE FIRST CYCLE OF SPEECHES

As noted in the prologue, the friends are silent as long as Job is silent. This is the appropriate protocol for mourning. The chief mourner must be the one to break the silence. Job has done just that with his personal lament of life. Now the friends are free to respond, and they do it in very definite order. While it is not explicitly stated, it is presumed that Eliphaz is the elder for he is the first to speak, followed by Bildad and Zophar. The content of his speech is far from consoling. It is more an instruction with a tone of condemnation. It is inappropriate to continue to refer to Eliphaz and his companions as comforters or consolers. An examination of their message will show that they are advocates of a point of view that will be fervently and consistently rejected by Job. Each attempts to point out Job's error. Each exhortation is followed by a response from Job which may or may not be related to what had just been spoken. With the exception of the third series of speeches, the interaction between Job and his three companions constitutes three balanced cycles.

Eliphaz

JOB'S LIFE, PAST AND PRESENT
Job 4:1-6

> **4** Then Eliphaz the Temanite answered:
> ²"If one ventures a word with you, will you be offended?
>   Yet who can keep from speaking?
> ³Behold, you have instructed many,
>   and you have strengthened the weak hands.
> ⁴Your words have upheld him who was stumbling,
>   and you have made firm the feeble knees.
> ⁵But now it has come to you, and you are impatient;
>   it touches you, and you are dismayed.
> ⁶Is not your fear of God your confidence,
>   and the integrity of your ways your hope?

Eliphaz begins with a polite question. Realizing that Job is under profound strain he wonders whether interrogation will further weaken the man. Yet he feels compelled to speak. With Job having broken the silence he is free to try to throw some light on the situation, to remind Job of the wisdom and justice of the theory of retribution and the consistency with which it is administered, and to help him to recognize the fairness of his plight. One immediately perceives that Eliphaz intends to instruct and persuade rather than encourage and console. He does praise Job's former teaching to others. In the past Job had strengthened the weak, upheld the stumbling, and made firm the feeble. He had been a true pillar of the community. He always knew how to explain and to encourage. One would think that he could apply some of that wisdom to his own case. Or is he unable to do this because his teaching was empty and devoid of solid tradition? Has personal misfortune brought him to a different understanding of suffering in life? Is he unwilling or unable to answer his own questions with the very solutions he had previously offered to others?

Eliphaz does not really accuse Job of hypocrisy. Quite the contrary. Verse 6 contains some encouragement and an indirect acknowledgement of Job's righteousness. In several earlier passages (cf. 1:1; 8; 2:3) Job was described in technical wisdom language as blameless and fearing God. Eliphaz uses the very same vocabulary with no shade of sarcasm. He exhorts Job to trust. If his proclaimed righteousness is authentic, he has nothing to fear and every reason to be confident. His confidence will ultimately be rewarded. Job lacks patience. His present dismay indicates a lack of confidence in his professed convictions. In the long run, the good will be rewarded. If Job is a man of true integrity, he should have nothing to fear. This counsel from Eliphaz leads naturally into a short discourse on the theory of retribution.

THE THEORY OF RETRIBUTION
Job 4:7-11

> [7]"Think now, who that was innocent ever perished?
>   Or where were the upright cut off?
> [8]As I have seen, those who plow iniquity
>   and sow trouble reap the same.
> [9]By the breath of God they perish,
>   and by the blast of his anger they are consumed.
> [10]The roar of the lion, the voice of the fierce lion,
>   the teeth of the young lions, are broken.
> [11]The strong lion perishes for lack of prey,
>   and the whelps of the lioness are scattered.

There are basically two ways of living. One can search for and discover the proper order of things and move in harmony with life, or one can refuse to do so and live in dissonance. This arrangement is inevitable as are the respective consequences. Eliphaz asks Job to reflect on his own knowledge. The innocent do not perish. The upright are not cut off. This must have been some of the teaching that Job used in former times to instill confidence in those who turned to him. It is the same teaching that must now bring Job either to trust in the eventual resolution of his dilemma or to repent of his transgressions.

Eliphaz next searches his own experience. The wicked will indeed be punished. The order perceived in the natural world is employed to emphasize the certitude of this tenet. What is plowed and sown will eventually be reaped. It may take time, but there is a determinancy here that cannot be ignored. This agricultural image is juxtaposed with another example of nature's conformity to fundamental laws. Verses 10-11 contain five different words for lion. Fierce as it is, it, too, perishes. Throughout the scriptures the wicked are often referred to as lions (cf. Ps 22:13; 21; Prov 28:15). The same verb is used in these verses to speak of the fate of the lion and the fate of the wicked. Such is not the fate of the innocent. It is obvious that all die - the lion, the wicked and the innocent, as well. Therefore, the word *perish* has a slightly different nuance when referring to one's lot in life. In that context it must mean to live in dissonance or conflict as the wicked are destined to do.

The theory of retribution is twofold with concern for the fate of the righteous as well as that of the guilty. Yet, after acknowledging the integrity of Job and exhorting him to confidence, Eliphaz not only reminds him of the final ruin of the wicked but elaborates his point with examples from nature. Such an explanation is superfluous when directed toward a man who is struggling with a sense of meaningless suffering in a life of proclaimed innocence. Is it possible that the Temanite doubts Job's integrity? Does he question the truth of Job's claims? Are his thoughtfulness and consideration only apparent, while his true disposition is self-righteousness and accusatory? The answer to those questions will become obvious as the speech unfolds.

THE NIGHT VISION
Job 4:12-21

> [12]"Now a word was brought to me stealthily,
>   my ear received the whisper of it.
> [13]Amid thoughts from visions of the night,
>   when deep sleep falls on men,
> [14]dread came upon me, and trembling,
>   which made all my bones shake.
> [15]A spirit glided past my face;
>   the hair of my flesh stood up.
> [16]It stood still,
>   but I could not discern its appearance.
>   A form was before my eyes;
>   there was silence, then I heard a voice:
> [17]'Can mortal man be righteous before God?
>   Can a man be pure before his Maker?
> [18]Even in his servants he puts no trust,
>   and his angels he charges with error;
> [19]how much more those who dwell in houses of clay,
>   whose foundation is in the dust,
>   who are crushed before the moth.
> [20]Between morning and evening they are destroyed;
>   they perish for ever without any regarding it.
> [21]If their tent-cord is plucked up within them,
>   do they not die, and that without wisdom?'

Wisdom is achieved through a profound and consistent reflection on life and the movements that constitute and determine its course. How strange, then, that at the very beginning of an explanation of the inevitable consequences of certain behavior, necessary knowledge about human beings should be communicated from a source outside of human experience. Perhaps certain things cannot be understood through mere reflection and discernment. Without

realizing it, Eliphaz may be telling Job that some enlightenment from another realm is indispensible if one is to grasp
what is not immediately perceptible. It is obvious that this is
not the conscious intent of Eliphaz. He has been using the
authority of knowledge acquired through a vision to
authenticate his own views and the judgments that would
flow from them. Nor has Job realized the implications of the
need of a kind of revelation in order to grasp some of the
dimensions of life. It will take an encounter of a totally
different nature to bring him to this awareness.

The nocturnal visit itself is rather curious. It takes place
during a deep sleep which is often associated with an
encounter with God, as was the case with Adam (cf. Gen
2:21) and Abram (cf. Gen 15:12). Three words, each with its
own meaning and tradition, are used to relate the experience. The man claims to have received a word, the same
claim made by the prophets. Is he suggesting that his message is of divine origin and has the strength and validity of a
prophetic utterance? How could anyone possibly question a
conclusion that was derived from divine revelation? The
word translated as *vision* would be better translated as
nightmare for it is more of a disquieting occurrence than an
ecstatic disclosure. Finally, there is a hush and he hears a
voice. This is reminiscent of the hush that brought the
communication of God to the prophet Elijah (cf. 1 Kgs
19:12). It is like a calm that follows a storm, an apt image in
both cases mentioned. The description of this unearthly
event is intended to convince Job of the other-worldly origin
of the message, for it is the message that is important for
Eliphaz's argument.

Verses 17-19b comprise a tightly constructed poetic form
which appears again in 15:14-16 and 25:4-6. These latter
passages will be treated at those points in the commentary.
The few verses here are key for an understanding of the
frame of reference of Eliphaz and for a later comparison of
this viewpoint with that of Job. For this reason, a careful
and detailed analysis of the form and the words seems to be
required.

Each of the three major verses contains internal parallelism, a characteristic of Hebrew poetry. The second half of a verse repeats, although in different language, the thought of the first half. Thus verse 17a has three major concepts: *mortal man, righteous* and *God.* Parallel to this in verse 17b are found: *strong man, pure* and *maker.* Verses 18 and 19 follow the same poetic rule and yield: *servants, no trust* parellel to *angels, error; dwell in* and *clay* parallel to *foundation in* and *dust.* This poetic technique adds a quality to the description and extends the meaning of an idea by saying it in different ways.

Besides the parallelism inherent in each verse, the progression of thought contained within the three verses together follows à principle of argumentation known as *minori ad maius,* from the light or less important to the heavy or more important. This form is an example of such an argument.

The specific type of Hebrew interrogative that introduces verse 17 indicates that the question is meant to be rhetorical with an implied negative response. The language also has four terms that one can translate *man.* Two of these terms are used here. The first means a mortal or vulnerable man while the other refers to a strong man. The second elements of the parallel form have varied meanings. *Pure* in verse 17b ususally, though not exclusively, appears in a cultic context. However, because it is in parallel construction with *righteousness,* a word whose meaning is broader than the merely cultic, here it is understood in the moral sense. The verb forms indicate that the actions have not been completed but are still in progress. The question stated in verse 17 is thus twofold: "Is it possible for a person to be righteous?" "And if one can be righteous now, can this person continue to be righteous in the future?" As stated above, this rhetorical question has an implied negative answer. It is not possible for a human to be righteous now nor in the future. Why should Eliphaz make such a statement and how can be prove its truth?

The argument is found in verses 18 and 19 and is introduced by the word *if*. There is nothing to indicate the identity of the *servants,* but the fact that the word is parallel with *angels* suggests that they are on a level higher than human. *Error* is understood in a moral sense. This is further substantiation for reading *pure* in a moral rather than a cultic sense. Verse 18 declares that beings that are more exalted than humans lack moral integrity.

If God mistrusts the integrity of those beings that are superior to humans, *how much more* he will mistrust humans. Verse 19 contains allusions to the makeup of humankind—perishable clay and dust. The remainder of the chapter continues the theme of the perishability of humans and the short duration of their lives. The parallelism of verses 19c and 20a points to the frailty and brevity of life. Each image found in the concluding verses furthers the description. Calling attention to human physical instability, Eliphaz returns to the idea of moral weakness. Physical imperfections and the fleeting nature of life prevent people from attaining wisdom.

The entire unit is a poetic declaration of the inability of humans, precisely because they are human, to be righteous before God. Their very mortality, expressed by means of the clay motif, seems to be the reason for this. If higher beings are not free of error, perishable humans, because of their perishability, are even less apt to be so.

Eliphaz does not have a very exalted opinion of humans. He does not seem to share the same view as God, who "saw everything that he had made, and behold, it was very good" (cf. Gen 1:31). It is obvious what answer he would give to the question, "Why do the innocent suffer?" "There are no innocent!"

THE FATE OF THE FOOL
Job 5:1-7

> **5** "Call now; is there any one who will answer you?
> To which of the holy ones will you turn?

²Surely vexation kills the fool,
    and jealousy slays the simple.
³I have seen the fool taking root,
    but suddenly I cursed his dwelling.
⁴His sons are far from safety,
    they are crushed in the gate,
    and there is no one to deliver them.
⁵His harvest the hungry eat,
    and he takes it even out of thorns;
    and the thirsty pant after his wealth.
⁶For affliction does not come from the dust,
    nor does trouble sprout from the ground;
⁷but man is born to trouble
    as the sparks fly upward.

Many people of the Ancient Near East believed in personal patron gods. It was to one such god that an individual could turn when in great need or looking for protection or assistance. Eliphaz has just insisted that these 'lesser gods' cannot be trusted and so it would be foolish of Job to turn to one of them for consolation or direction.

The teaching of the wise moves freely from explicit moral exhortation to everyday common sense. In its earliest development, there may have been some clearer distinctions between the two. In a late work such as Job, these distinctions fade and the ideas of 'wise' and 'good' become interchangeable categories as do 'fool' and 'sinner'. In the first part of his speech, Eliphaz used terms that have moral nuances. Here his words are taken from the wisdom tradition.

A classic example of a proverb is found in verse 2. In poetic parallelism the fate of the fool is declared. Although it may appear that the fool enjoys prosperity, this is only short-lived. In time the inevitable destiny will overtake anyone who is foolish enough to depart from the set rules of fortune. The apparent prosperity of the wicked has always been a problem for people who hold to some form of the theory of retribution. If it is true that the good or wise will enjoy the fruits of right living and the wicked or foolish will suffer the consequences of their disregard of universal rules, how does one explain situations where the reverse seems to be the case? Eliphaz is saying that in due time the forces that are released by one's behavior will accomplish their own inner purposes and the appropriate fate will win out. This might happen gradually or it could be a sudden about-face. It could come upon the very one whose actions are the cause or it could spill over into the next generation who will then suffer the effects of the foolishness or sin. Whichever the case may be, the power that is set in motion by human action will ultimately work its way to completion and its consequences will be felt.

This description of the fool ends in the same way as it began, with a proverb in parallel style. In 4:8 Eliphaz used agricultural imagery to account for the problems of the wicked. The same words appear here and once again within an agrarian context. He wants to show that trouble does not just happen; it is caused. In the earlier verse it was clear that the wicked are responsible for their own hardships. Here the topic is hardship in general. Verses 6 and 7 should be read together for they comprise a literary continuity. *Trouble* appears in both verses. *Ground* is closely associated with *adam* (man). *Adam, ground* and *dust* all belong to the creation theme of Genesis 2:7, a text which is concerned with the creation of all humankind and not merely one couple. The use of this vocabulary suggests that Eliphaz is also speaking of humankind in general and not just about some specific person or persons.

Eliphaz's meaning is clear. Affliction does not just happen. People, all people, are responsible for it. While verse 7 may read, ". . . man is born to trouble," it can also be read, "Man begets trouble." The second reading is more in keeping with the thought of the speaker. In either reading, the truth of the relationship is compared with the certainty of sparks flying upward.

This short passage reveals once more the negative view of humankind held by Eliphaz. Humans, not specifically mortal or strong as earlier but precisely as human, are the source of trouble. They are not only victims of hardship, but the cause of it as well. Such a point of view can hardly offer much consolation to Job who insists that he is an innocent sufferer.

RECOURSE TO GOD
Job 5:8-16

> 8"As for me, I would seek God,
>   and to God would I commit my cause;
> 9who does great things and unsearchable,
>   marvelous things without number:
> 10he gives rain upon the earth
>   and sends waters upon the fields;
> 11he sets on high those who are lowly,
>   and those who mourn are lifted to safety.
> 12He frustrates the devices of the crafty,
>   so that their hands achieve no success.
> 13He takes the wise in their own craftiness;
>   and the schemes of the wily are brought to a quick end.
> 14They meet with darkness in the daytime,
>   and grope at noonday as in the night.
> 15But he saves the fatherless from their mouth,
>   the needy from the hand of the mighty.
> 16So the poor have hope,
>   and injustice shuts her mouth.

Having criticized the way of the wicked and the fool, Eliphaz praises the power that God has over all things, but not before he has confessed that God is his own source of refuge. Let others turn to 'lesser patron gods'. Eliphaz judges himself to be righteous. He knows in whose hands are found all wisdom and power and final destinies. In his praise of the wonders of God, he admits that there are some things that are beyond our comprehension. However, this point is merely mentioned. Had he developed it, he would have had to admit that Job is not the only one from whom the mysteries of life are held. He, too, is incapable of understanding and judging certain realities. His confession of the marvels of God is sincere. It is God who sends the miracle of rain, who relieves the distress of the lowly, and who thwarts the evil designs of those who refuse to live in accord with the order of the universe. Only God has such power and, for that reason, only God should be invoked. Why should Eliphaz go to such pains to remind Job of the governance of God? Does he suspect that Job has forgotten this? Has he understood Job's complaint, found in Chapter Three, to be a denial of the wisdom and power of God? At any rate, he seems intent upon his confession and will urge Job to place his trust in the very wisdom and power that he is extolling.

THE DISCIPLINE OF SUFFERING
Job 5:17-27

[17]"Behold, happy is the man whom God reproves;
therefore despise not the chastening of the Almighty.
[18]For he wounds, but he binds up;
he smites, but his hands heal.
[19]He will deliver you from six troubles;
in seven there shall no evil touch you.
[20]In famine he will redeem you from death,
and in war from the power of the sword.
[21]You shall be hid from the scourge of the tongue,
and shall not fear destruction when it comes.
[22]At destruction and famine you shall laugh,
and shall not fear the beasts of the earth.
[23]For you shall be in league with the stones of the field,
and the beasts of the field shall be at peace with you.
[24]You shall know that your tent is safe,
and you shall inspect your fold and miss nothing.
[25]You shall know also that your descendants shall be many,
and your offspring as the grass of the earth.

26You shall come to your grave in ripe old age,
as a shock of grain comes up to the threshing floor in its
season.
27Lo, this we have searched out; it is true.
Hear, and know it for your good."

The final bit of advice that Eliphaz has to offer is that Job
should look upon his suffering as a form of divine discipline.
Even if it is a punishment it has potential value as a corrective. God is able to draw tremendous good out of the
hardships that Job must endure. If he accepts this and learns
the lessons that are to be learned, he will indeed be happy in
the long run. Eliphaz admits that the adversity comes from
the hand of God. "... he wounds... he smites..." But "... he
binds up . . . his hands heal . . ." as well. If Job accepts this
chastisement, he will not only be relieved of the burden of
misfortune but will also be rewarded in his own life and on
into the lives of his descendants. There is another example
of how things are in the hands of God. One might be
tempted to consider his explanation of suffering less abrasive than any brought forward thus far. However, whether
one considers adversity a punishment or a discipline, either
one presumes that the one undergoing the hardship is guilty
of misconduct. The only difference between these two theories is that the latter tries to derive good from a painful
experience. Neither addresses the possibility of innocent
suffering.

The speech closes with an appeal to the authority of
tradition. Eliphaz is not alone in what he has espoused here.
He claims that he is a spokesman for the other two men as
well as for the entire wisdom tradition. The three have
searched it out and have found it to be true. Presumably the
tradition gained its validity from the best teacher humankind has — experience. If he is wise, Job has but one course
to follow. He must listen to this teaching and take it to heart
for his own good.

Exactly what has Eliphaz told him? He has reiterated the
theory of retribution. It is a proven fact that the good are

rewarded and the evil are punished. If for a time this principle appears to be suspended, it is either only an apparent
suspension or a temporary one. This is the traditional teaching of the sages and Eliphaz is true to it. Therefore, he
deserves to be called a wise man. But he says more. He
introduces the possibility of the disciplinary value of misfortune. While this idea does not alter the theory of just recompense, it admonishes the sufferer to derive as much benefit
from justified punishment as possible. Not once does Eliphaz hint at the prospect of adversity that is not inherently
linked to misconduct. All misfortune is caused and it is
caused by human beings.

What is in all probability most significant about the
speech is the underlying anthropology that is expressed.
Eliphaz contends that it is not possible for humans to be
righteous. This position eliminates the very question of
innocent suffering. There are no innocent.

Job

Were this a true response to Eliphaz, Job would have
attended to specific points of the argument. As it is, there is
hardly an exchange between the two men. Job directs his
outbursts, for that is what they are, toward God. It might be
truer to the structure of the dialogues to call them speeches
with very little continuity.

COMPLAINT AGAINST GOD
Job 6:1-13

> **6** Then Job answered:
> [2]"O that my vexation were weighed,
>   and all my calamity laid in the balances!
> [3]For then it would be heavier than the sand of the sea;
>   therefore my words have been rash.
> [4]For the arrows of the Almighty are in me:
>   my spirit drinks their poison;
>   the terrors of God are arrayed against me.

>⁵Does the wild ass bray when he has grass,
>   or the ox low over his fodder?
>⁶Can that which is tasteless be eaten without salt,
>   or is there any taste in the slime of the purslane?
>⁷My appetite refuses to touch them;
>   they are as food that is loathsome to me.
>⁸"O that I might have my request,
>   and that God would grant my desire;
>⁹that it would please God to crush me,
>   that he would let loose his hand and cut me off!
>¹⁰This would be my consolation;
>   I would even exult in pain unsparing;
>for I have not denied the words of the Holy One.
>¹¹What is my strength, that I should wait?
>   And what is my end, that I should be patient?
>¹²Is my strength the strength of stones,
>   or is my flesh bronze?
>¹³In truth I have no help in me,
>   and any resource is driven from me.

The insistence upon the justice of God affords Job little comfort. Eliphaz may be a guardian and proponent of the traditional teaching of the wisdom school, but Job speaks from the truth of experience. He knows the extent of his anguish and the sense of being the object of God's relentless attacks.

In his actual complaint against God, he uses some of the imagery that is characteristic of the patriarchal tradition. According to God's promise to Abraham, the innumerable sands of the sea are a sign of the prodigality of the blessing of God that will unfold in the future (cf. Gen 22:17). Job focuses on the immeasurability of the sand of the sea and its weightiness when wet to describe the magnitude of the burden that has been laid upon him. The name Almighty is a favorite patriarchal title. The earlier traditions present God the Almighty in the role of protector and guide. Job claims that this protecting God has turned against him and, because God is almighty, Job is helpless to defend himself.

The traditional God has shown himself the enemy of a righteous man.

A short digression might be in order here. The classical literary form of the wisdom school is the proverb. It can consist of one line or of a progression of several lines. Most proverbs are somewhat poetic in style, a sign that they are the product of repeated use and constant refinement. They continue in use because of the bits of truth that they incorporate, truth that has been gleaned from experience and has proven to be universally applicable. The movements of the universe, inanimate and animate nature, and human behavior are the primary observable phenomena from which proverbial wisdom springs. Patterns of regularity discerned in nature are presumed to be underlying principles of order. An understanding of how things proceed develops into a body of knowledge or traditions of wisdom. Knowledge of the operation of one realm of action becomes the guide for understanding the behavior in another. The sage is fond of calling attention to what is obvious in nature in order to point to something about human life. Proverbs are significant, therefore, not merely for their artistic crispness of style nor for their accuracy in description. It is because they are axiomatic and presume universal validity that they have endured as wisdom. This very point is at the heart of the struggle of the book of Job and of the focus of this commentary.

The major concern is order or regularity. Principles of order are expressed in proverbs. The question arises: Does this order allow for exception? Does an obvious exception falsify the rule? If rules are not really universal, is there anything that can be depended upon for stability? It is with this understanding that one must appreciate the force of proverbial argumentation as carried on in the book.

Job has bewailed his position and has maintained that God is responsible for it. He turns to nature to explain his complaint. The animals do not cry out when their basic needs have been met. Carrying the image of food further, he compares the tastelessness of Eliphaz's counsel with insipid food. The proverbs describe indisputable reactions. Job's response should be seen in the same light.

What follows is the first real appeal from Job. He does not ask to be relieved of his suffering: nor does he seek an explanation. He wants to die. A request of this nature belies the possibility of explanation or vindication, either because these do not appear to be forthcoming or because Job does not think that he can last much longer under the weight of his calamity. He is afflicted by the hand of God; let God slay him. He will die knowing that he has not betrayed God even though it would appear that God has betrayed him.

This lament reveals a man who is versed in the wisdom of his tradition. He knows how to learn from the patterns in nature. He also confesses the authority of God in the determination of the life of a human being. His personal experience of adversity is meaningless within this tradition. He can no longer endure the struggle and its incomprehensibility and so he pleads for death. He does not contemplate taking his own life, but looks to his God for ultimate release.

COMPLAINT AGAINST HIS COUNSELORS
Job 6:14-30

> 14"He who withholds kindness from a friend
>   forsakes the fear of the Almighty.
> 15My brethren are treacherous as a torrent-bed,
>   as freshets that pass away,
> 16which are dark with ice,
>   and where the snow hides itself.
> 17In time of heat they disappear;
>   when it is hot, they vanish from their place.
> 18The caravans turn aside from their course;
>   they go up into the waste, and perish.
> 19The caravans of Tema look,
>   the travelers of Sheba hope.
> 20They are disappointed because they were confident;
>   they come thither and are confounded.
> 21Such you have now become to me;
>   you see my calamity, and are afraid.

22Have I said, 'Make me a gift'?
    'Or, 'From your wealth offer a bribe for me'?
23Or, 'Deliver me from the adversary's hand"?
    Or, 'Ransom me from the hand of oppressors'?
24"Teach me, and I will be silent;
    make me understand how I have cried.
25How forceful are honest words!
    But what does reproof from you reprove?
26Do you think that you can reprove words,
    when the speech of a despairing man is wind?
27You would even cast lots over the fatherless,
    and bargain over your friend.
28"But now, be pleased to look at me;
    for I will not lie to your face.
29Turn, I pray, let no wrong be done.
    Turn now, my vindication is at stake.
30Is there any wrong on my tongue?
    Cannot my taste discern calamity?

Job turns to his companions and reviles them for their violation of friendship. He had a right to expect steadfast loyalty from them. They had come to him when they heard of the evil that had befallen him. They had remained with him in silent support. Now that one of them opens his mouth, Job discovers that their solace was momentary and their trustworthiness superficial. Their dependability is no surer than that of the desert watercourses that give the appearance of bounty and refreshment but in reality are shallow and quickly dry up. Travelers depend upon them for sustenance only to be disappointed when they are in greatest need. Such are the friends of Job who turn out to be falsehearted.

What has Job ever required of them? He never asked them to come. He does not expect them to negotiate for his release. The accusation brought against them is that they withheld kindness. The word kindness has covenantal connotations. It implies loyalty that is enduring in spite of misfortune. These would-be friends have turned against Job in his

time of need. If they were such God-fearing men they would
have remained true to their commitment to Job even if he
had been false to them or to God, neither of which is the
case.

Job is open to whatever can be offered as explanation for
his plight. If they can show how he has sinned and made
himself deserving of what he must now endure, he will be
silent and listen. All that he has heard has been condemnation and reproof. He has nothing to learn from this but that
they are faithless and more concerned with their own prestige than with his welfare. He makes another appeal to
them. "Turn" — return or repent! He begs them to stand by
him, believing what he tells them about his own experience.
He is not asking that they trust in some speculation. He
previously enjoyed the reputation of being an upright man.
He was trusted then; he asks for the same consideration
now.

A DESCRIPTION OF LIFE
Job 7:1-6

7   "Has not man a hard service upon earth,
     and are not his days like the days of a hireling?
²Like a slave who longs for the shadow,
     and like a hireling who looks for his wages,
³so I am allotted months of emptiness,
     and nights of misery are apportioned to me.
⁴When I lie down I say, 'When shall I arise?'
     But the night is long,
     and I am full of tossing till the dawn.
⁵My flesh is clothed with worms and dirt;
     my skin hardens, then breaks out afresh.
⁶My days are swifter than a weaver's shuttle,
     and come to their end without hope.

Human life, as Job sees it and experiences it, is burden-
some. It is like hard military service, like the days of a

hireling or a slave. It is fraught with misery and trouble and quickly slips by, devoid of hope. This description is stated as an accomplished fact. It is introduced by a particlar inter-rogative form, the use of which expresses the conviction that the statement is an acknowledged truth known to the hearer. Eliphaz has earlier advanced a belief about the moral deficiency of humankind. Job's axioms relate to the experience of life as lived, an experience which is character-ized as an enslavement. Job does not say that he *is* a slave, or that his life *is* the life of a hireling. The whole tenor of his protestation is that he is being treated in a manner that ill suits him. He is being treated like something that he is not. Although the Babylonian literature depicts humans as slaves of the god(s), Job rejects this kind of anthropology. He was not made for oppressive servitude. Nor was he created to be manipulated by a capricious deity. He had been fashioned and nurtured with loving care and, there-fore, had no reason to expect later rejection. This is the basis of his complaint against God who appears to be acting out of character.

There is mention of a possible reason for this state of existence. Before he turns to his own specific distress, he claims that this condition is common to all. He first empha-sizes the misery of life and then directs his attention to its transitory nature. This latter theme is picked up and deve-loped further in the following verses.

LIFE IS FLEETING
Job 7:7-21

> [7]"Remember that my life is a breath;
> my eye will never again see good.
> [8]The eye of him who sees me will behold me no more;
> while thy eyes are upon me, I shall be gone.
> [9]As the cloud fades and vanishes,
> so he who goes down to Sheol does not come up;
> [10]he returns no more to his house,
> nor does his place know him any more.

11"Therefore I will not restrain my mouth;
   I will speak in the anguish of my spirit;
   I will complain in the bitterness of my soul.
12Am I the sea, or a sea monster,
   that thou settest a guard over me?
13When I say, 'My bed will comfort me,
   my couch will ease my complaint,'
14then thou dost scare me with dreams
   and terrify me with visions,
15so that I would choose strangling
   and death rather than my bones.
16I loathe my life; I would not live for ever.
   Let me alone, for my days are a breath.
17What is man, that thou dost make so much of him,
   and that thou dost set thy mind upon him,
18dost visit him every morning,
   and test him every moment?
19How long wilt thou not look away from me,
   nor let me alone till I swallow my spittle?
20If I sin, what do I do to thee, thou
   watcher of men?
   Why hast thou made me thy mark?
   Why have I become a burden to thee?
21Why dost thou not pardon my transgression
   and take away my iniquity?
   For now I shall lie in the earth;
   thou wilt seek me, but I shall not be."

Job turns from those around him and addresses God. Life is so brief and there is no return after death, so if God is going to set things right he will have to do something soon. What does Job have to lose if he complains to God? As it is, he is stripped of all. For the first time he cries out directly to God about the mistreatment he is undergoing at the hand of the Almighty.

The fate of a person after death was a question that vexed the ancient world. Each society wrestled with the problem and most of them arrived at an idea of some kind of abode of the dead. This concept might be well or ill defined, but it usually took the form of an underworld dwelling. The concept of Sheol belongs to this complex of ideas. Early traditions merely referred to this place with little or no detail. It was a shadowy region and those who were there led a kind of inanimate existence. There was no reward but there was no punishment either. While it appears that existence there is meaningless, the fact that it was conceived at all indicates that the ancients did not believe that death was the definitive termination of all forms of life. They may not have developed this idea very specifically, but the seed was there for future germination.

For Job, Sheol was a refuge from the terrors of life. He may not be able to communicate with anyone or with God for that matter, but he would be free from torment.

The tone of verse 11 is obvious. Reverence for the majesty of God does not temper Job's emotional outburst. His desperate situation has brought him to the point of disregard for religious conventions. Who would fault him under the circumstances? It is his faith in God as architect and guardian of world order that moves him to direct his complaint to God himself. God is the one who has either done this to Job or allowed it to happen to him and, therefore, the one to whom the protest should be directed.

The first figure of speech (v. 12) comes from the mythological imagery of the ancient Near East. There one finds myths of creation which tell of the god of chaos, characterized as the sea or a sea monster, in battle with the mighty god who is responsible for order. This theme appears in other places within the tradition of Israel as well (cf. Isa 27:1; 51:9; Ps 74:13). By suggesting this imagery the author is once again calling attention to the underlying theme: order versus chaos. Here Job wonders if God is treating him as if he, Job, were the source of disorder so that God is constrained to conquer him. This may be God's duty in some other situation, but Job is guilty of no flagrant violation. He complains of being treated as if he were. There is no escape for Job. God's harassment is unrelenting. He pursues Job even into the world of sleep. The only release is death.

A second figure of speech that Job uses is also taken from creation theology. Psalm 8 is a hymn that praises God for the marvels of creation, in particular for the wonder of humankind. While the psalmist goes on to describe human dignity, Job seems to imply that humans are too insignificant for God to stalk them as he does (v. 17). God should not be so affected by human behavior (v. 20). Job's application of the theme from Psalm 8 underlines his accusation of inconsistency in God's treatment. Provident care has given way to unreasonable surveillance. In the psalm, God visited humankind for the purpose of blessing; here it is in order to test. Having taken such great pains to create, God appears to have turned against this special creature. The look of love has become a fierce penetrating stare unyielding in its intensity.

Job ends his cry to God with a plea that any transgression that he might have indeed committed be pardoned and that God let him alone to die in peace. If God is as merciful as Job's religious tradition holds, he should be willing to forgive the minor offenses of a fundamentally righteous man. Time is short: Job's end is imminent. God will have to pardon him now before it is too late. There is no thought of vindication after death. It must take place now or not at all.

Bildad

THE TWO WAYS
Job 8:1-7

8 Then Bildad the Shuhite answered:
²"How long will you say these things,
    and the words of your mouth be a great wind?
³Does God pervert justice?
    Or does the Almighty pervert the right?
⁴If your children have sinned against him,
    he has delivered them into the power of their transgression.

5If you will seek God
and make supplication to the Almighty,
6if you are pure and upright,
surely then he will rouse himself for you
and reward you with a rightful habitation.
7And though your beginning was small,
your latter days will be very great.

The second man who has come to comfort and counsel Job begins his speech by condemning Job and criticizing his outcry. Bildad actually taunts Job, revealing that he, like Eliphaz, is more a critic than a friend and his words are scornful rather than consoling.

He begins his argument with a poetic statement affirming the justice of God (v. 3). Once again the rhetorical question can only be answered in the negative. Of course God cannot pervert! The Almighty cannot pervert what is right. If such were the case, where would one turn? Whom could one trust? Such a thought cannot possibly be entertained. Regularity, inevitability, even determinism dominate the structures of reality. If there is sin, there will be restitution (v. 4). If there is righteousness or repentance, there will be final reinstatement (vv. 5-7). It is as simple as that and for Job even to question the certainty of this arrangement is foolish, a challenge to God, and proof of his culpability.

Even as Bildad describes the good fortune in store for Job if he would only seek God and be pure and upright, the implication is that Job has not yet done this and hence he is presently in distress. Bildad speaks from the same worldview as did Eliphaz. According to that model, a tormented Job is a guilty Job.

AN APPEAL TO TRADITION
Job 8:8-19

8"For inquire, I pray you, of bygone ages,
and consider what the fathers have found;

⁹for we are but of yesterday, and know nothing,
    for our days on earth are a shadow.
¹⁰Will they not teach you, and tell you,
    and utter words out of their understanding?
¹¹"Can papyrus grow where there is no marsh?
    Can reeds flourish where there is no water?
¹²While yet in flower and not cut down,
    they wither before any other plant.
¹³Such are the paths of all who forget God;
    the hope of the godless man shall perish.
¹⁴His confidence breaks in sunder,
    and his trust is a spider's web.
¹⁵He leans against his house, but it does not stand;
    he lays hold of it, but it does not endure.
¹⁶He thrives before the sun,
    and his shoots spread over his garden.
¹⁷His roots twine about the stoneheap;
    he lives among the rocks.
¹⁸If he is destroyed from his place,
    then it will deny him, saying, 'I have never seen you.'
¹⁹Behold, this is the joy of his way;
    and out of the earth others will spring.

Everyone recognizes the role that experience plays in the acquisition of wisdom and all societies have held their past learning in highest esteem. It stands to reason that they would look to the elders for guidance and to the wisdom of the past for direction. Bildad appeals to the proven wisdom of the past which has stood the test of time and is trustworthy. Conversely, Job and his companions are short-lived and know so little. To presume to contest the accumulated wisdom of the ancients and to advance one's own views in their place is unthinkable. The consistency in nature should be an example of the irrefutability of the laws of human behavior.

Plants cannot survive without water; humans cannot endure without God. The one dictum is as true as the other.

Things may appear to be thriving, but death and corrosion will finally take over and the true state of affairs will become apparent to all. One is a fool to trust in what has no substance (vv. 14-15). Bildad is not only predicting the ultimate downfall of the godless but he is also ridiculing one who relies on anything of questionable dependability. He has already explicitly reproached Job for his empty words (v. 2), and reminded him of the limited knowledge that one can acquire during one's lifetime (v. 9). Now he is suggesting that if Job depends only upon his own insight he resembles a fool who trusts in what has no substance.

RESTATEMENT OF RETRIBUTION
Job 8:20-22

> [20]"Behold, God will not reject a blameless man,
>   nor take the hand of evildoers.
> [21]He will yet fill your mouth with laughter,
>   and your lips with shouting.
> [22]Those who hate you will be clothed with shame,
>   and the tent of the wicked will be no more."

Bildad straightforwardly expresses the theory of retribution. He chooses one of the very words that the Lord used to describe Job — blameless. If such an affirmation is intended to console Job, it misses the mark. Job's complaint is that God has done just exactly what Bildad says will not happen. Bildad insists that in the end, if he is truly blameless, Job will know joy and those who have hated him will experience shame. The wicked will be taken to task.

The speech of Bildad has added nothing to the debate. He has convinced Job of nothing. He has made no positive contribution to the testimony of Eliphaz. He has shown no understanding, no sympathy. It is no wonder that Job rejects the judgment and advice that is offered to him.

Job

THE POWER OF THE CREATOR
Job 9:1-13

9   Then Job answered:
²"Truly I know that it is so:
But how can a man be just before God?
³If one wished to contend with him,
  one could not answer him once in a thousand times.
⁴He is wise in heart, and mighty in strength
—who has hardened himself against
  him, and succeeded?—
⁵he who removes mountains, and they know it not,
  when he overturns them in his anger;
⁶who shakes the earth out of its place,
  and its pillars tremble;
⁷who commands the sun, and it does not rise;
  who seals up the stars;
⁸who alone stretched out the heavens,
  and trampled the waves of the sea;
⁹who made the Bear and Orion,
  the Pleiades and the chambers of the south;
¹⁰who does great things beyond understanding,
  and marvelous things without number.
¹¹Lo, he passes by me, and I see him not;
  he moves on, but I do not perceive him.
¹²Behold, he snatches away; who can hinder him?
  Who will say to him,'What doest thou?'
¹³"God will not turn back his anger;
  beneath him bowed the helpers of Rahab.

   The pattern of the second response is similar to that of the first. At times Job addresses his companions and at other times he speaks directly to God. It is not always clear to which man he is speaking for he does not refute their accusations in any orderly manner. This becomes clear as one reads his second reply which follows a harangue by Bildad but reiterates a phrase spoken by Eliphaz (cf. 4:17a). How can a mortal be just?

Once again the issue is order. To be righteous means to be in right relationship with the righteous God who is responsible for the origin of the world and its government. The creative power and the wise governance of God are perceived as inter-related. The vocabulary suggests a court scene where the charge of injustice is brought. The plantiff, Job, hopes to bring the accused, God, to justice and force reinstatement of order. He realizes that his case is hopeless because God is also the judge and he, Job, is powerless to force a verdict of "guilty". Job is no match for the wisdom and power of this God, a wisdom and power that is now described.

Much of the poetry of ancient Israel praises God for the glories of creation (cf. Ps 104:1-9). Later in the book of Job itself (38:4-9) the scope of this power and wisdom is brought forth to argue for the mystery in creation. Here Job acknowledges it but charges that it has been turned against the very creation that it has produced. The mountains that had been set up are overturned; the pillars that support the earth are threatened; even the sun fails to rise. This cataclysm can only mean that chaos reigns. It is the creator alone who can do this. Repeating the words of Eliphaz, regarding the god "who does great things beyond understanding, and marvelous things without number" (v. 10; cf. 5:9), Job blames God for anarchy in the world.

His argument is not merely a twisting of words. A constituent dimension of the wisdom approach to understanding life is the observation of the regularity in the natural world whereby one attempts to discern the underlying principles of order. Men and women looked to nature in order to discover a comparable pattern in human matters. Job does just that but discovers disorder rather than order. This dissonance is also present in Job's own life. The argument from creation proposed by the wisdom school does not refute Job's stance but supports it. There is no question here of a denial of the divine might and of the resulting creation.

The claim is that this same provident God can in anger convert the creative power into a destructive force and turn it against the universe. Job sees himself as an innocent and unsuspecting victim of this wrath, unable to understand this anger and incapable of staving off its fury. Even the forces of chaos, "the helpers of Rahab", are helpless before such rage. Job does not accuse God of powerlessness in the face of chaos but of capriciousness in the use of power.

DISPUTE WITH AN ARBITRARY GOD
Job 9:14-24

> ¹⁴How then can I answer him,
>   choosing my words with him?
> ¹⁵Though I am innocent, I cannot answer him;
>   I must appeal for mercy to my accuser.
> ¹⁶If I summoned him and he answered me,
>   I would not believe that he was listening to my voice.
> ¹⁷For he crushes me with a tempest,
>   and multiplies my wounds without cause;
> ¹⁸he will not let me get my breath,
>   but fills me with bitterness.
> ¹⁹If it is a contest of strength, behold him!
>   If it is a matter of justice, who can summon him?
> ²⁰Though I am innocent, my own mouth would condemn me;
>   though I am blameless, he would prove me perverse.
> ²¹I am blameless; I regard not myself;
>   I loathe my life.
> ²²It is all one; therefore I say,
>   he destroys both the blameless and the wicked.
> ²³When disaster brings sudden death,
>   he mocks at the calamity of the innocent.
> ²⁴The earth is given into the hand of the wicked;
>   he covers the faces of its judges—
>   if it is not he, who then is it?

Job's argument again takes the form of a legal dispute. Initially Job was the plaintiff and God the accused. Now

Job is the one on trial. He must respond to questioning and plead for mercy and even then he will not be able to prove his innocence (vv. 14-16). The proverb in verse 19 once again juxtaposes strength and justice showing the close relationship that exists between them. Job claims that God uses this power to subvert justice. He insists on his innocence (vv. 15a: 20a) and uses the technical term *blameless* to describe himself (vv. 20b: 21a). God seems to disregard justice for "he destroys both the blameless and the wicked."

What is one to do before such a tyrannical God? Escape is impossible; relief is not in sight; there is no one to whom to turn; even innocence is perverted. For one whose worldview is so ordered and predictable, there is but one explanation for this. God has relinquished the rule of the universe. He has allowed pernicious forces to upset the balance in the cosmos and has handed the world over to the wicked. Little does Job know that this is exactly what has happened. In the prologue the reader was informed of this. God has surrendered control of Job's fortunes and had allowed them to disintegrate. Job errs in concluding that it is out of wrath and injustice that this has occurred.

HELPLESSNESS BEFORE GOD
Job 9:25-35

> [25]"My days are swifter than a runner;
>   they flee away, they see no good.
> [26]They go by like skiffs of reed,
>   like an eagle swooping on the prey.
> [27]If I say, 'I will forget my complaint,
>   I will put off my sad countenance,
>   and be of good cheer,'
> [28]I become afraid of all my suffering,
>   for I know thou wilt not hold me innocent.
> [29]I shall be condemned;
>   why then do I labor in vain?
> [30]If I wash myself with snow,
>   and cleanse my hands with lye,

> [31]yet thou wilt plunge me into a pit,
>   and my own clothes will abhor me.
> [32]For he is not a man, as I am, that I might answer him,
>   that we should come to trial together.
> [33]There is no umpire between us,
>   who might lay his hand upon us both.
> [34]Let him take his rod away from me,
>   and let not dread of him terrify me.
> [35]Then I would speak without fear of him,
>   for I am not so in myself.

Three figures of speech are used to describe the fleeting nature of life. Each image provides a different nuance to the sketch. Although the runner may be swift, there is a strength or endurance present. This feature is countered by the image of a skiff constructed of reeds that is delicate and easily damaged. The final figure, that of the eagle seizing its prey, speaks of brutal and unexpected tragedy. This is how Job views his life. It runs by rapidly, is always in danger of being destroyed and will be cruelly snatched from him.

In describing his powerlessness, Job alternates between bemoaning his fate to those around him and complaining directly to God. There is absolutely no way for him to set the situation right. Even if he stops complaining, God will either hold him guilty (vv. 28-29) or make him guilty (vv. 30-31). Job is no match for God. A resolution would be possible only if there were someone who could act as an unprejudiced arbitrator, an umpire, who would be able to decide the case impartially. Verse 33 is the first of three passages which reveal Job's longing for a patron whose authority is powerful enough to vindicate him (cf. 16:19; 19:25). There was a belief in the Ancient Near Eastern world that each person had such a patron god who would intercede for the petitioner before the divine council. The umpire referred to here must have authority independent of either of the disputants in order to act without prejudice. But who has authority over God? And the court before which Job must stand is the court of God. Under such circumstances, what kind of impartiality can Job expect? Who could Job's umpire be? His only patron is God. Could Job possibly be asking God to judge in his, Job's, favor before God, against God? Job doubts that he can expect a fair hearing.

JOB'S LAMENT
Job 10:1-7

> **10** "I loathe my life;
> I will give free utterance to my complaint;
> I will speak in the bitterness of my soul.
> ²I will say to God, Do not condemn me;
>   let me know why thou dost contend against me.
> ³Does it seem good to thee to oppress,
>   to despise the work of thy hands
>   and favor the designs of the wicked?
> ⁴Has thou eyes of flesh?
>   Dost thou see as man sees?
> ⁵Are thy days as the days of man,
>   or thy years as man's years,
> ⁶that thou dost seek out my iniquity
>   and search for my sin,
> ⁷although thou knowest that I am not guilty,
>   and there is none to deliver out of thy hand?

Once again anguish and despair threaten to swallow Job in their wake and he cries out in agony. This hopeless situation has also stripped him of all his restraint and so once again he hurls his torment directly at God. As before (cf. 7:11f), he prefaces his lament with an exclamation of utter desperation. His complaint erupts from the midst of the irrepressible turmoil deep within him. "WHY?"

Job challenges God's management of the works of creation. Having made things as they are and continuing to have control over them, why should he delight in tormenting them? He accuses God of behaving in a very irresponsible way, with limited perspective and total incompetence. Is he so myopic that all that interests him is ferreting out Job's failures, disregarding Job's intrinsic adherence to justice? Job cannot fathom what appears to be obvious disdain for creatures by the very creator, God. This piercing lament is followed by a beautiful poetic description of Job's creation.

CREATION AND MISUSE
Job 10:8-22

8Thy hands fashioned and made me;
and now thou dost turn about and destroy me.
9Remember that thou has made me of clay;
and wilt thou turn me to dust again?
10Didst thou not pour me out like milk
and curdle me like cheese?
11Thou didst clothe me with skin and flesh,
and knit me together with bones and sinews.
12Thou hast granted me life and steadfast love;
and thy care has preserved my spirit.
13Yet these things thou didst hide in thy heart;
I know that this was thy purpose.
14If I sin, thou dost mark me,
and dost not acquit me of my iniquity.
15If I am wicked, woe to me!
If I am righteous, I cannot lift up my head,
for I am filled with disgrace
and look upon my affliction.
16And if I lift myself up, thou dost hunt me like a lion,
and again work wonders against me;
17thou dost renew thy witnesses against me,
and increase thy vexation toward me;
thou dost bring fresh hosts against me.
18"Why didst thou bring me forth from the womb?
Would that I had died before any eye had seen me,
19and were as though I had not been,
carried from the womb to the grave.
20Are not the days of my life few?
Let me alone, that I may find a little comfort
21before I go whence I shall not return,
to the land of gloom and deep darkness,

[22]the land of gloom and chaos,
  where light is as darkness."

Verses 8 and 9 express the same idea but employ different words. The first part of each verse speaks of Job's creation while the final theme is of his death. After having fashioned Job with great care, God hardly would take his life now. The theme of creation is further developed in verses 10-12. Two new images, one from dairying and the other from the art of weaving, point to the craft involved in the act of creation and the intricacy of the development of the fetus. The mystery of embryonic growth elicited reverence and awe from the ancient Israelites and caused them to wonder at the loving providence of the creator. A manifestation of divine care and artistry has here been added to the tradition of God the maker. This is not the scene of the creation of humankind in general, but of the intimacy of life within the womb. If God has gone to such lengths in making Job, why destroy him now? And if destruction was part of God's original intent, why did he take such great pains in creating him in the first place?

The covenantal word *steadfast love* describes faithful commitment to one's covenant partner. It is ususally used in reference to God's attitude toward humankind. Here, along with life and care, it has been given to Job by God. Because it follows immediately upon creation imagery, one could say that Job is reminding God of the covenant commitment made with him before he was born. This thought is not unique with Job, for the prophet Jeremiah tells of being called from his mother's womb (cf. Jer 1:5). Whether this pledge was made with Job before he was born or later in life, the issue remains the personal devotedness of God.

Returning to the themes of creation and birth, he ends his long lament with the same sentiments expressed in his first speech (cf. 3:1-16). If this is the only prospect that life has to offer, why was he even born in the first place? Having been born, why doesn't God just let him alone? Life is so short. All he asks is a brief reprieve before he is plunged into death which for him will be utter gloom and ultimate chaos.

A comparison of Job's speeches shows that Job is becoming bolder and bolder in his complaints and accusations. At first (chapter 3) he speaks generally, crying out but accusing no one. Next (chapters 6-7) he questions God and demands some explanation. Now his address is filled with denunciation. Eliphaz and Bildad represent the traditional religious perspective which Job held previously without recognizing its inadequacy. Unexplained misfortune has exposed another side of the theory and another side of Job.

Zophar

A TAUNT
Job 11:1-12

11   Then Zophar the Naamathite answered:
²"Should a multitude of words go unanswered,
    and a man full of talk be vindicated?
³Should your babble silence men,
    and when you mock, shall no one shame you?
⁴For you say, 'My doctrine is pure,
    and I am clean in God's eyes.'
⁵But oh, that God would speak,
    and open his lips to you,
⁶and that he would tell you the secrets of wisdom!
    For he is manifold in understanding.
    Know then that God exacts of you less than your guilt
    deserves.
⁷"Can you find out the deep things of God?
    Can you find out the limit of the Almighty?
⁸It is higher than heaven—what can you do?
    Deeper than Sheol—what can you know?
⁹Its measure is longer than the earth,
    and broader than the sea.
¹⁰If he passes through, and imprisons,
    and calls to judgment, who can hinder him?
¹¹For he knows worthless men;
    when he sees iniquity, will he not consider it?

¹²But a stupid man will get understanding,
when a wild ass's colt is born a man.

From the outset, Zophar shows no sympathy for Job's exclamations and considers them little more than babbling. He does not even attempt to persuade Job to relinquish his pretext of innocence but launches immediately into a taunt. He takes issue with two claims made by Job: that what Job has said is true; that Job is a man of integrity (v. 4). The error of the second assertion is quite clear. Were he guiltless he would not be suffering as he is. It is understandable that he would concoct some notion about his own innocence and God's guilt in order to exonerate himself. Any fabrication of this sort deserves to be ridiculed. There is a reason for his predicament. There are also things that Job does not comprehend.

Earlier Eliphaz had touched on the possibility of mystery. Zophar does the same here. His conception of it is far from consoling. He insists that there are serious sins of which Job is unaware and it is for these that he is now in torment. Job is correct in asking for an explanation for his straits, but in error in thinking that this information will vindicate him. It will simply illuminate his deeper sinfulness and his outrageous arrogance.

Verses 7-9 consist of a paean to the incomparability of God. There is no limit to the Almighty or to the divine wisdom or power. No one and nothing can calculate the height, the depth, the length or the breadth of God. Once again Zophar merely brushes past the question of mystery in his rush to indict Job. Recognition of God's mysteriousness could instill wonder and awe and even trust, but instead Zophar proposes it as something to fear (vv. 10-11). It is an unnecessary argument on his part for this is exactly how Job views God — as one having unspeakable power whereby he scrutinizes in order to punish and with no cause.

The proverb with which he ends his taunt epitomizes Zophar's impression of Job who has rejected the wisdom of the tradition and has replaced it with a doctrine of his own.

To pretend that this is wisdom is ridiculous. If Job has sunk to such depths of foolishness then it is unlikely that he has any kind of understanding at all, and the chance of acquiring some is as slim as the prospect of the colt of a wild ass being born human.

DOCTRINE OF THE TWO WAYS
Job 11:13-20

> 13"If you set your heart aright,
>   you will stretch out your hands toward him.
> 14If iniquity is in your hand, put it far away,
>   and let not wickedness dwell in your tents.
> 15Surely then you will lift up your face without blemish;
>   you will be secure, and will not fear.
> 16You will forget your misery;
>   you will remember it as waters that have passed away.
> 17And your life will be brighter than the noonday;
>   its darkness will be like the morning.
> 18And you will have confidence, because there is hope;
>   you will be protected and take you rest in safety.
> 19You will lie down, and none will make you afraid;
>   many will entreat your favor.
> 20But the eyes of the wicked will fail;
>   all way of escape will be lost to them,
>   and their hope is to breathe their last."

It is clear that Zophar does not believe Job's avowal of righteousness. He continually urges Job to turn away from iniquity and to return to the Lord, and he holds out the promose of reinstatement and happiness as reward. His arguments flow from the traditional theory of retribution, a theory that has become a millstone around Job's neck pulling him further and further into despair. All of the advice that has been offered by him presumes sinfulness. He paints a picture of the lot of the sinner using some of the very colors which Job used when depicting his affliction. There is no escape for the wicked and the only hope for release is death.

Remorse and conversion will reestablish order in his life and the reputation that he once enjoyed (v. 19).

Job

DEFENSE OF HIS WORLDVIEW
Job 12:1-12

12 Then Job answered:
2"No doubt you are the people,
and wisdom will die with you.
3But I have understanding as well as you;
I am not inferior to you.
Who does not know such things as these?
4I am a laughingstock to my friends;
I, who called upon God and he answered me,
a just and blameless man, am a laughingstock.
5In the thought of one who is at ease
there is contempt for misfortune;
it is ready for those whose feet slip.
6The tents of robbers are at peace,
and those who provoke God are secure,
who bring their god in their hand.
7"But ask the beasts, and they will teach you;
the birds of the air, and they will tell you;
8or the plants of the earth, and they will teach you;
and the fish of the sea will declare to you.
9Who among all these does not know
that the hand of the LORD has done this?
10In his hand is the life of every living thing
and the breath of all mankind.
11Does not the ear try words
as the palate tastes food?
12Wisdom is with the aged,
and understanding in length of days.

Job's final reply in the first cycle is a refutation of the charges of all three of his companions. At times, in defending himself, he employs the very arguments which were posed against him by one or the other of his antagonists.

As Zophar began his reproof with a taunt, so Job resorts to the same tactic (vv. 1-2). All three men have chided Job as if they alone possessed wisdom and Job was bereft of it. They seem to have forgotten that previously Job too had enjoyed the reputation for wisdom. In fact, he surpassed "all the people of the east" (cf.1:3). There is nothing that they have told him about order and harmony and life that is new to him. He was imbued with the tradition of the ancients, proficient in the art of discovering the laws that govern reality, and steadfast in his adherence to both. It is not that he has forfeited his understanding. Quite the contrary! This miserable situation has given him a new insight into life and how God controls it. Job does not know less than his companions; he knows something that they cannot possibly comprehend.

Never doubting his own ability to interpret correctly, Job defends the reliability of the perspective that he has gained from his own experience. Using wisdom vocabulary, he describes himself as just and blameless, and this should make him deserving of respect and praise. Instead, he has become a laughingstock. This state of affairs is an indictment of those who disparage the helpless and afflicted rather than comfort and assist them in accordance with the tradition of Israel. The prosperous who do nothing to aid the needy are now guilty of disdain as well as neglect.

These three spokesmen of wisdom have called on natural phenomena to instruct the erring Job, hence he now does the same. Nature teaches that there is a fundamental order, but it also reveals destructive forces over which one has no control. All living things know this (vv. 7-10) for all life is in the hand of God and subject to the divine will. Life and breath are given and taken away (cf. Ps 104:29) and no one knows how or why.

Job ridicules their claim to wisdom (vv. 11-13). A person knows by experience, by tasting, whether or not the food is palatable. Job's own practical knowledge has judged their counsel and has found it distasteful. They disprove the old adage that wisdom comes with age. Perhaps one has more opportunity to learn if one lives a long life, but there is no guarantee that this will happen. Besides, if it is primarily life experience that teaches, then the lessons that suffering has to offer have been lost on these men.

GOD'S ABILITY TO OVERTURN
Job 12:13-25

13"With God are wisdom and might;
  he has counsel and understanding.
14If he tears down, none can rebuild;
  if he shuts a man in, none can open.
15If he withholds the waters, they dry up;
  if he sends them out, they overwhelm the land.
16With him are strength and wisdom;
  the deceived and the deceiver are his.
17He leads counselors away stripped,
  and judges he makes fools.
18He looses the bonds of kings,
  and binds a waistcloth on their lions.
19He leads priests away stripped,
  and overthrows the mighty.
20He deprives of speech those who are trusted,
  and takes away the discernment of the elders.
21He pours contempt on princes,
  and looses the belt of the strong.
22He uncovers the deeps out of darkness,
  and brings deep darkness to light.
23He makes nations great, and he destroys them:
  he enlarges nations, and leads them away.
24He takes away understanding from the
  chiefs of the people of the earth,
  and makes them wander in a pathless waste.
25They grope in the dark without light;
  and he makes them stagger like a drunken man.

Job has defended his own wisdom and has challenged that of his associates, but he does proclaim the unparallelled wisdom and power of God. The negative character of his proclamation is striking. He states categorically that no one can reverse the decisions of this power even when the results may be ruinous. God can destroy, cause draught or flood, and manipulate whomever he wishes. The very pillars of society — the counselors, judges, kings, princes and priests — are helpless in his hand. Even the sages are stripped of their effectiveness. If this is the case, then society itself is insecure and its basic fabric can unravel at any time. The destructive force of God is evident in creation.

The ancient worldview postulated an interrelatedness between the broader universe and the arena of human endeavor. The same laws governed both realms; the same divine wisdom was the foundation of the order perceived. It is out of this framework that Job develops his own argument. He moves from the cosmic sphere (v. 15) to the societal setting (vv. 17-21). Then using mythological imagery, he reminds his listeners of the omnipotence before which they are insignificant (v. 22; cf. 3:4-5; 10:21-22). Great nations have been formed by him and are dependent upon divine favor for continued prosperity. Leaders are successful only at his bidding and can be reduced to shambles with no recourse if this is his desire.

As Job describes conditions that all know to be true, he makes no mention of the cause of such reversal of fortune. He never questions God's abilities. What he denounces is the paradigm of strict retribution posed as the only explanation for what has occurred. Either this worldview is correct and God is at fault, or the theory is significantly deficient as a description of the meaning of events.

APPEAL WILL BE MADE TO GOD
Job 13:1-19

13 "Lo my eye has seen all this,
  my ear has heard and understood it.

2What you know, I also know;
  I am not inferior to you.
3But I would speak to the Almighty,
  and I desire to argue my case with God.
4As for you, you whitewash with lies;
  worthless physicians are you all.
5Oh that you would keep silent,
  and it would be your wisdom!
6Hear now my reasoning,
  and listen to the pleadings of my lips.
7Will you speak falsely for God,
  and speak deceitfully for him?
8Will you show partiality toward him,
  will you plead the case for God?
9Will it be well with you when he searches you out?
  Or can you deceive him, as one deceives a man?
10He will surely rebuke you
  if in secret you show partiality.
11Will not his majesty terrify you,
  and the dread of him fall upon you?
12Your maxims are proverbs of ashes,
  your defenses are defenses of clay.
13"Let me have silence, and I will speak,
  and let come on me what may.
14I will take my flesh in my teeth,
  and put my life in my hand.
15Behold, he will slay me; I have no hope?
  yet I will defend my ways to his face.
16This will be my salvation,
  that a godless man shall not come before him.
17Listen carefully to my words,
  and let my declaration be in your ears.
18Behold, I have prepared my case;
  I know that I shall be vindicated.
19Who is there that will contend with me?
  For then I would be silent and die.

The first two verses of the chapter are a continuation of
the previous theme. Job's own observation of life has shown

him the truth of what he has claimed. He has perceived it
and understood its meaning. In words identical with those
of chapter 12 (v. 3b) he insists that he is as wise as they are
and that his words should be heeded.

He has listened to them long enough. They have consistently refused to credit Job with proof of the accuracy of his
point of view. They have preferred empty rhetoric rather
than truth, and they have misrepresented God. Such flimsy
polemic weakens the strength of their case for it does not
take into account any flexibility in worldview and it confines God to a limited and predestined manner of activity.
For this reason, Job will take his case to the divine tribunal.

In his earlier retorts, he criticized the empty advice of his
companions as well as their insensitivity toward him. Now
he denounces them as worthless and deceitful. If they were
authentic champions of truth they would be more effective
in their defense of God. He reproaches them with his challenging interrogation. He threatens them with the bane of
the same theory that they are advancing. Their representation of God is in error and they will suffer the consequences
of their folly. He concludes his tirade with a proverb describing the futility of their words. They have no substance
and they have no future.

There is no other avenue open to Job but to summon God
to court. He realizes the risk that he runs in doing this, but
he trusts in his own integrity. It is the one certainty that he
will not relinquish. Just as his initial period of mourning
demanded their silence, so does this decision. There is
nothing they can say that will deter him nor can they resolve
the dispute. Job is ready for his lawsuit. He is confident of
vindication (v. 18). Verse 19a is the opening formula of the
plaintiff in a suit. If God refuses him a hearing he is lost and
there is nothing left for him but death.

JOB'S APPEAL TO GOD
Job 13:20-28

> [20]Only grant two things to me,
>   then I will not hide myself from thy face:

21withdraw thy hand far from me,
and let not dread of thee terrify me.
22Then call, and I will answer;
or let me speak, and do thou reply to me.
23How many are my iniquities and my sins?
Make me know my transgression and my sin.
24Why dost thou hide thy face,
and count me as they enemy?
25Wilt thou frighten a driven leaf
and pursue dry chaff?
26For thou writest bitter things against me,
and makest me inherit the inquities of my youth.
27Thou puttest my feet in the stocks,
and watchest all my paths;
thou settest a bound to the soles of my feet.
28Man wastes away like a rotten thing,
like a garment that is moth eaten.

At last Job turns to God. In addition to demanding that God come to court with him, Job begs for two favors. He asks to be released from the stranglehold that God has on him and he begs for relief from the intimidation that is incapacitating him. His yearning to meet God in court is so great that he is willing to be the defendant rather than the plaintiff if this will guarantee a hearing. If God would see fit to name his transgressions Job would accept the allegation and any just sentence that would be passed. What he can no longer tolerate is silence from God. He storms the heavens with appeals and denunciations and to no avial. If only God would answer! As it is, Job remains locked in his agony, a slave to his pain with no recourse and no relief in sight.

THE FUTILITY OF LIFE
Job 14:1-6

14 "Man that is born of a woman is of few days, and full of trouble.
2He comes forth like a flower, and withers;
he flees like a shadow, and continues not.

> ³And dost thou open thy eyes upon such a one
>   and bring him into judgment with thee?
> ⁴Who can bring a clean thing out of an unclean?
>   There is not one.
> ⁵Since his days are determined,
>   and the number of his months is with thee,
>   and thou hast appointed his bounds
>   that he cannot pass,
> ⁶look away from him and desist,
>   that he may enjoy, like a hireling, his day.

Verse 28 of the preceding chapter probably belongs to this section as well. Job laments the conditions of human existence. He has moved from a consideration of his personal plight to a reflection on the common state of all. He struggled with this same idea earlier (cf. 7:1-6). Then the emphasis was on the misery that all must suffer during a brief life span. Here the focus is more on the brevity than on the affliction. He takes examples from nature to describe the transitoriness of mortal life. Why does God take such unfair advantage of this fleeting creature? Since it is God who has determined the swift course of life, he should at least allow for a bit of relative peace. Is it perhaps that God disdains humankind, agreeing with Eliphaz that men and women are essentially evil with few redeeming qualities (cf. 4:17)? Job cannot believe this and dismisses the idea. Yet again he pleads for deliverance, asking for no more than the rights assured a hired laborer. After performing his assigned task he can delight in rest from his drudgery.

DISCOURSE ON HOPE
Job 14:7-22

> ⁷"For there is hope for a tree,
>   if it be cut down, that it will sprout again,
>   and that its shoots will not cease.
> ⁸Though its root grow old in the earth,
>   and its stump die in the ground,

⁹yet at the scent of water it will bud
   and put forth branches like a young plant.
¹⁰But man dies, and is laid low;
   man breathes his last, and where is he?
¹¹As waters fail from a lake,
   and a river wastes away and dries up,
¹²so man lies down and rises not again;
   till the heavens are no more he will not awake,
   or be roused out of his sleep.
¹³Oh that thou wouldest hide me in Sheol,
   that thou wouldest conceal me until thy wrath be past,
   that thou wouldest appoint me a set time and
   remember me!
¹⁴If a man die, shall he live again?
   All the days of my service I would wait,
   till my release should come.
¹⁵Thou wouldest call, and I would answer thee;
   thou wouldest long for the work of thy hands.
¹⁶For then thou wouldest number my steps,
   thou wouldest not keep watch over my sin;
¹⁷my transgression would be sealed up in a bag,
   and thou wouldest cover over my iniquity.
¹⁸"But the mountain falls and crumbles away,
   and the rock is removed from its place;
¹⁹the waters wear away the stones;
   the torrents wash away the soil of the earth;
   so thou destroyest the hope of man.
²⁰Thou prevailest for ever against him,
   and he passes;
   thou changest his countenance, and
   sendest him away.
²¹His sons come to honor, and he does not know it;
   they are brought low, and he perceives it not.
²²He feels only the pain of his own body,
   and he mourns only for himself."

Job turns from pondering the brevity of life to a consideration of its futility. True to the wisdom style of discernment, he probes the functioning of nature in order to learn something of the fundamental principles of reality. Cursory observation reveals that even after a tree has been felled, there is a possibility that it can revive. Water, the source of life, continues to pull it out of the shadows of decay into the light of new growth. Humans do not enjoy the prospect of a comparable restoration. When a man or woman dies, life is over. There is no hidden source of revitalization, no underground stream to promise new life. All of the living waters have been dried up.

At a last resort, Job longs to be delivered from his wretchedness and detained in Sheol until that time when God will vindicate him. He is not proposing some kind of resuscitation or resurrection but is expressing his hope for a hearing even if it will only take place after his death (v. 15a; cf. 13:22a). Job knows that his request is within God's power to fulfill. Not doubting the all-encompassing and unlimited supremacy of God, he wonders about divine willingness. The request is extraordinary, but so is the situation. He has been forced to his limits and so he is suggesting the preposterous. Even this prospect offers little hope because the most formidable examples of stability fall to pieces. If the mighty mountains are vulnerable, solid rock can be displaced and impenetrable stone can erode, should one wonder at the deterioration of human hope which is fragile by nature? Creation has some very painful lessons to teach. Those very elements to which one looks for life also possess destructive power and have often caused ruin and disaster. Without betraying the wisdom school's method of understanding, one can justifiably infer that the same twofold manner of operation is characteristic of the God that Job has come to know. In the past Job had been beneficiary of divine benevolence. Now he is the victim of God's malevolent shadow side. It is understandable that human hope would crumble when the same God who had created and sustained the person turns out to be a mortal enemy.

The first cycle of speeches ends on a note of despair. It has become clear that the companions of Job all represent the same traditional view of retribution pushed to its rigid extreme. Their conception of the world and of human life within it is inflexible as is their conception of God. Job is a man steeped in the same tradition, with the identical view of the universe, but whose present state of life defies explanation. Refusing to deny the truth of his integrity, how can he remain committed to his tradition and accept the conventional worldview? None of his counselors will consider his righteousness, hence they all refuse to modify their position. Steadfast to their theory of harmony and determinism, they vilify humankind. The order of the universe is not suspect, the human person is. No wonder that the theological debate is at an impasse. The rudimentary anthropological outlooks are radically opposed to each other. The altercation is doomed to failure from the start.

CHAPTER THREE
SECOND AND THIRD CYCLES
OF SPEECHES

The first cycle of speeches has substantially disclosed the theological position of those men who came to offer assistance and counsel to Job. They have couched their advice in words that reveal self-righteous and patronizing attitudes as well as anger and disdain rather than solace and understanding. One, Eliphaz, has also been perfectly clear about the anthropological presuppositions from which these theological admonitions flow. Job too has described his dilemma in unmistakable terms, insisting upon the irreconcilability of his predicament with the traditional answers given as explanation. The identical arguments continue throughout the second and third cycles of speeches with very little divergence on either side. If there is a change it is merely a reinforcement of the particular man's stand and a hardening in his resistance to any other point of view. This is as true of Job as it is of the others. The repetition of the arguments and the reiteration of the literary forms, style and imagery employed heighten the tension between the two sides, underscore the deadlock to which the controversy has come, and dramatize the unyielding adherence of the disputants to their respective stands. Commentary on the remaining speeches will concentrate on those features which add a new dimension or nuance to the already clearly delineated outlooks.

THE SECOND CYCLE OF SPEECHES

Eliphaz

TAUNTS AGAINST JOB
Job 15:1-16

15 Then Eliphaz the Temanite answered:
²"Should a wise man answer with windy knowledge,
and fill himself with the east wind?
³Should he argue in unprofitable talk,
or in words with which he can do no good?
⁴But you are doing away with the fear of God,
and hindering meditation before God.
⁵For your iniquity teaches your mouth,
and you choose the tongue of the crafty.
⁶Your own mouth condemns you, and not I;
your own lips testify against you.
⁷"Are you the first man that was born?
Or were you brought forth before the hills?
⁸Have you listened in the council of God?
And do you limit wisdom to your self?
⁹What do you know that we do not know?
What do you understand that is not clear to us?
¹⁰Both the gray-haired and the aged are among us,
older than your father.
¹¹Are the consolations of God too small for you,
or the word that deals gently with you?
¹²Why does your heart carry you away,
and why do your eyes flash,
¹³that you turn your spirit against God,
and let such words go out of your mouth?
¹⁴What is man, that he can be clean?
Or he that is born of a woman, that he can be righteous?

> ¹⁵Behold, God puts no trust in his holy ones,
>   and the heavens are not clean in his sight;
> ¹⁶how much less one who is abominable and corrupt,
>   a man who drinks iniquity like water!

The first part of Eliphaz's second discourse contains three distinct insulting criticisms (vv. 2-6; 7-10; 11-13) and a second anthropological axiom that asserts inherent human culpability (vv. 14-16). Gone are his courteous manner and conciliatory tone. Mockery and derision mark the style of this representative of the religious traditions of the people. He counters Job's claim of having gained incontrovertible insights contrary to conventional dicta by characterizing his protestations as empty wind that can effect no good. Job is not only a fool but he is also a perverter of righteousness. As has been pointed out several times, the perfect sage was one who feared the Lord. Here Job is accused of doing away with that fear. His arrogant obstinancy is evidence of this attitude. *It* condemns him, Eliphaz does not. Job has indeed admitted to former failures (cf. 13:26). He has also maintained, however, that even though innocent, he would be compelled by God to admit guilt. Eliphaz is not referring to this particular aspect of the dispute. He means, rather, that if Job were truly innocent of any evil that might have precipitated his present affliction, his refusal to accept the situation and his persistance in reproaching God is itself reprehensible. He is condemned by his very assertions of innocence. Thus Eliphaz scorns Job's supposed wisdom.

The taunt found in verses 7 and 8 refers to the theme of the 'First Human'. The allusion is to a primordial person not merely to the firstborn of the race. The ancients believed that this primeval being was the crown of wisdom and perfection, beloved of God, present at creation (cf. Prov 8:25), and had access to the council of God. The tradition that was common among the cultures of the time pictured this first and wisest person as superhuman with a unique relationship with the deity. From Eliphaz's perspective, by refusing to be satisfied with human understanding and common experience from which it was derived, Job is implying that he has superior wisdom, the source of which is beyond the realm of human endeavor. He deserves to be reproached for such an insinuation.

It is clear from verses 9 and 10 that the authoritative trustees of the wisdom of the people were the sages. Job has repeatedly rejected their wisdom and claimed to have something of which they are ignorant. The likelihood of his being the primordial sage has already been discounted, his haughtiness makes his deviant claims untenable, and Eliphaz becomes adamant in his own sense of superiority. While it may seem that this is merely a criticism of Job's lack of respect for the wisdom of the elders, it is a far more significant point in the argument of the book. The elders represent the tested and trustworthy store of learning and knowledge of the entire people. To challenge this wisdom is to question the basic framework of social mores. This is what Job is doing and, from the perspective of the guardians of society, he deserves to be condemned. In fact, not to condemn him is to endanger the security of the prevailing conventions.

The final taunting questions denounce Job for his impatience and the impudence that has been unleashed because of it. His dissatisfaction with God's management of the world and in particular with Job's own life has transformed him from a docile man of faith (cf. 1:21; 2:10) to an audacious rebel intent on authenticating his innocence regardless of the havoc wreaked in the process.

Eliphaz caps his reproach of Job with a second poetic statement which reveals his anthropological understanding. Identical in form and meaning to 4:17-19, verses 14-16 restate the negative view of humankind that underlies the admonitions of the principal spokesperson of the tradition (cf. pp. 47-49 above). The differences in the imagery of the two passages often reflect the specific context of the individual unit. Here Eliphaz uses the expression "born of a woman" to counter any suggestion of 'First Human' pretensions. Job is reminded that he is merely human, "born of a woman" like everyone else and not "the first man that was born. . . before the hills" (v. 7).

The assertions in verse 16 are moral in character. There is no reference to the perishability of humans as was the case in 4:19. Words like *abominable, corrupt, iniquity* emphasize the moral reprehensibility of humankind. Sating oneself with wickedness seems as natural as drinking water. Eliphaz is becoming more condemnatory as his argument with Job becomes more futile.

THE WICKED WILL PERISH
Job 15:17-35

> 17"I will show you, hear me;
>   and what I have seen I will declare
> 18(what wise men have told,
>   and their fathers have not hidden,
> 19to whom alone the land was given,
>   and no stranger passed among them).
> 20The wicked man writhes in pain all his days,
>   through all the years that are laid up for the ruthless.
> 21Terrifying sounds are in his ears;
>   in prosperity the destroyer will come upon him.
> 22He does not believe that he will return out of darkness,
>   and he is destined for the sword.
> 23He wanders abroad for bread, saying,
>   'Where is it?'
>   He knows that a day of darkness is
>   ready at his hand;
> 24distress and anguish terrify him;
>   they prevail against him, like a king
>   prepared for battle.
> 25Because he has stretched forth his hand against God,
>   and bids defiance to the Almighty,
> 26running stubbornly against him
>   with a thick-bossed shield;
> 27because he has covered his face with is fat,
>   and gathered fat upon his loins,

²⁸and has lived in desolate cities,
    in houses which no man should inhabit,
    which were destined to become heaps of ruins;
²⁹he will not be rich, and his wealth will not endure,
    nor will he strike root in the earth;
³⁰he will not escape from darkness;
    the flame will dry up his shoots,
    and his blossom will be swept
    away by the wind.
³¹Let him not trust in emptiness, deceiving himself;
    for emptiness will be his recompense.
³²It will be paid in full before his time,
    and his branch will not be green.
³³He will shake off his unripe grape, like the vine,
    and cast off his blossom, like the olive tree.
³⁴For the company of the godless is barren,
    and the fire consumes the tents of bribery.
³⁵They conceive mischief and bring forth evil
    and their heart prepares deceit."

The remainder of the chapter is taken up with one of Eliphaz's favorite themes, the ultimate fate of the wicked. Before he begins he reminds Job of the source of his knowledge. It came to him from a higher realm through the vehicle of a dream (cf. 4:12-16). The content of his doctrine is a distillation of the tradition of the ancients which is now taught by the sages. With all of this authority behind the teaching, how can Job presume to question its validity and universality?

What is the lot of the wicked? Suffering and pain. Eliphaz is not so naive as to be blind to the present prosperity of some of the evildoers. This fact is explained very simply as temporary success, hollow at best for they know that it is short-lived. Retribution will eventually come upon them and all of their wealth and good fortune will crumble before their very eyes. This ever-present realization deprives them of the enjoyment that fortune and comfort should afford them. Thus, even while they appear to be blessed, it is a blessing that oppresses as it bestows. In such a situation the wicked can hardly be envied for their affliction is in proportion to their well-being.

For Eliphaz to think that this rather strange argument would in any way influence Job is indicative of how oblivious he is of Job's perspective. In the first place, when Job was a man of means he was innocent of the kind of behavior that Eliphaz attributes to the sinner (vv. 25-28). Had he indulged in such a manner of life his current straits would be understandable. As it is, they are unintelligible, inappropriate, and unjust. This description of the fate of the wicked has no applicability in Job's case.

Secondly, to tell a man, who insists that he has been unjustly dispossessed, rejected and maligned, that the prosperious sinner is really tormented because of the fleeting nature of his good fortune is foolhardy. What possible comfort could that yield? This is but another instance of the irrelevance of the admonitions thrust upon the poor man.

Verses 29-35 specify the sufferings that will come upon the reprobate, sufferings flowing from the realization of the fears that had troubled them earlier. Sudden and furious reprisals will swoop down upon them and escape will be impossible. The fleetingness of ill-gotten gains will augment the sense of futility. The last ounce of payment will be demanded and finally collected. In his earlier speech, Eliphaz merely stated the principle of the retribution that is in store for the offender. Here, where his tone is sarcastic and his message is disheartening, he is more detailed in his characterization and increasingly unsympathetic in his assessment.

Job

INNOCENCE CRIES OUT
Job 16:1-22

16 Then Job answered:
2"I have heard many such things;
    miserable comforters are you all.

3Shall windy words have an end?
  Or what provokes you that you answer?
4I also could speak as you do,
    if you were in my place;
    I could join words together against you,
    and shake my head at you.
5I could strengthen you with my mouth,
    and the solace of my lips would
    assuage your pain.
6"If I speak, my pain is not assuaged,
    and if I forbear, how much of it leaves me?
7Surely now God has worn me out;
    he has made desolate all my company.
8And he has shriveled me up,
    which is a witness against me;
    and my leanness has risen up against me,
    it testifies to my face.
9He has torn me in his wrath, and hated me;
    he has gnashed his teeth at me;
    my adversary sharpens his eyes against me.
10Men have gaped at me with their mouth,
    they have struck me insolently upon the cheek,
    they mass themselves together against me.
11God gives me up to the ungodly,
    and casts me into the hands of the wicked.
12I was at ease, and he broke me asunder;
    he seized me by the neck and dashed me to pieces;
    he set me up as his target,
13   his archers surround me.
    He slashes open my kidneys, and does not spare;
    he pours out my gall on the ground.
14He breaks me with breach upon breach;
    he runs upon me like a warrior.
15I have sewed sackcloth upon my skin,
    and have laid my strength in the dust.
16My face is red with weeping,
    and on my eyelids is deep darkness;
17although there is no violence in my hands,
    and my prayer is pure.

> 18"O earth, cover not my blood,
>   and let my cry find no resting place.
> 19Even now, behold, my witness is in heaven,
>   and he that vouches for me is on high.
> 20My friends scorn me;
>   my eye pours out tears to God,
> 21that he would maintain the right of man with God,
>   like that of a man with his neighbor.
> 22For when a few years have come I shall go the way
> whence I shall not return.

There is nothing for Job to do but reiterate his declaration of integrity, bemoan the injustice of his affliction, and denounce the overbearing haughtiness of his false friends. As they have become adamant in their urging for his confession of guilt and repentance for sin, so he has been transformed to a noncompliant malcontent insisting on the truth of his case. This second reply to Eliphaz lacks internal unity and progression of thought. It is composed of complaints and supplications as well as an articulation of faith in the existence of justice that may presently be hidden.

Eliphaz had accused Job of "windy knowledge" (cf 15:2) and Job throws the same charge back (v. 3). There is nothing that he has been told that he could not have offered to the very men who are now preaching to him. He too is versed in the tradition. Were he in their place and they in his, he would be the one with the treasury of counsel to offer. Then they would know how empty their words are of meaning and how abrasive their attitudes of superiority and righteousness. What should have been solace to him has become an intolerable burden.

The rest of the speech is a collage of laments, supplications and descriptions of woes and tribulations. Job is obsessed with the fury of God that has been unleashed against him. To cry out in the face of it offers no relief, but no good comes from being silent either (v. 6). God is directly responsible for the suffering which is considered the very proof of Job's sinfulness (v. 8). There is no way that he can argue otherwise. God has deprived him of the acknowledged visible signs of his innocence which are his only grounds of defense.

He suffers at the hands of God as well as at the hands of other humans. Actually, others afflict him because he has been handed over to them by the Almighty. They merely follow divine directives. Even through them it is really God who is Job's adversary. If these human agents are called "ungodly." and "wicked", what is one to think of God who orchestrates such a production?

In spite of all of this persecution Job has not resorted to violence and retaliation. It is God who has been guilty of violence, tearing at Job, gnashing his teeth (v. 9), dispatching his archers against him (v. 13). Job's reaction has been one of mourning (vv. 15-18). Once again he casts himself in the role of the innocent sufferer and God in the role of the oppressor who has taken advantage of his unparalled superiority.

In the face of all of the apparent injustice, Job clings tenaciously to a belief in ultimate vindication. Blood that has been wrongfully shed cried out to heaven for vengeance. If the grievance is not rectified the earth itself will suffer the punishment for innocent bloodshed. He may not see the day of vindication, but he does not cease trusting that there will be such a day. He has begged for an arbitrator who would act impartially (cf. 9:33). Here (v. 19) he speaks with confidence of one who is even now a witness for his defense. The problem of identification is the same here as it was in 9:33 (cf. pp. 72-73). Both passages presume a court scene where Job longs that judgment be passed in his favor. It seems significant that as his situation appears more and more hopeless, his attitude toward ultimate vindication becomes more optimistic. Earlier he did not seem to believe that there was an umpire who could decide for him. Here he is confident that there is one who can speak in his defense. Is this witness God? If so, then God testifies against God and is adversary, witness and judge at the same time. But if not God, who else has the stature and authority to exert the necessary pressure on the unjust harasser of the defenseless?

The chapter ends with a reflection on the brevity of life and mindfulness of the finality that death brings. While alive, Job can still cry out for reinstatement, the hope of which he has really never relinquished. After he dies who will act on his behalf? Who will guarantee that he will be exonerated? If his own efforts appear in vain, no one else's will be any more effective. This realization contributes to the urgency of his plea.

NEITHER LIFE NOR DEATH OFFERS HOPE
Job 17:1-16

17 My spirit is broken, my days are extinct,
the grave is ready for me.
²Surely there are mockers about me,
and my eye dwells on their provocation.
³"Lay down a pledge for me with thyself;
who is there that will give surety for me?
⁴Since thou hast closed their minds to understanding,
therefore thou wilt not let them triumph.
⁵He who informs against his friends to
get a share of their property,
the eyes of his children will fail.
⁶"He has made me a byword of the peoples,
and I am one before whom men spit.
⁷My eye has grown dim from grief,
and all my members are like a shadow.
⁸Upright men are appalled at this,
and the innocent stirs himself up
against the godless.
⁹Yet the righteous holds to his way,
and he that has clean hands grows stronger and
stronger.
¹⁰But you, come on again, all of you,
and I shall not find a wise man among you.
¹¹My days are past, my plans are broken off,
the desires of my heart.
¹²They make night into day;
'The light,' they say, 'is near to the darkness.'

¹³If I look for Sheol as my house,
  if I spread my couch in darkness,
¹⁴if I say to the pit, 'You are my father,'
  and to the worm, 'My mother,' or 'My sister,'
¹⁵where then is my hope?
  Who will see my hope?
¹⁶Will it go down to the bars of Sheol?
  Shall we descend together into the dust?"

The first two verses of this chapter are a continuation of
the theme of the previous chapter. Death, which earlier was
viewed as the only possible deliverance from misery, now is
considered the cessation of life and of any hope of restoration or vindication that might still be forthcoming. This
difference of perspective explains why Job both longs for
and dreads death.

Once again Job turns his supplication to God (vv. 3-5).
Earlier in this speech (cf. 16:19) he confessed faith in a
witness in heaven who would be an advocate for him. Here
he implores God himself to supply the legal bond that is
demanded in this judicial case. The irony of the situation is
obvious. Job is initiating a case against God and yet Job is
the one whose innocence is questioned. He has asked for a
witness in heaven and it would seem that the only witness
available is God, the defendant who will scarcely testify
against himself. Now the plaintiff is called upon to provide
surety and the only source open to him is the very one he has
accused of injustice. It is no wonder that Job is utterly
frustrated. He is absolutely vulnerable and completely
dependent upon his adversary for a fair trial. The wonder is
that he has not simply abandoned all hope of achieving a
just resolution of his plight. Why does he persevere in his
hope? What is it that prevents him from despairing of the
existence of a righteous deity? The God whom he continues
to trust is the same one who has plunged him into this sea of
distress and has barred others from coming to his rescue.
Why does he persist?

Job is deeply grieved by the faithlessness of those who

were once thought to be friends and who should have remained at his side, steadfast in their loyalty (v. 5). It appears that everyone concludes to his guilt and treats him accordingly. The disdain that he experiences only compounds his already unbearable sufferings. In former times he had enjoyed the esteem of the righteous. Now he is the object of their contempt.

Job concludes his response by considering the various ways that people respond to distress. The righteous are appalled by it and react against the sufferer who is obviously responsible for it. Turning away from it as they do serves to strengthen them in their own righteousness (vv. 8-9). Friends and companions appear to abandon the sufferer. In Job's case, his companions lack sympathy and offer hollow platitudes (v. 10). As for Job himself, his affliction has brought him to the limits of hope and the brink of despair. He has done what he could to correct this miscarriage of justice. Not death nor Sheol nor the pit offer any glimmer of hope. This reply ends on a very bitter note.

Bildad

THE FATE OF THE WICKED
Job 18:1-21

> **18** Then Bildad the Shuhite answered:
> 2"How long will you hunt for words?
>   Consider, and then we will speak.
> 3Why are we counted as cattle?
>   Why are we stupid in your sight?
> 4You who tear yourself in your anger,
>   shall the earth be forsaken for you,
>   or the rock be removed out of its place?
> 5"Yea, the light of the wicked is put out,
>   and the flame of his fire does not shine.
> 6The light is dark in his tent,
>   and his lamp above him is put out.

⁷His strong steps are shortened
and his own schemes throw him down.
⁸For he is cast into a net by his own feet,
and he walks on a pitfall.
⁹A trap seizes him by the heel,
a snare lays hold of him.
¹⁰A rope is hid for him in the ground,
a trap for him in the path.
¹¹Terrors frighten him on every side,
and chase him at his heels.
¹²His strength is hunger-bitten,
and calamity is ready for his stumbling.
¹³By disease his skin is consumed,
the first-born of death consumes his limbs.
¹⁴He is torn from the tent in which he trusted,
and is brought to the king of terrors.
¹⁵In his tent dwells that which is none of his;
brimstone is scattered upon his habitation.
¹⁶His roots dry up beneath,
and his branches wither above.
¹⁷His memory perishes from the earth,
and he has no name in the street.
¹⁸He is thrust from light into darkness,
and driven out of the world.
¹⁹He has no offspring or descendant
among his people,
and no survivor where he used to live.
²⁰They of the west are appalled at his day,
and horror seizes them of the east.
²¹Surely such are the dwellings of the ungodly,
such is the place of him who knows not God."

Bildad's contempt for Job mounts as the dialogues progress. Like his first discourse which is predominantly accusatory in tone and lacking in encouragement, the present speech is devoid of any comfort or admonition. It appears that Bildad is not only convinced of Job's iniquity but offers nothing in the form of hope for reconciliation and reinstatement. He opens this tirade as he did the previous one, with a scornful rebuke of Job's personal defense (vv. 2-4). In his eyes Job is insolent in his refusal to acquiesce to traditional teaching and guidance and arrogant in presuming that his understanding is superior to one that has weathered the storm of time.

Job argues that the orders within the universe have been reversed or disrupted. He claims that chaos reigns and that justice is exercised arbitrarily. Bildad counters this allegation by ridiculing Job's demands. The reordering that this tormented man is clamoring for is, in reality, the upheaval in nature that he claims has already taken place. Because his world is chaotic, he would have all of nature rearranged so that it meet his design. There is no reasoning with this kind of thinking and so Bildad launches into a cataloging of the consequences of living an evil life.

Contrary to Job's insistence, there is harmony and predictable regularity in the universe. Circumstances and events are not haphazard occurrences but are the results of the unfolding effects of easily recognized causes. Compounding examples of this from the fortunes of the wicked, he sets out to illustrate the truth of what he believes.

Bildad is convinced of the inevitability of retribution. The sinner will not fare well for prosperity is the reward of the righteous alone. The incontestable principles of justice assure this. Light, the symbol of life, will be extinguished. Stumbling in darkness and being vulnerable to all of its dangers has long been regarded as an appropriate sentence for those who have spurned the light of righteousness. Sinners will surely be wrenched from the security of light and be thrust into deserved darkness where a miserable death awaits them (vv. 5-6; 18). The consequences of their misbehavior will eventually overtake the evildoers. They will be trapped in the very snares that their sins have produced (vv. 7-12). Knowing this they live in constant terror. How can one possibly envy their illusory well-being? The short-lived accomplishments of the ungodly are doomed (vv. 13-15). Their achievements will be consumed by violence. Nothing of the sinners will survive, neither descendants nor memory of their names (vv. 16-17; 19). The notion of community solidarity that was prevalent in the ancient world held that an individual shared in the fortunes of society and also effected the fortunes of the group. If one actually survived in one's descendants, to be denied offspring was to be cut off from the future and so this was viewed as the ultimate punishment.

Bildad continues his tirade by pointing to the widespread knowledge of and disdain for the misfortunes of the malefactor. There is no question in the minds of the observers as to the culpability of the wretched one. It is obvious that Bildad has been describing the misfortunes of Job for the poor man had lost his children, his fortune and his health. He is further terrified by the thought of darkness and death. Capitalizing on Job's total downfall, Bildad draws the conclusion that this personal catastrophe is just recompense which brings to light moral corruption that may have been concealed in former times. Job is surely a sinner who has finally been exposed.

Job

A LAMENT TO THOSE WHO WILL LISTEN
Job 19:1-29

19   Then Job answered:
2"How long will you torment me,
    and break me in pieces with words?
3These ten times you have cast reproach upon me;
    are you not ashamed to wrong me?
4And even if it be true that I have erred,
    my error remains with myself.
5If indeed you magnify yourselves against me,
    and make my humiliation and argument against me,
6know then that God has put me in the wrong,
    and closed his net about me.

⁷Behold, I cry out, 'Violence!' but I am not answered;
  I call aloud, but there is no justice.
⁸He has walled up my way, so that I cannot pass,
  and he has set darkness upon my paths.
⁹He has stripped from me my glory,
  and taken the crown from my head.
¹⁰He breaks me down on every side, and I am gone,
  and my hope has he pulled up like a tree.
¹¹He has kindled his wrath against me,
  and counts me as his adversary.
¹²His troops come on together;
  they have cast up siegeworks against me,
  and encamp round about my tent.
¹³"He has put my brethren far from me,
  and my acquaintances are wholly estranged from me.
¹⁴My kinsfolk and my close friends have failed me;
¹⁵ the guests in my house have forgotten me;
  my maidservants count me as a stranger;
  I have become an alien in their eyes.
¹⁶I call to my servant, but he gives me no answer;
  I must beseech him with my mouth.
¹⁷I am repulsive to my wife,
  loathsome to the sons of my own mother.
¹⁸Even young children despise me;
  when I rise they talk against me.
¹⁹All my intimate friends abhor me,
  and those whom I loved have turned against me.
²⁰My bones cleave to my skin and to my flesh,
  and I have escaped by the skin of my teeth.
²¹Have pity on me, have pity on me, O you my friends,
  for the hand of God has touched me!
²²Why do you, like God, pursue me?
  Why are you not satisfied with my flesh?
²³"Oh that my words were written!
  Oh that they were inscribed in a book!
²⁴Oh that with an iron pen and lead they were graven in
  the rock for ever!

²⁵For I know that my Redeemer lives,
and at last he will stand upon the earth;
²⁶and after my skin has been thus destroyed,
then from my flesh I shall see God,
²⁷whom I shall see on my side,
and my eyes shall behold, and not another.
My heart faints within me!
²⁸If you say, 'How we will pursue him!'
and, 'The root of the matter is found in him';
²⁹be afraid of the sword,
for wrath brings the punishment of the sword,
the you may know there is a judgment."

As Job resumes his solitary defense he borrows the introductory complaint heard from Bildad, "How long?" He accuses his companions of tormenting him with their accusations. Isn't it enough that he must endure affliction from the hand of God? Must they add to his distress with their abrasive words of condemnation? Surely they have wronged him with their false charges. Even if he is guilty of sin, and he has already admitted this, the magnitude of his punishment far outstrips the gravity or frequency of his misdeeds.

Job takes up their contention that his affliction is evidence of his guilt. He has consistently argued that his troubles are evidence of the disruption of order, and God, who is responsible for safeguarding this order, is answerable for its disintegration. Repeatedly Job has cried out for mercy and justice and understanding, but his cries have fallen on deaf ears (v. 7; cf. Jer 20:8). These sufferings have not grown out of human sinfulness. They are the results of direct intervention of a power that cannot be resisted. God not only allows trouble to fall upon him, he initiates it as well. He seems to be waging an unrelentless attack against a helpless creature (vv. 8-12). This particular argument is at the heart of the impasse between Job and his companions. All agree that trouble is caused by some kind of dissonance. But who is responsible for this dissonance? The defenders of conventional wisdom maintain that the one afflicted is chargeable.

Job refutes this and blames God for the situation. God has either succumbed to the power of an evil force or has himself inflicted unwarranted adversity on a previously favored devotee.

In addition to God's straightforward attack, he harasses Job by instigating persecution and oppression at the hands of others. Far from being a case of retaliation for past offenses, the people who have turned against Job are those who had previously enjoyed his friendship and graciousness. This makes the pain of their insincerity doubly hard to endure. The very ones who should comfort him are now in league with his adversaries. Once again Job is an innocent victim of the scorn and wrath of others. The soul-piercing cry of verse 21 has echoed and reechoed down through the ages as women and men have looked in vain for tenderness and support from those who should have remained steadfast in their commitment and friendship. His tortured appeal persists in claiming innocence and pleads with his hearers to call a halt to their own part in this travesty of justice.

Convinced that there will be no respite from God and no support or encouragement from those around him, Job makes a plea for final vindication (vv. 23-29). Let his story be permanently inscribed so that future generations will know of his plight in the face of innocence and will finally exonerate him.

Verses 25-27 are some of the most difficult of the book. There is no single interpretation of the ideas expressed. One reason for this is the variety of emendations that is proposed. Even the ancient versions differ on the arrangement of the verses. While there is general agreement on the interpretation of verse 25, the diversity of interpretations regarding when vindication will take place has caused some confusion. The best way to understand this troublesome passage is to read it within the purview of the book.

In ancient Israel a redeemer was usually a kinsman whose responsibility it was to ensure the integrity of the family and its possessions. This redeemer would reclaim what had been

lost because of bankruptcy or enslavement. Blood vengeance was another duty of the redeemer. It was just such a
liberator that Job proclaims. In spite of all of the rejection
that he experiences from every side, he tenaciously clings to
belief in a redeemer. Perseverance in holding to his inherent
integrity will not permit him to succumb to despair of all
hope. Nor has he given up on justice. It will come to pass and
without his compromising his position. The faith of this
man is so strong that he is confident that the one who will
deliver him is alive now and only waits for the right time to
act. What Job awaits is moral vindication, not necessarily
physical relief. The arbiter who would resolve the conflict
(cf. 9:33) and the witness who would speak in his behalf (cf.
16:19) were not expected to intervene with the same force as
that which this redeemer will wield. The identity of the
vindicator is as mysterious as was that of the arbiter and the
witness. Only God has the power and authority to accomplish what is desired, and yet God is the very one accused of
being responsible for Job's predicament. Such a situation
highlights the impossibility of Job's dilemma.

Because of the problems underlying the Hebrew text,
verse 26 has been translated in several ways. Some say that
without his flesh, Job will see God. Others read that with his
flesh (before death) he will see God. Still others understand
this to refer to a time after death when a risen Job, with new
flesh, will see God. A cursory reading of the text might lead
one to the erroneous conclusion that Job is looking for
vindication in some kind of afterlife. This does not coincide
with the major direction of the book. While he may have
exhausted all current avenues of thought and finds himself
bereft of any possible explanation, he does not not take the
decisive step into belief in the possibility of an afterlife as a
solution to his dilemma. At a later period within the biblical
tradition, others may take this step, but not Job and certainly not at this point.

This raises the question of Job's willingness to wait in
Sheol until God will vindicate him (cf. 14:13; 17:13-16).
Does this not presume hope in an afterlife? While some

might say yes, the position held here is that it does not. Immediately preceding the statement concerning the vindicator, Job pleaded that his story be preserved in stone that it be permanently remembered. His confidence is not in a future life but in future generations. He hopes that even though he has passed into that shadowy and empty state of Sheol, others will be informed of his plight, his innocence and his faithfulness and he will thereby be vindicated.

To suggest that the righteous will enjoy reward in an afterlife does not explain the origin of present suffering which is the crux of the struggle. The ambiguity of the present text can be explained by the absence of any conventional solution to the problem superimposed by Job's refusal to concede defeat. He will not relinquish his claim to integrity nor will he repudiate his faith in justice. This is indeed a man of immutable faith in the endurance of righteousness and a man of a resolute unwillingness to compromise in order to resolve what appears to be incomprehensible. This discourse illustrates the unyielding quality of Job's faith.

Zophar

THE DOCTRINE OF JUST PUNISHMENT
Job 20:1-29

> **20** Then Zophar the Naamathite answered:
> [2]"Therefore my thoughts answer me,
>   because of my haste within me.
> [3]I hear censure which insults me,
>   and out of my understanding a spirit answers me.
> [4]Do you not know this from of old,
>   since man was placed upon earth,
> [5]that the exulting of the wicked is short,
>   and the joy of the godless but for a moment?
> [6]Though his height mount up to the heavens,
>   and his head reach to the clouds,

⁷he will perish for ever like his own dung;
   those who have seen him will say,
   'Where is he?'
⁸He will fly away like a dream, and not be found;
   he will be chased away like a vision of the night.
⁹The eye which saw him will see him no more,
   nor will his place any more behold him.
¹⁰His children will seek the favor of the poor,
   and his hands will give back his wealth.
¹¹His bones are full of youthful vigor,
   but it will lie down with him in the dust.
¹²"Though wickedness is sweet in his mouth,
   though he hides it under his tongue,
¹³though he is loath to let it go,
   and holds it in his mouth,
¹⁴yet his food is turned in his stomach;
   it is the gall of asps within him.
¹⁵He swallows down riches and vomits them up again;
   God casts them out of his belly.
¹⁶He will suck the poison of asps;
   the tongue of a viper will kill him.
¹⁷He will not look upon the rivers,
   the streams flowing with honey and curds.
¹⁸He will give back the fruit of his toil,
   and will not swallow it down;
   from the profit of his trading
   he will get no enjoyment.
¹⁹For he has crushed and abandoned the poor,
   he has seized a house which he did not build.
²⁰"Because his greed knew no rest,
   he will not save anything in which he delights.
²¹There was nothing left after he had eaten;
   therefore his prosperity will not endure.
²²In the fulness of his sufficiency he will be in straits;
   all the force of misery will come upon him.
²³To fill his belly to the full
   God will send his fierce anger into him,
   and rain it upon him as his food.

> ²⁴He will flee from an iron weapon;
>   a bronze arrow will strike him through.
> ²⁵It is drawn forth and comes out of his body,
>   the glittering point comes out of his gall;
>   terrors come upon him.
> ²⁶Utter darkness is laid up for his treasures;
>   a fire not blown upon will devour him;
>   what is left in his tent will be consumed.
> ²⁷The heavens will reveal his iniquity,
>   and the earth will rise up against him.
> ²⁸The possessions of his house will be carried away,
>   dragged off in the day of God's wrath.
> ²⁹This is the wicked man's portion from God,
>   the heritage decreed for him by God."

The final contender adds little if anything to the dispute. Like his companions before him he introduces his reply with a taunt. (This has been the case in every instance with the exception of the first speech of Eliphaz.) The pattern demonstrates the true intentions of the companions. They have not taken Job's protestations seriously and, therefore, feel obliged to reprove him and force him to accept their perspectives and judgments. This is quite clear from Zophar's utterances.

The gist of his remarks is the sorry fate of the godless (vv. 5-11). He calls upon the authority of wisdom gleaned from the past to substantiate the validity of his doctrine. He does not concentrate on the fear of future tragedy that may consume the wicked even during good times. He admits that the happiness that others have called only apparent is not illusory but roundly enjoyed. The point made here is that the happiness lasts for only a short time and eventually hardship will snatch everything good from life.

What point could Zophar be trying to make? He insists that the well-being of sinners is only temporary. How can this console Job? It cannot be denied that one aspect of the theory of retribution is concerned with this matter. But Job's conflict is with the vexation of the innocent and more specifically with the reasons of the sufferings. More and more his demands proceed from a desire to understand the cause and to be found blameless in the sight of others. The arguments of these three men are not only devoid of comfort and enlightenment, they are also irrelevant to the major point in question. Nonetheless, Zophar proceeds with his reflections.

The use of food imagery (vv. 12-18) illustrates well the idea of inner determinism that was an important pillar in the structure of the theory of retribution. It was not so much that God acted as watchman and judge monitoring the behavior of humans, ready to punish any infraction of the law. Rather, goodness and evil were forces within behavior itself that were released in the execution of the act. These forces advanced toward the inherent fruition of the act. Therefore, even though wickedness may be sweet to the taste, it can only result in evil consequences. It is quite clear that in some cases it is easier to recognize this cause and effect relationship. Understanding this principle has enabled women and men to gain insight into some of the laws of the universe. To insist, however, that the principles that human beings have reached are applicable in every situation with absolutely no exceptions is to presume a comprehensive mastery of the laws of the universe and of the God who is its creator. The speeches of the companions of Job betray precisely this attitude.

Returning to the food imagery, Zophar gives examples of the malice practiced by these people (vv. 19-21). They have no one to blame but themselves when the evil they have perpetrated returns to wreak its vengeance on them. They will be overwhelmed by affliction within themselves (vv. 22-25) as well as from outside terrors (vv. 26-28). Zophar seems to be following Bildad in his cataloging of woes that will come up on the wicked (cf. 18:13-19) for he too highlights many of the adversities that have rained down upon Job. If it is their intention to parallel the straits of the wicked with those of Job in order to force him to capitulate, their efforts are in vain. Job may have resembled the man of this description in his wealth and accomplishments, but certainly not in his pride, misuse of power and exploitation of the helpless which are the reasons given for his downfall. These arguments lack substance and truth and are nothing but false accusations. Zophar ends his speech on the same negative note with which he began it.

Job

PROSPERITY OF THE WICKED
Job 21:1-34

21   Then Job answered:
²"Listen carefully to my words,
  and let this be your consolation.
³Bear with me, and I will speak,
  and after I have spoken, mock on.
⁴As for me, is my complaint against man?
  Why should I not be impatient?
⁵Look at me, and be appalled,
  and lay your hand upon your mouth.
⁶When I think of it I am dismayed,
  and shuddering seizes my flesh.
⁷Why do the wicked live,
  reach old age, and grow mighty in power?
⁸Their children are established in their presence,
  and their offspring before their eyes.
⁹Their houses are safe from fear,
  and no rod of God is upon them.
¹⁰Their bull breeds without fail;
  their cow calves, and does not cast her calf.
¹¹They send forth their little ones like a flock,
  and their children dance.
¹²They sing to the tambourine and the lyre,
  and rejoice to the sound of the pipe.
¹³They spend their days in prosperity,
  and in peace they go down to Sheol.

¹⁴They say to God, 'Depart from us!
  We do not desire the knowledge of thy ways.
¹⁵What is the Almighty, that we should serve him?
  And what profit do we get if we pray to him?
¹⁶Behold, is not their prosperity in their hand?
  The counsel of the wicked is far from me.
¹⁷"How often is it that the lamp of the wicked is put out?
  That their calamity comes upon them?
  That God distributes pains in his anger?
¹⁸That they are like straw before the wind,
  and like chaff that the storm carries away?
¹⁹You say, 'God stores up their iniquity for their sons.'
  Let him recompense it to themselves,
  that they may know it.
²⁰Let their own eyes see their destruction,
  and let them drink of the wrath of the Almighty.
²¹For what do they care for their houses after them,
  when the number of their months is cut off?
²²Will any teach God knowledge,
  seeing that he judges those that are on high?
²³One dies in full prosperity,
  being wholly at ease and secure,
²⁴his body full of fat
  and the marrow of his bones moist.
²⁵Another dies in bitterness of soul,
  never having tasted of good.
²⁶They lie down alike in the dust,
  and the worms cover them.
²⁷"Behold, I know your thoughts
  and your schemes to wrong me.
²⁸For you say, 'Where is the house of the prince?
  Where is the tent in which the wicked dwelt?'
²⁹Have you not asked those who travel the roads,
  and do you not accept their testimony
³⁰that the wicked man is spared in the day of calamity,
  that he is rescued in the day of wrath?
³¹Who declares his way to his face,
  and who requites him for what he has done?

> 32When he is borne to the grave,
>   watch is kept over his tomb.
> 33The clods of the valley are sweet to him;
>   all men follow after him,
>   and those who go before him are innumerable.
> 34How then will you comfort me with empty nothings?
>   There is nothing left of your answers but falsehood."

Job's final reply of the second cycle of speeches, like its counterpart of the first cycle, is a refutation of the theory put forth by his three associates. They have invoked the authoritative character of the traditional teaching to affirm the validity of their instruction. Job speaks from the certainty of personal experience. They believe that what they profess is correct; he knows the truth of which he speaks, hence his daring. He begins by justifying his persistent complaints (vv. 2-3). His argument is not with mere people who are incapable of comprehending the order of the world much less directing it. He is in a contest with the author of the universe who refuses to throw any light on the mystery that Job's troubles have produced. It is easy for them to demand that he remain silent and submissive. Life is not an enigma for them and, therefore, they are in no position to advise him.

The focus of his rebuttal is a protrayal of the good fortune and tranquil life of the wicked. All three of his critics have assured him that the prosperity of the wicked is short-lived. They die in agony and disgrace and their children are thrust into lives of hardship as a result of parental sin. Job rejects this unconditionally. Rather, their lives are lived in comparative peace surrounded by loved ones, possessions and wealth. Even death is without terror for them and they pass tranquilly into Sheol (vv. 7-13). Far from fearing the reversal of fotunes of which the companions speak, they are so secure in their prosperity that they see no need to serve God. They do not consider wealth as God's reward for righteous living but rather as the fruits of their own toil, be it honest or unlawful.

Having described the lives of sinners in this way, Job

challenges the case put forward by the others. How often have they seen their claims of retributive punishment come to pass? There is no certain calamity for the wicked (vv. 17-18). As for the belief that the sins of one generation are visited upon the next (vv. 19-21), what affliction does this cause the sinner? The post-exilic understanding of retribution placed responsibility on the shoulders of the individual concerned and not on the descendants or other family members. Justice should be meted out to the guilty ones. This argument is ineffectual.

There can be no denial, death does not have favorites. All alike lie down in the dust. However, there appears to be gross inequity during the life that precedes death. When one scours the wisdom tradition in an effort to discover an explanation for this state of affairs, one is left without an answer. Job is confronted with the mysteries of human destiny and acknowledges his inability to discover their secrets. It will take an experience of the deity for him to stand in awe of this incomprehensible wonder. For now he is left with a sense of powerlessness as he grapples with that which is unfathomable.

The burden of the reproaches of Job's colleagues had been an insistence on the hardships in store for the godless. They are arguing from principles while Job challenges them to look honestly at experience. Ask anyone who has observed life. They will attest to the good fortune as well as the good reputation of the wicked. There is no assurance of final recompense. If one hopes to savor vindication in this way, disappointment looms on the horizon. Job rejects the views of these companions because they guarantee a final punishment that does not come about. Even if it did, what comfort could that afford a man who claims that his affliction is undeserved? How does that shed light on the puzzle of innocent suffering, which is Job's dilemma? A second cycle of speeches ends without one step being taken toward a reconciliation or solution.

THIRD CYCLE OF SPEECHES

Many biblical scholars agree that it is a misnomer to refer to chapters 22-27 as a cycle in the full sense of that word. The definite interchange of speeches between Job and his visitors that made up the earlier chapters is absent here. Bildad's discourse is abbreviated and Zophar's is missing. Job's replies are inordinately long and often contain material that is at variance with his basic stance. Scholars have reconstructed some of the third cycle and explained the remaining discrepancies as the result of the loss of some of the material. While this commentary will follow the arrangement of the *Revised Standard Version* translation and deal with the disparities as they appear in the text, it might be useful to transpose some of these discrepancies and provide an alternate arrangement of texts.

There is general agreement that Chapters 22 and 23 pose no major problems. Although several scholars suggest a reordering of verses in Chapter 24, most hold that, with the exception of verses 18-25, it is a Joban reply. Bildad's third speech is comprised of 25:1-6 and 26:5-14 and is followed by Job's response in 26:1-4 and 27:1-10. What remains, 27:11-23 and 24:18-25, is considered the third speech of Zophar. If scholars are correct in believing that the present text is out of order then this textual disarray is ancient, for the order that has come down to us is in general agreement with a version of the book found at Qumran and dated about the second century B.C.E. (Before the Common Era).

Eliphaz

THE FINAL ASSAULT
Job 22:1-14

> **22** Then Eliphaz the Temanite answered:
> ²"Can a man be profitable to God?
>   Surely he who is wise is profitable to himself.

³Is it any pleasure to the Almighty if you are righteous,

or is it gain to him if you make your ways blameless?

⁴Is it for your fear of him that he reproves you, and enters into judgment with you?

⁵Is not your wickedness great? There is no end to your iniquities.

⁶For you have exacted pledges of your brothers for nothing,

and stripped the naked of their clothing.

⁷You have given no water to the weary to drink, and you have withheld bread from the hungry.

⁸The man with power possessed the land, and the favored man dwelt in it.

⁹You have sent widows away empty, and the arms of the fatherless were crushed.

¹⁰Therefore snares are round about you, and sudden terror overwhelms you;

¹¹your light is darkened, so that you cannot see, and flood of water covers you.

¹²"Is not God high in the heavens? See the highest stars, how lofty they are!

¹³Therefore you say, 'what does God know? Can he judge through the deep darkness?

¹⁴Thick clouds enwrap him, so that he does not see,

and he walks on the vault of heaven.'

The final speech of Eliphaz shows that the man has not moved one inch from the position that he held at the beginning of his dialogues with Job. He has heard all of the claims of Job as well as his defenses and has remained unconvinced of Job's virtue and of the scandal of his predicament. Rather, he has alternated from respectful admonition to outright accusation and condemnation. His counsel has turned to derision and his elucidation of the circumstances of Job's situation is really an indictment of guilt. In spite of the extremely pessimistic view of humankind that he entertains, this visitor does conclude his conversation with the tormented man on a note of hope. He may be deaf to Job's cries and may completely mistake the reasons for his agony, but he does encourage Job to seek what is believed to be the only course of action that will lead to reconciliation and peace.

Eliphaz's first argument seems rather strange. He insists that God derives no benefit from human righteousness. One wonders whether this is a polemic against something that Job has said or implied, or a last ditch effort to use every scrap of doctrine in a futile attempt to force Job to recant. Such an argument can be used against the traditional position as well. If God is impervious to human righteousness, He is impervious as well to malice and sinfulness. Unaffected by any kind of behavior, the deity would be concerned with neither reward nor punishment. Were this the case Job could not accuse God of afflicting him with unmerited chastisement, but then neither could those around him defend God's right to punish.

Having said this, Eliphaz launches into his concluding attack on Job's integrity. His allegations all presume that Job was a man of means and guilty of exploiting his position of power and influence by withholding the essentials of life from the vulnerable people within society who rightfully turned to him for assistance (vv. 6-9). The authentically righteous person was blameless and upright (cf. 1:1; 8; 2:3) acting as protector and benefactor of the helpless. Job is charged with behaving in just the opposite manner, exploiting rather than protecting, taking or holding back rather than giving. The tribulations that have come upon him are the just deserts of his insensitivity toward and callous treatment of others (vv. 10-11). Eliphaz persists in his verdict. Job's dire straits are evidence of his gross misconduct. There can be no other explanation for his sorry state.

The loftiness of God, admitted by all, has been advanced as a reason for believing either that God has preeminent control over the universe or that his distance precludes direct involvement or interest in its operations. Eliphaz erroneously asserts that Job espouses the second view (vv. 13-14). This would explain Job's former life lived in disregard of the most high God who would eventually take him to task for his wrongdoing, as well as his present false contention that God is disinterested in executing justice. Far from denying God's involvement in the world, Job asserts that it is this ever-scrutizing eye of God that refuses to grant him any semblance of respite. Job does not question whether or not God *can* judge from afar, but the manner and equity of God's judging. Therefore, this assertion is false and adds nothing to the allegations.

THE TWO WAYS
Job 22:15-30

> ¹⁵Will you keep to the old way
>   which wicked men have trod?
> ¹⁶They were snatched away before their time;
>   their foundation was washed away.
> ¹⁷They said to God, 'Depart from us,'
>   and 'What can the Almighty do to us?'
> ¹⁸Yet he filled their houses with good things—
>   but the counsel of the wicked is far from me.
> ¹⁹The righteous see it and are glad;
>   the innocent laugh them to scorn,
> ²⁰saying, 'Surely our adversaries are cut off,
>   and what they left the fire has consumed.'
> ²¹"Agree with God, and be at peace;
>   thereby good will come to you.
> ²²Receive instruction from his mouth,
>   and lay up his words in your heart.
> ²³If you return to the Almighty and humble yourself,
>   if you remove unrighteousness far from your tents,
> ²⁴if you lay gold in the dust,
>   and gold of Ophir among the stones
>   of the torrent bed,

[25]and if the Almighty is your gold,
and your precious silver;
[26]then you will delight yourself in the Almighty,
and lift up your face to God.
[27]You will make your prayer to him,
and he will hear you;
and you will pay your vows.
[28]You will decide on a matter, and it will
be established for you,
and light will shine on your ways.
[29]For God abases the proud,
but he saves the lowly.
[30]He delivers the innocent man;
you will be delivered through the cleanness of your
hands."

After reiterating the contrast between the way of the wicked and the way of the just, Eliphaz exhorts Job to choose the latter (vv. 15-30). Adherence to God will guarantee a life of peace; repentance will be rewarded. This is the classical admonition of the wisdom tradition put forward by Eliphaz from the beginning to the end of his debate. He had not deviated from this stand. In fact, he appears unable to appreciate that an admission of human limitation would provide an invitation to new depths of faith and trust. A world view that does not make room for realities beyond human comprehension is narrow and confining and denies the governance of a transcendent God of mystery. Job may have reached only the frontiers of this experience, but Eliphaz, because of his self-righteousness, cannot even envision its possibility. A regretable state of affairs has come to pass when one disregards the very experience from which wisdom is gleaned in favor of static principles of interpretation. Practical knowledge ceases to be of any value when it clashes with formulaic statements and life is defined and determined by set patterns of behavior and consequences. The well regulated and circumscribed view of life and the universe that characterizes the moralizing of Eliphaz impedes any serious communication with one who has been hurled into a maelstrom of confusion and upheaval. The dialogue between Eliphaz and Job has brought them to a cul-de-sac.

Job

A TRIAL FOR ACQUITTAL
Job 23:1-7

> **23**   Then Job answered:
> 2"Today also my complaint is bitter,
>   his hand is heavy in spite of my groaning.
> 3Oh, that I knew where I might find him,
>   that I might come even to his seat!
> 4I would lay my case before him
>   and fill my mouth with arguments.
> 5I would learn what he would answer me,
>   and understand what he would say to me.
> 6Would he contend with me in the
>   greatness of his power?
>   No; he would give heed to me.
> 7There an upright man could reason with him,
>   and I should be acquitted for ever
>   by my judge.

It is truly remarkable that Job perseveres in his faith in the ultimate justice of God. He seems to have exhausted every argument in his own defense, failing dismally in his attempts to persuade his companions of his innocence. Yet he remains steadfast in his certainty of acquittal if only he could meet God in court. Although he admits bitterness (v. 2a) he has not despaired of final vindication. Never deviating from his initial claim that God is the cause of his affliction (v. 2b), he does not believe that the divine power will be pitted against him forever nor that it will crush him at the time of his trial (v. 6). Unlike his accusers, Job is not willing to compromise what he knows to be true in order to uphold the traditional world view. Nor will he relinquish his trust in a God whom his religious tradition reveres as wise and just. When the experience of life and the tenets of religion appear to be in serious conflict, Job does not repudiate one in favor of the other but struggles with the tension of the unresolved paradox and looks to God for some kind of response.

HUMAN HELPLESSNESS
Job 23:8-17

8"Behold, I go forward, but he is not there;
  and backward, but I cannot perceive him;
9on the left hand I seek him, but I
  cannot behold him;
  I turn to the right hand, but I cannot see him.
10But he knows the way that I take;
  when he has tried me, I shall come forth as gold.
11My foot has held fast to his steps;
  I have kept his way and have not turned aside.
12I have not departed from the commandment of his lips;
  I have treasured in my bosom the
  words of his mouth.
13But he is unchangeable and who can turn him?
  What he desires, that he does.
14For he will complete what he appoints for me;
  and many such things are in his mind.
15Therefore I am terrified at his presence;
  when I consider, I am in dread of him.
16God has made my heart faint;
  the Almighty has terrified me;
17for I am hemmed in by darkness,
  and thick darkness covers my face.

Throughout the complaints of God it has been increasingly clear that the suffering that Job has encountered because of calamity or personal misfortune is overshadowed by the dark cloud of its incomprehensibility. He alternates between concluding that he is a victim of injustice and searching desperately for some other explanation for the dilemma. He clings tenaciously to the belief that God is in control but he feels that he is dangling in mid air because of God's inaccessibility. He is confident that could he but reach God, all things would be put in right order. It seems, however, that God is beyond Job's reach and is unwilling to bridge the chasm that yawns between them.

Job has consistently questioned the reason for his misfortune. In verses 10-12 he recognizes, if only for a brief moment, the true character of his plight. He is being tested. He may not know the circumstances of the trial, but he admits that it is a trial and he knows that he will meet the challenge and emerge faithful and proven. The technical word *way* is used here. Job chooses the right *way,* which is the way of the just. Thus he identified himself with the truly wise.

Confessing all of this does not in any way change the situation and Job knows this. God is free and will do what he wants (vv. 13-14). Again, without pursuing this point, Job has touched on a central issue of the book, the freedom of God. From Job's perspective, this freedom seems to be exercised haphazardly, i.e., with little or no regard for the established orders. The truth of the matter is, however, that the all-wise and all-powerful God is not bound to rules and regulations devised by human beings in their attempt to understand the workings of the universe. God is indeed free, but with a freedom that transcends rather than violates the human point of view. Because Job cannot appreciate the terms of this freedom, he is terrified by it. His ordered world has been disrupted. The darkness of chaos holds sway.

THE INDIFFERENCE OF GOD
Job 24:1-17

> **24**   "Why are not times of judgment
> kept by the Almighty,
> and why do those who know him never see his days?

²Men remove landmarks;
  they seize flocks and pasture them.
³They drive away the ass of the fatherless;
they take the widow's ox for a pledge.
⁴They thrust the poor off the road;
  the poor of the earth all hide themselves.
⁵Behold, like wild asses in the desert
  they go forth to their toil,
    seeking prey in the wilderness
    as food for their children.
⁶They gather their fodder in the field
  and they glean the vineyard of the wicked man.
⁷They lie all night naked, without clothing,
  and have no covering in the cold.
⁸They are wet with the rain of the mountains,
  and cling to the rock for want of shelter.
⁹(There are those who snatch the fatherless
  child from the breast,
    and take in pledge the infant of the poor.)
¹⁰They go about naked, without clothing;
  hungry, they carry the sheaves;
¹¹among the olive rows of the wicked they make oil;
  they tread the wine presses, but suffer thirst.
¹²From out of the city the dying groan,
  and the soul of the wounded cries for help;
    yet God pays no attention to their prayer.
¹³"There are those who rebel against the light,
  who are not acquainted with its ways,
    and do not stay in its paths.
¹⁴The murderer rises in the dark,
  that he may kill the poor and needy;
    and in the night he is as a thief.
¹⁵The eye of the adulterer also waits for the twilight,
  saying, 'No eye will see me';
    and he disguises his face.
¹⁶In the dark they dig through houses;
  by day they shut themselves up;
    they do not know the light.

17For deep darkness is morning to all of them;
     for they are friends with the terrors of deep darkness.

The only norms for judging at Job's disposal are human and according to these norms God is either unjust or indifferent. Job gives examples of serious violations of fundamental social law and of the ease with which these offenses are committed (vv. 2-4a). Each crime is perpetrated against the defenseless of society, the very ones who were thought to enjoy special protection from God. It would appear that their trust in the Almighty was ill-placed. God does not seem to intervene in any way to defend them from exploitation. Job adds example upon example of the suffering that they endure in order to emphasize the neglect of which God is guilty. He is blind to their affliction and deaf to their cries.

The three crimes of murder, adultery and burglary are offered as examples of deeds committed under the cover of darkness when the criminals are less likely to be detected. Actually, Job is arguing that all crime is a rebellion against the light. Yet it appears that God treats the evil as though it were hidden from all eyes since he does nothing about it and the evildoers continue in their ways without fear of reprisal.

PUNISHMENT OF THE WICKED
Job 24:18-25

18"You say, 'They are swiftly carried
     away upon the face of the waters;
     their portion is cursed in the land;
     no treader turns toward their vineyards.
19Drought and heat snatch away the
     snow water;
     so does Sheol those who have sinned.
20The squares of the town forget them;
     their name is no longer remembered;
     so wickedness is broken like a tree.'
21"They feed on the barren childless woman,
     and do no good to the widow.

²²Yet God prolongs the life of the
   mighty by his power;
   they rise up when they despair of life.
²³He gives them security, and they are supported;
   and his eyes are upon their ways.
²⁴They are exalted a little while, and then they are gone;
   they wither and fade like the mallow,
   they are cut off like the heads of grain.
²⁵If it is not so, who will prove me a liar,
   and show that there is nothing in what I say?"

The Hebrew text at this point is very difficult to translate.
While the passage is found within the speech of Job, the
content more appropriately belongs to an argument of one
of the visitors. Translations have handled this problem in
various ways. Some, such as the *New American Bible,* omit
the most difficult verses and provide an explanation in a
footnote. Others, including the *Jerusalem Bible,* transfer
this section to the end of Chapter 27 and consider it part of
the third speech of Zophar. The present translation explains
the discontinuity by suggesting that Job is quoting one of
the companions only to refute the ideas, hence the introductory phrase, "You say" is added. There seems to be no
totally satisfactory solution. This, along with the fact that
the section itself is a confusion of statements, explains some
of the diversity of interpretation.

Verses 18-20 and 24 support the prevailing theory of
retribution while verses 21-23 challenge the universality of
its scope. The latter do reflect the mind of Job even though
the former do not. Whichever position of interpretation is
espoused, all commentators agree that insistence upon
eventual retribution of the wicked is the view of the companions and not of Job.

Bildad

THE GOD OF HIGH HEAVEN
Job 25:1-6

> **25**   Then Bildad the Shuhite answered:
> ²"Dominion and fear are with God;
>   he makes peace in his high heaven.
> ³Is there any number to his armies?
>   Upon whom does his light not arise?
> ⁴How then can man be righteous before God?
>   How can he who is born of woman be clean?
> ⁵Behold, even the moon is not bright
>   and the stars are not clean in his sight;
> ⁶how much less man, who is a maggot,
>   and the son of man, who is a worm!"

The need to transpose certain passages becomes more evident as the third cycle of speeches unfolds. First of all, unlike every other speech directed toward Job, this one does not begin with a personal attack agains the protagonist. There is an abruptness as Bildad launches immediately into his defense of God. A second indication of the need to reorder the text is the brevity of this last reply of Bildad, only six verses. Most scholars believe that the speech that begins in Chapter 25 has been interrupted by 26:1-4, a passage consistent with the arguments of Job, and continues through to the end of Chapter 26. This arrangement would not only provide a response more in keeping with the earlier ones of Bildad, but also explain the incongruity of some of the motifs of the chapter. It would also shorten the otherwise unusually long speech of Job.

The imagery of the chapter is celestial. God is described as the royal conqueror of the cosmos, who has secured peace through military prowess. One thinks of the ancient myth of creation where the great warrior is victorious over chaos, establishes peace, and stations the heavenly bodies in their appointed places. At the heart of Bildad's use of this imagery is an argument supporting the claim of a cosmic order guaranteed by God and corresponding to historical harmony in the lives of women and men. If there is any disruption of this order it is not the fault of God but should be ascribed to perverse human freedom.

An explanation of the admitted disharmony is given in verses 4-6. The poetic construction is the third of its kind, identical in form and meaning to those found in 4:17-19b and 15:14-16 (cf. pages 47-49; 93). The celestial imagery here is in accord with the overall cosmic theme of the chapter. The description of humankind is the strongest and most derogatory of the three passages. Both *worm* and *maggot* are associated with the reality of death and the fate that awaits each person. The contrast between the triumphant God of the universe and the despicable human destined to decay is striking. Another significant point to be noted is the relationship between the lack of moral virtue and the inevitable corruptibility of humans. Like Eliphaz, Bildad implies that there is no possibility that mortal humankind can ever be truly upright. As has been seen earlier, this anthropological position does not allow for the question of innocent suffering, for no one is totally innocent.

Job

RIDICULE OF THE CLAIM TO WISDOM
Job 26:1-4

26 Then Job answered:
²"How you have helped him who has no power!
How you have saved the arm that has no strength!
³How you have counseled him who has no wisdom,
and plentifully declared sound knowledge!
⁴With whose help have you uttered words,
and whose spirit has come forth from you?

Once again Job taunts his visitors. They have claimed to be guardians of tradition and spokesmen of its wisdom.

What counsel have they been able to provide that has comforted or enlightened him? Job marshals forceful wisdom vocabulary against his antagonists who have been ineffective in their attempts at persuasion. In fact, they have even denied some of the facts of the situation and have thereby become perverters of the truth. They cannot possibly claim to speak in the name of God who would not lie.

THE COSMIC POWER OF GOD
Job 26:5-14

> 5The shades below tremble,
>   the waters and their inhabitants.
> 6Sheol is naked before God,
>   and Abaddon has no covering.
> 7He stretches out the north over the void,
>   and hangs the earth upon nothing.
> 8He binds up the waters in his thick clouds,
>   and the cloud is not rent under them.
> 9He covers the face of the moon,
>   and spreads over it his cloud.
> 10He has described a circle upon the face of the waters
>   at the boundary between light and darkness.
> 11The pillars of heaven tremble,
>   and are astounded at his rebuke.
> 12By his power he stilled the sea;
>   by his understanding he smote Rahab.
> 13By his wind the heavens were made fair;
>   his hand pierced the fleeing serpent.
> 14Lo, these are but the outskirts of his ways;
>   and how small a wisper do we hear of him!
> But the thunder of his power who can understand?"

As noted earlier (cf. p. 118), these verses fit much better in a speech of one of the three men who have come to counsel Job than in a speech of Job himself. Because of the commonality of themes in this section with that of the answer of Bildad (25:1-6), the remainder of this chapter is viewed, by most commentators today, as the conclusion of Bildad's third reply. True, Job could very well praise the creative power of God, but when Job speaks of cosmic wonders and the deity responsible for their splendor he usually emphasizes their crushing might and destructive force. That is not the tone of this passage.

Verses 5 and 6 describe the authority that God has over the underworld. Unlike other Ancient Near Eastern religions, Israel believed that her God held exclusive and universal dominion over all corners of the universe. There was no region too remote from him and no power strong enough to challenge his rule. Humans may be helpless in the face of death, but the realm of the dead was exposed to his view and subservient to his command.

Now begins one of the most powerful descriptions of the creation of the cosmos. Similar portraits are found in Psalm 104, Proverbs 8 and other isolated sections of the prophets. In this book it is rivaled only by the magnificent speech of Yahweh (38:1-38). There are so many references to Babylonian cosmology that a brief summary of this complex of thought would serve as background for appreciating the passage under discussion.

According to the Babylonian myth *Enuma Elish,* a great cosmic battle was waged between the forces of chaos, personified as the sea or a sea monster, and a valiant young warrior god, who had only the four winds to accompany him as he went out to meet his enemy. When the dragon opened her mouth to devour him, the warrior drove the winds into her body. Their expanding force incapacitated her enabling the young god to slay her with his sword. The carcass of the monster was then sliced horizontally, the upper half forming the vault of the heavens and the lower half becoming the earth. This victory also led to the setting of boundaries for the chaotic sea lest it overwhelm the universe once more. The latter image admits that the sea is restrained and not destroyed and that the return of chaos is a constant threat. With the creation of the heavens and the earth from the remains of the monster, a palace was set up in the heavens from which the conqueror god could rule and where he could receive the homage and praise that were his due. This myth appears in several and sometimes fragmentary forms but the essence of the story is quite clear. One god is triumphant over the forces of evil and establishes order in the heavens and on the earth. The foundation of this order is divine and cosmic and all of creation is under his dominion.

Returning to the passage in Job, references to this mythic perception are numerous. The ancients believed that the great god dwelt in the north, the same place where God stretches out his dwelling as one would stretch out a tent (v. 7a). The pillars of the earth were conceived as fixed in the waters (v. 7b). God is the one who has stored the waters in the clouds until he sees fit to send the rains (v. 8) and he has decided the place of the moon (v. 9). Having split chaos in two he has fashioned a horizon upon which appear both the light of dawn and the darkness of dusk (v. 10). The cosmic might of the warrior is felt when he thunders through the heavens (v. 11). A recounting of the actual defeat is found in verses 12 and 13. Rahab is a name given to this sea monster in other places of the Hebrew tradition (cf. 9:13; Ps 89:10; Isa 51:9).

The passage ends with an acknowledgement of the splendor of this God of creation. The use of the technical wisdom word *ways* (v. 14) underscores the definitiveness of the statement. The *way* is the established pattern of operation. Used within the context of cosmic activity it refers to the inexorable nature of these works. The design has been determined and the pattern has been set in perpetuity. Even though chaos may be a constant threat, it is under the watchful control of God and there is no chance that it might burst its bonds and gain ascendency. The text claims that these marvels are only peripheral to the divine cosmic plan. It is far beyond human powers even to speculate about the scope of God's *ways* much less presume to be able to plumb their depths.

Here is an argument that might have been acceptable to Job had the speaker moved from the admission of the mystery of God to an admonition to trust in him. Several times the participants of the dialogues have come to the brink of this summons to trust. But each time they have retreated from it. Each time that it has been broached it was for the purpose of ridiculing Job and calling attention to his limited knowledge rather than suggesting that the God who so painstakingly set up the universe and its principles of harmony should be trusted when the magnitude of this world exceeds the powers of human comprehension. It is left to Yahweh to teach this lesson.

DEFENSE OF INNOCENCE
Job 27:1-6

> **27**   And Job again took up his discourse, and said:
> 2"As God lives, who has taken away my right,
>   and the Almighty, who has made my soul bitter;
> 3as long as my breath is in me,
>   and the spirit of God is in my nostrils;
> 4my lips will not speak falsehood,
>   and my tongue will not utter deceit.
> 5Far be it from me to say that you are right;
>   till I die I will not put away my integrity from me.
> 6I hold fast my righteousness, and will not let it go;
>   my heart does not reproach me for any of my days.

The chapter begins with a rather curious verse. In none of the previous replies of Job is there an identification of the speaker within the speech itself. This may be another indication of the disarrangement of the text or of an insertion by a later editor who felt it necessary to break up an otherwise exceptionally long discourse. This commentary holds the view that 27:1-6 follows immediately upon the Joban material in 26:1-4.

The introduction is followed by an oath of innocence by the afflicted man. He swears by the God who lives, the very one he has accused as his oppressor, the one who has deprived him of the good fortune that he deserves. He uses the very general Canaanite title El (God) as well as the specifically patriarchal name Shaddai (Almighty). If there was ever any doubt about the identity of the God to whom Job is directing his claims and his demands, they are dismissed here. Job is a devotee of Yahweh, believing as the Yahwist taught that he lives by the very breath of God. As long as he has life in him he will remain true to his integrity and will not compromise in order to conform to the ideology that these men have tried to force upon him. He has been righteous and it would be a breach of loyalty to deny this. He will go to his death insisting on this fashion. From the way he speaks it appears that to admit otherwise would be deceitful. The God of truth and righteousness would never ask this of Job. Such a thought could only come from foolish misguided men who are intent on their myopic point of view and impervious to any new perspective.

THE FATE OF THE WICKED
Job 27:7-10

> ⁷"Let my enemy be as the wicked,
>   and let him that rises up against me
>   be as the unrighteous.
> ⁸For what is the hope of the godless
>   when God cuts him off,
>   when God takes away his life?
> ⁹Will God hear his cry,
>   when trouble comes upon him?
> ¹⁰Will he take delight in the Almighty?
>   Will he call upon God at all times?

It is very difficult to interpret verse 7. The tone places it in the mouth of Job, but thematically it is out of place. Although some commentators include it with Job's oath of innocence that precedes it (27:1-6), others consider it the introduction to the theme of this unit, the fate of the wicked. The latter choice has been made in this study. The verse is in parallel construction and calls down punishment upon those who have risen up against Job.

Although the remainder of the section continues the theme of deserved chastisement, the emphasis is in accord with the orthodox position rather than the radical challenge of Job. Perhaps it is even directed against Job, for the patriarchal name Shaddai is employed again and the sense of the passage deals with the hopelessness of the wicked who are separated from God and, therefore, do not call upon him. Here too, God seems to be deaf to the cries of the sufferer. It is especially when on feels cut off from God and in danger of losing one's life that the pleas grow louder and more frequent.

EXPERIENTIAL WISDOM
Job 27:11-23

> [11] I will teach you concerning the hand of God;
> what is with the Almighty I will not conceal.
> [12] Behold, all of you have seen it yourselves;
> why then have you become altogether vain?
> [13] "This is the portion of a wicked man with God,
> and the heritage which oppressors
> receive from the Almighty:
> [14] If his children are multiplied, it is for the sword;
> and his offspring have not enough to eat.
> [15] Those who survive him the pestilence buries,
> and their widows make no lamentation.
> [16] Though he heap up silver like dust,
> and pile up clothing like clay;
> [17] he may pile it up, but the just will wear it,
> and the innocent will divide the silver.
> [18] The house which he builds is like a spider's web,
> like a booth which a watchman makes.
> [19] He goes to bed rich, but will do so no more;
> he opens his eyes, and his wealth is gone.
> [20] Terrors overtake him like a flood;
> in the night a whirlwind carries him off.
> [21] The east wind lifts him up and he is gone;
> it sweeps him out of his place.

22It hurls at him without pity;
  he flees from its power in headlong flight.
23It claps its hands at him,
  and hisses at him from its place.

The final section of this chapter, along with 24:18-25, may well be the lost third reply of Zophar. Scholars agree that, despite the fact that the present arrangement of the text suggests that this is a Joban reply, the sentiments are contrary to Job's but similar to Zophar's (cf. Chapter 20). Some commentaries begin this unit with verse 8 rather than verse 11. The present commentary considers verse 11 more appropriate as an introductory line.

The speaker assumes the role of a teacher of wisdom (v. 11). True to the tradition, this wisdom has been gleaned from experience and is a treasure available to all who are willing to search for it. One needs only to observe life and its secrets will be revealed. The use of plural pronouns (vv. 11-12) might lead one to think that Job is addressing his visitors, but what follows contradicts this. The speaker argues that experience proves that the evildoers will meet with a miserable end. What appears to be an advantage is really added suffering in disguise. The ancients looked upon children as a blessing, but in poverty a large family simply means more hunger. At times one survives only to die a far worse death. This particular discourse introduces a new dimension to the thinking. The prosperous will not only be prevented from enjoying their wealth, but it will be the just who will benefit from it. They will be awarded the spoils at the demise of the rich. The speech ends with the oft-repeated description of the fall of the wicked. This surely does not express the sentiments of Job.

HYMN TO WISDOM
Job 28:1-28

28 "Surely there is a mine for silver,
  and a place for gold which they refine.

²Iron is taken out of the earth,
and copper is smelted from the ore.
³Men put an end to darkness,
and search out to the farthest bound
the ore in gloom and deep darkness.
⁴They open shafts in a valley away from where men live;
they are forgotten by travelers,
they hang afar from men, they swing to and fro.
⁵As for the earth, out of it comes bread;
but underneath it is turned up as by fire.
⁶Its stones are the place of sapphires,
and it has dust of gold.
⁷"That path no bird of prey knows,
and the falcon's eye has not seen it.
⁸The proud beasts have not trodden it;
the lion has not passed over it.
⁹"Man puts his hand to the flinty rock,
and overturns mountains by the roots.
¹⁰He cuts out channels in the rocks,
and his eye sees every precious thing.
¹¹He binds up the streams so that they do not trickle,
and the thing that is hid he brings forth to light.
¹²"But where shall wisdom be found?
and where is the place of understanding?
¹³Man does not know the way to it,
and it is not found in the land of the living.
¹⁴The deep says, 'It is not in me,'
and the sea says, 'It is not with me.'
¹⁵It cannot be gotten for gold,
and silver cannot be weighed as its price.
¹⁶It cannot be valued in the gold of Ophir,
in precious onyx of sapphire.
¹⁷Gold and glass cannot equal it,
nor can it be exchanged for jewels of fine gold.
¹⁸No mention shall be made of coral or of crystal;
the price of wisdom is above pearls.
¹⁹The topaz of Ethiopia cannot compare with it,
nor can it be valued in pure gold.

20"Whence then comes wisdom?
  And where is the place of understanding?
21It is hid from the eyes of all living,
  and concealed from the birds of the air.
22Abaddon and Death say,
  'We have heard a rumor of it with our ears.'
23"God understands the way to it,
  and he knows its place.
24For he looks to the ends of the earth,
  and sees everything under the heavens.
25When he gave to the wind its weight,
  and meted out the waters by measure;
26when he made a decree for the rain,
  and a way for the lightning of the thunder;
27then he saw it and declared it;
  he established it, and searched it out.
28And he said to man,
  'Behold, the fear of the Lord, that is wisdom;
  and to depart from evil is understanding.' "

This hymn is an independent piece of poetry which breaks the flow of the dialogue. Reflecting neither the thoughts of Job nor those of his companions, it treats the same theme which is later developed in the Yahweh speeches, viz., the inaccessibility of wisdom. The authorship of this piece is often disputed among scholars, but no one doubts the quality of the poetry nor the relevance of the motif. It is a motif that appears with various nuances in other places of the Hebrew Scriptures. Proverbs 8:22-31 praises wisdom present at creation while Baruch 3:9—4:6 and Sirach 24 applaud the Law as the dwelling place of wisdom.

The first section of the poem (vv. 1-6) highlights two extraordinary characteristics of the human spirit, the insatiable desire to search out treasures and the extremes to which people will go in order to procure them. Silver, gold, iron and copper as well as precious stones have been prized from very earliest times, valued for their brilliance as well as for their usefulness. In their search to discover more and more of the secrets of the world and its riches humans have uncovered the hidden places wherein these treasures are to be found and have devised techniques for extracting them. No hardship is too great to endure, no danger too threatening for one in the quest. Neither the remoteness of the site nor the depth of the descent can dissuade those intend on the possession of the wealth that the earth has to offer. Human ingenuity is credited for the discovery and the conquest of this treasure.

Although certain animals have always been noted for highly esteemed characteristics (vv. 7-8), humans have still been able to see what birds with the sharpest eyesight have not perceived. They have conquered regions of the earth far beyond the domain of the animal kingdom. Here is an instance where the beasts, those usually called upon to instruct humankind in the mysteries of the world, have been far outstripped by those eager to learn. Such is the capacity of the human spirit that has peered into the bowels of the mountains, controlled the forces of the streams, and brought to light the hidden treasures of the earth.

Possessing all of the skill needed to uncover the wonders of the world, humankind is still incapable of knowing where wisdom is to be found and is unequal to the task of achieving it. The basic question is asked in verse 12 and again in verse 20 and every corner of creation must confess ignorance of the answer. Neither humans (v. 13) nor the cosmos (v. 14) nor living things (v. 21) nor even death (v. 22) can claim knowledge of the dwelling place of wisdom. It cannot be mined like precious ores or gems, the value of which pales when compared to this coveted understanding. It is the treasure par excellence, universally desired and yet beyond the reach of all.

The rest of the poem develops the theme of the relationship of God with wisdom. Only God knows its proper place and the *way* (again the technical term) to it. The divine gaze is all-encompassing, capturing the entire scope of creation. A brief mention of God's creative activity (vv. 25-26) is followed by an unusual reference to wisdom which seems to be present within creation rather than preceding it. This resembles the image of Lady Wisdom of the Book of Proverbs (cf Pro 8:1-21) who calls out to humankind, inviting all to seek her and to plumb the depths of her mysteries. The message of this poem is quite clear. No human quest regardless of its scope, intensity, or duration will result in the acquisition of the secrets of the created order. This supernal wisdom, which continually invites pursuit is known by God alone.

This is the first explicit development of a theme that was briefly mentioned several times throughout the dialogues, viz., the theme of the elusive nature of wisdom or the inability of humans to grasp the vast sweep of its mysteries. Were the poem to end with verse 27, some might say that the situation is a hopelessly frustrating one of desiring what is outside of one's reach. Should one be satisfied with the search and find fulfillment in it? Or is this but another example of God toying with women and men who are unequal to divine caprice? Because of a significant change in literary characteristics, some feel that a later editor added verse 28 to the poem. Whether this be the case or not, this verse transforms the quest for wisdom into a challenge well within human reach. Even though divine wisdom may be impossible to attain, fidelity to piety will assure one of a kind of practical wisdom. The theme of fearing the Lord and avoiding evil has appeared time and again as part of the classical description of the wise person (cf. 1:1; 8; 2:3; Pro 3:7; etc.). Here it is held out as the only way that humans can attain wisdom. This may very well be the traditional teaching, but that does not invalidate it in the eyes of the Joban poet who has just acknowledged, in a supremely artistic manner, the inaccessible nature of wisdom. While they may long for a deeper comprehension, humans must realistically strive for and be satisfied with piety and morality.

Job's Soliloquy

LAMENTING THE LOSS OF THE PAST
Job 29:1-25

29   And Job again took up his discourse, and said:
2"Oh, that I were as in the months of old,
   as in the days when God watched over me;
3when his lamp shone upon my head,
   and by his light I walked through darkness;
4as I was in my autumn days,
   when the friendship of God was upon my tent;
5when the Almighty was yet with me,
   when my children were about me;
6when my steps were washed with milk,
   and the rock poured out for me streams of oil!
7When I went out to the gate of the city,
   when I prepared my seat in the square,
8the young men saw me and withdrew,
   and the aged rose and stood;
9the princes refrained from talking,
   and laid their hand on their mouth;
10the voice of the nobles was hushed,
   and their tongue cleaved to the roof of their mouth.
11When the ear heard, it called me blessed,
   and when the eye saw, it approved;
12because I delivered the poor who cried,
   and the fatherless who had none to help him.
13The blessing of him who was about to perish came upon
   me, and I caused the widow's heart to sing for joy.
14I put on righteousness, and it clothed me;
   my justice was like a robe and a turban.
15I was eyes to the blind,
   and feet to the lame.
16I was a father to the poor,
   and I searched out the cause of him whom I did not
   know.
17I broke the fangs of the unrighteous,
   and made him drop his prey from his teeth.

¹⁸Then I thought, 'I shall die in my nest,
   and I shall multiply my days as the sand,
¹⁹my roots spread out to the waters,
   with the dew all night on my branches,
²⁰my glory fresh with me,
   and my bow ever new in my hand.'
²¹"Men listened to me, and waited,
   and kept silence for my counsel.
²²After I spoke they did not speak again,
   and my word dropped upon them.
²³They waited for me as for the rain;
   and they opened their mouths as for the spring rain.
²⁴I smiled on them when they had no confidence;
   and the light of my countenance they
   did not cast down.
²⁵I chose their way, and sat as chief,
   and I dwelt like a king among his troops,
   like one who comforts mourners.

Remembrance of days gone by has an added pathos for Job for in the past he knew the watchful eyes of God and felt the security of divine protection. The images that he used to depict this period are warm and familial and portray Job as a man enjoying the peace and prosperity of friendship with God (vv. 2-6). Then he was a man respected by the young and by the old alike. He appears to have exercised some authority at the gate where legal cases were often decided and to have won the esteem of the leaders of the community as well (vv. 7-10). Job next enumerates some of the good works he performed that brought him to the exalted station which he held in the past. Part of Israel's prophetic picture of the truly righteous person was the concern shown to those within society who had no legal rights. This care was directed especially toward the widowed, the orphaned and those aliens within the community who had no one to intercede for them when they were most vulnerable. By listing just such behavior, Job is sketching a portrait of himself as the model Israelite, the very first theme developed in the Prologue (cf. 1:1-5). There the concentration was on the good fortune that he enjoyed, here it is on the good life that he lived. He was not isolated in his prosperity, blind and deaf to the needs of others. On the contrary, he was the champion of righteousness and the advocate of the helpless. He rightly expected to enjoy the well-earned rewards of godly living. Job has gone into great detail in this recounting of former days in order to dramatize the stark contrast between that stage of life and his present predicament.

DISDAINED BY THE OUTCAST
Job 30:1-14

30   "But now they make sport of me,
    men who are younger than I,
    whose fathers I would have disdained
    to set with the dogs of my flock.
²What could I gain from the strength of their hands,
    men whose vigor is gone?
³Through want and hard hunger
    they gnaw the dry and desolate ground;
⁴they pick mallow and the leaves of bushes,
    and to warm themselves the roots of the broom.
⁵They are driven out from among men;
    they shout after them as after a thief.
⁶In the gullies of the torrents they must dwell,
    in holes of the earth and of the rocks.
⁷Among the bushes they bray;
    under the nettles they huddle together.
⁸A senseless, a disreputable brood,
    they have been whipped out of the land.
⁹"And now I have become their song,
    I am a byword to them.
¹⁰They abhor me, they keep aloof from me;
    they do not hesitate to spit at the sight of me.
¹¹Because God has loosed my cord and humbled me,
    they have cast off restraint in my presence.

12On my right hand the rabble rise,
    they drive me forth,
    they cast up against me their ways of destruction.
13They break up my path,
    they promote my calamity;
    no one restrains them.
14As through a wide breach they come;
    amid the crash they roll on.

Job who had been a prominent member of the community and preeminent for his philanthropic endeavors has become the butt of the ridicule of the very dregs of society. He had been revered by the great ones of the world and is now scorned by a segment of the community with which he would not have had any dealings in the past. These people are not only destitute but despicable as well. That even they have been let loose against Job illustrates the depths to which he has been cast and the total defenselessness that he endures. All of this has come upon him because God has unleashed the forces of chaos and destruction and has allowed Job to fall victim to their fury. He who had stood as a refuge for the weak is naked and alone in his time of peril and there is no one to blame but God.

JOB'S TERROR AND THE CRUELTY OF GOD
Job 30:15-31

15Terrors are turned upon me;
    my honor is pursued as by the wind,
    and my prosperity has passed away
    like a cloud.
16"And now my soul is poured out within me;
    days of affliction have taken hold of me.
17The night racks my bones,
    and the pain that gnaws me takes no rest.
18With violence it seizes my garment;
    it binds me about like the collar of my tunic.
19God has cast me into the mire,
    and I have become like dust and ashes.

²⁰I cry to thee and thou dost not answer me;
  I stand, and thou dost not heed me.
²¹Thou hast turned cruel to me;
  with the might of thy hand thou dost persecute me.
²²Thou liftest me up on the wind, thou
  makest me ride on it,
  and thou tossest me about in the roar of the storm.
²³Yea, I know that thou wilt bring me to death,
  and to the house appointed for all living.
²⁴"Yet does not one in a heap of ruins
  stretch out his hand,
  and in his disaster cry for help?
²⁵Did not I weep for him whose day was hard?
  Was not my soul grieved for the poor?
²⁶But when I looked for good, evil came;
  and when I waited for light, darkenss came.
²⁷My heart is in turmoil, and is never still;
  days of affliction come to meet me.
²⁸I go about blackened, but not by the sun;
  I stand up in the assembly, and cry for help.
²⁹I am a brother of jackals,
  and a companion of ostriches.
³⁰My skin turns black and falls from me,
  and my bones burn with heat.
³¹My lyre is turned to mourning,
  and my pipe to the voice of those who weep.

Stripped of his honor and his security, Job's inner anguish is likened to a complete emptying of his soul. He is propelled to the brink of death symbolized by *mire* and *dust* and *ashes*. This will be Job's last opportunity at self-defense and so he turns once again to God (v. 20) and accuses him of desertion at a time when Job most needed assistance. No one will be able to find any evidence that this pitiful man has ever turned away from God. He has remained faithful even when God has made a plaything of him in the midst of a tempest. To the end Job acknowledges God's sovereignty and power over life and death, still insisting on his own integrity and on divine inconsistency. In the face of all of this Job continues to cry to the Almighty. He will not relinguish his belief in God's presence and his confidence in God's fundamental solicitude despite the fact that he is denied every attention that he formerly gave to others and any glimmer of hope that things will eventually be resolved.

JOB'S INNOCENCE
Job 31:1-40

31 "I have made a covenant with my eyes;
how then could I look upon a virgin?
²What would be my portion from God above,
and my heritage from the Almighty on high?
³Does not calamity befall the unrighteous,
and disaster the workers of iniquity?
⁴Does not he see my ways,
and number all my steps?
⁵"If I have walked with falsehood,
and my foot has hastened to deceit;
⁶(Let me be weighed in a just balance,
and let God know my integrity!)
⁷if my step has turned aside from the way,
and my heart has gone after my eyes,
and if any spot has cleaved to my hands;
⁸then let me sow, and another eat;
and let what grows for me be rooted out.
⁹"If my heart has been enticed to a woman,
and I have lain in wait at my neighbor's door;
¹⁰then let my wife grind for another,
and let others bow down upon her.
¹¹For that would be a heinous crime;
that would be an iniquity to be punished by the judges;
¹²for that would be a fire which consumes unto Abaddon,
and it would burn to the root all my increase.
¹³"If I have rejected the cause of my
manservant or my maidservant,
when they brought a complaint against me;

14what then shall I do when God rises up?
    When he makes inquiry, what shall I answer him?
15Did not he who made me in the womb make him?
    And did not one fashion us in the womb?
16"If I have withheld anything that the poor desired,
    or have caused the eyes of the widow to fail,
17or have eaten my morsel alone,
    and the fatherless has not eaten of it
18(for from his youth I reared him as a father,
    and from his mother's womb I guided him);
19if I have seen any one perish for lack of clothing,
    or a poor man without covering;
20if his loins have not blessed me,
    and if he was not warmed with the fleece of my sheep;
21if I have raised my hand against the fatherless,
    because I saw help in the gate;
22then let my shoulder blade fall from my shoulder,
    and let my arm be broken from its socket.
23For I was in terror of calamity from God,
    and I could not have faced his majesty.
24"If I have made gold my trust,
    or called fine gold my confidence;
25if I have rejoiced because my wealth was great,
    or because my hand had gotten much;
26if I have looked at the sun when it shone,
    or the moon moving in splendor,
27and my heart has been secretly enticed,
    and my mouth has kissed my hand;
28this also would be an iniquity to be
    punished by the judges,
    for I should have been false to God above.
29"If I have rejoiced at the ruin of him that hated me,
    or exulted when evil overtook him
30(I have not let my mouth sin
    by asking for his life with a curse);
31if the men of my tent have not said,
    'Who is there that has not been filled with this meat?'
32(the sojourner has not lodged in the street;
    I have opened my doors to the wayfarer);

³³if I have concealed my transgressions from men,
   by hiding my iniquity in my bosom,
³⁴because I stood in great fear of the multitude,
   and the contempt of families terrified me,
   so that I kept silence, and did not go out of doors—
³⁵Oh, that I had one to hear me!
   (Here is my signature! let the Almighty answer me!)
   Oh, that I had the indictment written by my adversary!
³⁶Surely I would carry it on my shoulder;
   I would bind it on me as a crown;
³⁷I would give him an account of all my steps;
   like a prince I would approach him.
³⁸"If my land has cried out against me,
   and its furrows have wept together;
³⁹if I have eaten its yield without payment,
   and caused the death of its owners;
⁴⁰let thorns grow instead of wheat,
   and foul weeds instead of barley."
The words of Job are ended.

Job has come to the end of his defense. There is no more disputing with those around him, no more lamenting his lot, no more accusing or pleading with God. In his final soliloquy he outlines the rules of conduct that have governed his behavior and calls for either vindication or, if guilt can be found in him, punishment. The standards by which Job wishes to be judged are all ethical and deal more with honor and integrity than with outright violation of a law code. He has been more than righteous, he has been exemplary in his conduct. Having begged, and then demanded, that God meet him in court, Job solemnly pronounces his innocence and calls upon God to answer him.

He begins by reaffirming the orthodox position (vv. 1-3) which he has always upheld. Punishment will come upon those who have transgressed. Had he not believed this his dilemma would not have been so perplexing. He has always travelled the *way* of righteousness rather than the *way* of falsehood. Job is so confident of his virtue that he calls chastisement upon himself if iniquity can be found in him.

He is actually putting God to the test by this challenge. If God is truly just and Job is culpable then disciplinary measures will have to be taken. If he has strayed from the *way* of order and righteousness (vv. 4-7) then let God punish him, but let God first stipulate the offenses. He asserts that he has kept himself far from lust (vv. 9-12), from exploitation of subordinates (vv. 13-15), from insensitivity to the needy (vv. 16-23), from avarice (vv. 24-25) and forms of idolatry and superstition (vv. 26-28), from vengeance (vv. 29-30), inhospitality (vv. 31-32), and deception (vv. 33-34). This code of conduct and honor describes Job as a man of integrity with impeccable social morality. The weightiness of this oath and of its ramifications becomes clear as one looks closely at Job's claims and his suggested penalty for possible negligence in the respective areas.

Progeny was more than the hope of the future. It was a sign of God's favor and the assurance of the survival of one's name and memory. Knowing that his morality was irreproachable, Job could confidently propose total annihilation of his posterity if even the slightest doubt could be raised about his virtue (v. 12b).

Belief in the fundamental equality of all humankind is clearly articulated in verse 15. Job acknowledges that all have been created by the same God in the same manner. Though there may be diversity in social status, all deserve the same respect because of their common origin. To find such an insight in an ancient writer is remarkable when one remembers how long it has taken Western civilization and American law to admit the full personhood of women, of blacks and of other minorities.

The social covenantal law of ancient Israel called the people to a higher form of societal consciousness than merely avoiding explicit crimes against others. Fidelity to the covenant also meant assuming responsibility for the care and protection of those who were unable to provide for themselves. This was usually taken care of within the confines of the family, clan or tribe. Situations did arise when one was bereft of the security that such a social group guaranteed. Legal rights were exercised by the adult male of the society and those related to him shared in his privileges. Those within the community, especially widows and orphans and resident aliens, who were outside of the patronage of a man were often subject to exploitation, abuse and neglect. Convinced that his is a caring God and that covenantal union expects that he show the same solicitude, Job insists that he was the benefactor of the needy. His social consciousness had achieved the level of refinement expected of a truly righteous Israelite.

Even though the theory of retribution stated that justice will be rewarded and injustice will be punished, Job denies even having taken undue pleasure in his own good fortune or in the ill fortune of those who have turned against him. Because of the extreme hardship suffered during travel, hospitality was indispensible and was bestowed on all regardless of their loyalties. Even one's enemy was protected while under the mantle of hospitality. Social virtue and honor were often gauged according to the quality of this trait. Job has taken great pride in his reputation for cordiality and generosity as well as for his honesty and straightforwardness.

The chapter ends with one last expression of regret that God never responded to Job's attempt to bring legal action against him (vv. 35-37). His final action is, then, to affix his signature to this statement of innocence and await God's reply. In any court of law, the adversary would now be forced to produce a copy of the indictment. If God would only so act, Job would gladly display this document for all to see. He would quite proudly wear it on his shoulder or on his forehead for he is confident that it would be a statement of vindication. Job's oath of innocence is an attempt to force the hand of God. False testimony would result in divine sanctions, while silence on God's part would be interpreted as vindication of Job. One might argue that Job is already suffering the chastisement and is thereby condemned. However, this thought could be countered by the fact that the oath has just been pronounced and calls for future response.

Is Job perhaps merely using God's continued silence to his own advantage? The reader will never know because later Yahweh does indeed respond. The text is very clear at this point. "The words of Job are ended."

CHAPTER FOUR
ELIHU

Job has solemnly closed his defense. One would now expect a reply from God. Instead a fourth man appears on the scene. There has been no preparation for his appearance nor any indication of his presence during the exchange that has transpired between the participants of the debate. He is not mentioned in the Prologue nor will he be included in the Epilogue. Whence does he come? What role does he play in the drama? How does he add to the argument of either side? Questions such as these have plagued scholars over the years and have been variously answered by them.

Some believe that the Elihu speeches represent a later literary and theological development of the original author. While there may be significant differences between this section and the material that preceded it, there remains an underlying correspondence with the earlier material. It is not uncommon to find a work of art comprised of parts which represent different stages in the development of the artist's thinking. This could be the case here.

Other authors hold that the Elihu speeches are the work of a second writer, one who felt that there was another explanation for Job's suffering that had not yet been explored. Their objections to the authenticity of this material are based on differences in literary style as well as on the diverging theological explanations.

Whether one considers these speeches as a product of the original author, or of another poet, they constitute a significant part of the received text and provide a slightly different nuance to the argument against Job and in favor of God.

DEFENDING AN INTRUSION
Job 32:1-22

32 So these three men ceased to answer Job, because he was righteous in his own eyes. ²Then Elihu the son of Barachel the Buzite, of the family of Ram, became angry. He was angry at Job because he justified himself rather than God; ³he was angry also at Job's three friends because they had found no answer, although they had declared Job to be in the wrong. ⁴Now Elihu had waited to speak to Job because they were older than he. ⁵And when Elihu saw that there was no answer in the mouth of these three men, he became angry.

⁶And Elihu the son of Barachel the Buzite answered:
"I am young in years,
and you are aged;
therefore I was timid and afraid
to declare my opinion to you.
⁷I said, 'Let days speak,
and many years teach wisdom.'
⁸But it is the spirit in a man,
the breath of the Almighty, that
makes him understand.
⁹It is not the old that are wise,
nor the aged that understand what is right.
¹⁰Therefore I say, 'Listen to me;
let me also declare my opinion.'
¹¹"Behold, I waited for your words,
I listened for your wise sayings,
while you searched out what to say.

¹²I gave you my attention,
  and, behold, there was none that confuted Job,
  or that answered his words, among you.
¹³Beware lest you say, 'We have found wisdom;
  God may vanquish him, not man.'
¹⁴He has not directed his words against me,
  and I will not answer him with your speeches.
¹⁵"They are discomfited, they answer no more;
  they have not a word to say.
¹⁶And shall I wait, because they do not speak,
  because they stand there, and answer no more?
¹⁷I also will give my answer;
  I also will declare my opinion.
¹⁸For I am full of words,
  the spirit within me constrains me.
¹⁹Behold, my heart is like wine that has no vent;
  like new wineskins, it is ready to burst.
²⁰I must speak, that I may find relief;
  I must open my lips and answer.
²¹I will not show partiality to any person
  or use flattery toward any man.
²²For I do not know how to flatter,
  else would my Maker soon put an end to me.

The Elihu speeches begin with a prose introduction (vv. 1-6a) wherein the young man is identified and his anger is described. In the earlier chapters only the origins of the other men had been given, but here also the lineage of Elihu is carefully spelled out. His anger is twofold: it is directed against Job because the poor man insisted upon his own innocence and thereby accused God of injustice; it is also directed against the other visitors who were unable to convince Job of his guilt or to bring forth evidence of his sinfulness. Being an adherent of the theory that claimed wisdom for the elders, Elihu was diappointed that they had failed to demonstrate the validity of this theory.

The presumption that wisdom comes with age is the theme that is further developed as the poetic speeches continue. However, as Elihu speaks to his elders (vv. 6b-10) he explains that he has respected their years but has been disappointed with their performance as sages. He had expected them to confound Job and they had failed. This fact has lead him to the conclusion that it is not age and experience but the breath of the Almighty that gives wisdom. He is saying this in order to justify his own disagreement with the others. He gives no evidence of intending to use this argument in defense of Job, although it could very well be so used. If Elihu is going to insist that special insight has been bestowed upon him, insight that differs from the teaching of the representatives of the tradition, a case could be made in favor of Job as well. Elihu does not even consider this possibility.

The young man continues to chide the others (vv. 13-14). He criticizes them for giving up in their dispute and for claiming that only God can prove Job's error. Without resorting to their arguments, which have been empty, he himself will be successful where they have failed.

He then turns to Job and contends that the inadequacy of the others should not be a reason for silencing him (vv. 15-16). His message is new and comes not from experience and tradition but from the spirit within him. His speech cannot be constrained anymore than prophetic words can be curbed or the fermentation of new wine can be suppressed. He is compelled to speak regardless of the consequences. The truth of his words is no respecter of age or social status.

Is this young man merely a brash upstart? Is his insistence on unique understanding simply arrogant boasting? If the author of the Elihu intended to introduce a new insight into the dilemma of the book, why not include it in one of the earlier speeches? The answer to these questions is clear. If the author's purpose is to show that wisdom is not the prerogative of the elders, then the new insight should not come from one of them. Nor should it come from Job for that would imply that human experience is indeed the source of all wisdom. The conclusion of the Dialogue will show that this is not the answer that the author wishes to put forward. The only way to suggest that humans can propose another viewpoint is to introduce another person, and this after the traditional stance has been both defended and challenged.

SPEECH TO JOB

JOB IS IN ERROR
Job 33:1-11

> **33** "But now, hear my speech, O Job,
>   and listen to all my words.
> ²Behold, I open my mouth;
>   the tongue in my mouth speaks.
> ³My words declare the uprightness of my heart,
>   and what my lips know they speak sincerely.
> ⁴The spirit of God has made me,
>   and the breath of the Almighty gives me life.
> ⁵Answer me, if you can;
>   set your words in order before me;
>   take your stand.
> ⁶Behold, I am toward God as you are;
>   I too was formed from a piece of clay.
> ⁷Behold, no fear of me need terrify you;
>   my pressure will not be heavy upon you.
> ⁸"Surely, you have spoken in my hearing,
>   and I have heard the sound of your words.
> ⁹You say, 'I am clean, without transgression;
>   I am pure, and there is no iniquity in me.
> ¹⁰Behold, he finds occasions against me,
>   he counts me as his enemy;
> ¹¹he puts my feet in the stocks,
>   and watches all my paths.'

Elihu directs his first speech to Job. He has already defended his right to speak and has explained his delay in doing so. Now he demands Job's attention by repeating the theory of the origin of his wisdom and, therefore, the validity of his words (vv. 1-5). He is concerned that Job not be intimidated by him and so he goes to great lengths to show that he has no advantage over Job. Rather he is Job's peer (vv. 6-7). Twice he alludes to the Yahwistic creation account found in Genesis 2:7, referring to Job's and his common origin from clay and to their subsequent quickening by the breath of God. He speaks in this way in order to underscore his contention that human resources have little to do with his exceptional insight. Job can listen to his message with a certain amount of assurance that the wisdom to be given is of divine origin.

There are three basic claims that Job has made and to which he has tenaciously clung. Elihu recalls them there. Job has continually insisted upon his innocence (v. 9), has accused God of perverting justice by allowing him to suffer for no reason (v. 10), and has further accused God of standing by and watching a righteous man in agony without heeding his cries for help or coming to his aid (v. 11). A refutation of each of these claims in reverse can be found in the remainder of this chapter as well as in the two chapters that follow.

THE NIGHT VISION
Job 33:12-18

> [12]"Behold, in this you are not right.
>   I will answer you.
>   God is greater than man.
> [13]Why do you contend against him,
>   saying, 'He will answer none of my words'?
> [14]For God speaks in one way,
>   and in two, though man does not perceive it.
> [15]In a dream, in a vision of the night,
>   when deep sleep falls upon men,
>   while they slumber on their beds,

¹⁶then he opens the ears of man,
   and terrifies them with warnings,
¹⁷that he may turn man aside from his deed,
   and cut off pride from man;
¹⁸he keeps back his soul from the Pit,
   his life from perishing by the sword.

Elihu begins with a denunciation of Job's allegations and a counterstatement proclaiming the irreprehensibility of God. He insists that God is greater than Job (v. 12). This is not a new idea, for Job himself has argued in this way in several places earlier in the Dialogue (cf. 9:2-4; 19). Contrary to Job who has charged that God has used superior power to the disadvantage of humankind, Elihu maintains that no human can presume to relate to God as an equal by demanding that God conform to human expectations. Would that Elihu had developed the theme of the superiority of God one step further. He might have arrived at the threshhold of the mystery of God and the incomprehensibility of the divine ways. Like the speakers before him, he merely mentions this idea and then quickly moves on to the point that he wants to make.

Elihu next addresses one of Job's specific allegations, that God is apparently disinterested in the affliction of women and men, especially of those who are innocent of serious wrongdoing. God has not been deaf to the cries of the sufferer nor blind to the real needs of human beings. He does visit them, primarily in two different ways (v. 14): in dreams or night visions (vv. 15-18) and by means of affliction itself (vv. 19-22).

In the very first speech to Job, Eliphaz told of a night vision wherein he received a special message (cf. 4:12ff). He described: ". . . visions of night when deep sleep falls on men." In both instances the vision or dream is more like a nightmare because of the fear that is instilled and the seriousness of the communication received. Elihu is returning to this theme in his rebuttal of Job. While the depiction of the experience is identical with that of Eliphaz, the message conveyed is quite different. The earlier counselor contended that his nocturnal experience was the vehicle through which he acquired his particular anthropological insight (cf. page 47). Elihu on the other hand regards these communications as warnings. The terror that is instilled is for the sake of deterrence, to dissuade one from evil ways. The implication is that the individual is either already on the path that leads to evil and destruction or is likely to enter upon that way very shortly. God's interest and concern are demonstrated by the fact that these fearful occurrences are meant to preserve the individual from ruin, from the "Pit", the abode of the dead.

At the outset Elihu has exposed his basic assumption. The explanation that is given presumes guilt on the part of the recipient of the communication (vv. 17-18). He offers this as an insight to a man who asserts that his plight is unintelligible and his previous life was one of fidelity.

It is as empty as the arguments of the elders that he has called ineffective and inept. The only difference between his words and those of the others is his contention that God warns the person before the wrongdoing occurs and that this warning should prevent the deed.

VISITATION BY ILLNESS
Job 33:19-33

> ¹⁹"Man is also chastened with pain upon his bed,
>   and with continual strife in his bones;
> ²⁰so that his life loathes bread,
>   and his appetite dainty food.
> ²¹His flesh is so wasted away that it cannot be seen;
>   and his bones which were not seen stick out.
> ²²His soul draws near the Pit,
>   and his life to those who bring death.
> ²³If there be for him an angel,
>   a mediator, one of the thousand,
>   to declare to man what is right for him;

24and he is gracious to him, and says,
  'Deliver him from going down into the Pit,
  I have found a ransom;
25let his flesh become fresh with youth;
  let him return to the days of his youthful vigor';
26then man prays to God, and he accepts him,
  he comes into his presence with joy.
  He recounts to men his salvation,
27 and he sings before men, and says:
  'I sinned, and perverted what was right,
  and it was not requited to me.
28He has redeemed my soul from going down into the Pit,
  and my life shall see the light.'
29"Behold, God does all these things,
  twice, three times, with a man,
30to bring back his soul from the Pit,
  that he may see the light of life.
31Give heed, O Job, listen to me;
  be silent, and I will speak.
32If you have anything to say, answer me;
  speak, for I desire to justify you.
33If not, listen to me;
  be silent, and I will teach you wisdom."

The second way that God visits humankind is by means of physical illness, which is not always merely a punishment but has disciplinary and pedagogical value as well (vv. 19-22). It often brings the person to the brink of death, the "Pit", and forces one to look at life and the current manner of living in an entirely new way. It is meant to be a corrective. As with the example above, this interpretation of suffering does not speak to Job's situation. It either presumes culpability or, if it does not, it ignores the pressing question of innocent suffering. Elihu may very well be offering a nuanced explanation of appropriate chastisement, but he missed the mark in Job's regard.

Continuing his consideration of illness, he states that the afflicted one is only brought to the brink of death and is there snatched from ruin by an angel, a mediator, a deliverer (vv. 23-24). Job has pleaded for an umpire who would decide impartially (cf. 9:33), a witness in heaven who would speak in his behalf (cf. 6:19), and a redeemer who would ultimately vindicate him (cf. 19:25). In each case, however, Job steadfastly maintained that he was blameless, remaining confident that these advocates would show him to be so. The agents that Elihu describes act as rescuers from trouble. They in no way promise to exonerate the tormented individual. Elihu does not offer hope for vindication but suggests resignation and submission that will be rewarded by deliverance. An essential ingredient in this deliverance is an admission of guilt from the afflicted one who thus acknowledges that the mercy of God saves, not from suffering, but from total destruction.

He ends his first discourse to Job with another exhortation to listen. He asserts that he would prefer to find Job righteous, but if this is not the case Job should be silent and heed the wisdom that Elihu will impart. The tenor of this advice betrays a self-righteous attitude on the part of Elihu. He is no different from the others who are convinced of Job's sinfulness and the justice of his predicament. While he may not attack Job with the harshness of the others, his kindness is patronizing and his concern is a veneer. He ends his remarks in a way that is similar to the taunts with which the others began some of their speeches (cf. 4:2; 18:2; 20:2-3).

SPEECH TO COMPANIONS

JOB'S ERROR IS DESCRIBED
Job 34:1-9

> **34** Then Elihu said:
> ²"Hear my words, you wise men,
>   and give ear to me, you who know;
> ³for the ear tests words
>   as the palate tastes food.

⁴Let us choose what is right;
   let us determine among ourselves what is good.
⁵For Job has said, 'I am innocent,
   and God has taken away my right;
⁶in spite of my right I am counted a liar;
   my wound is incurable, though I am
   without transgression.'
⁷What man is like Job,
   who drinks up scoffing like water,
⁸who goes in company with evildoers
   and walks with wicked men?
⁹For he has said, 'It profits a man nothing
   that he should take delight in God.'

The self-assured Elihu turns from Job and speaks to the others whose wisdom he had previously questioned but here affirms. The use of the proverb in verse 3 illustrates the flexibility of the wisdom tradition. Job employed the same image to bear out the validity of his claim (cf. 12:11). Experience will demonstrate the attractiveness or repugnance of something. While Job was arguing for the negative evaluation Elihu is presuming the positive. They, he and the others, know what is right and so he accords them the prerogative of deciding and passing judgment on Job whose humble state itself is evidence of his unworthiness. Verse 5 expresses the second assertion of Job that Elihu will contest. Job's persistent claim to virtue is an implied condemnation of God who has allowed calamity to befall a righteous man. The bulk of the chapter is a defense of God and the divine sovereignty. Here Job is simply criticized for the allegation.

The picture of Job is harsh and uncompromising. Borrowing an image from one of the very negative anthropological statements of Eliphaz (cf. 15:16), Elihu pictures him as drinking in iniquity. The Hebrew word for *man* that is used refers to a strong gallant individual, an image different from the one being drawn. Job contends that he is noble and stalwart, yet his actions belie this assertion; hence the taunt. He is an associate of the wicked and is being treated as such.

The proof of this charge is that Job denies the reliability of retribution (v. 9). At the heart of the argument is the claim that there is no guaranteed future reward for fidelity to God. To hold to this is to undermine the basic order of the universe. This in itself is evidence of Job's waywardness.

THE JUST CREATOR
Job 34:10-20

10"Therefore, hear me, you men of understanding,
  far be it from God that he should do wickedness,
  and from the Almighty that he should do wrong.
11For according to the work of a man he will requite him,
  and according to his ways he will make it befall him.
12Of a truth, God will not do wickedly,
  and the Almighty will not pervert justice.
13Who gave him charge over the earth
  and who laid on him the whole world?
14If he should take back his spirit to himself,
  and gather to himself his breath,
15all flesh would perish together,
  and man would return to dust.
16"If you have understanding, hear this;
  listen to what I say.
17Shall one who hates justice govern?
  Will you condemn him who is righteous and mighty,
18who says to a king, 'Worthless one,'
  and to nobles, 'Wicked man';
19who shows no partiality to princes,
  nor regards the rich more than the poor,
  for they are all the work of his hands?
20In a moment they die;
  at midnight the people are shaken and pass away,
  and the mighty are taken away by no human hand.

Although he is speaking to the elders, Elihu's defense of God is a rebuttal to Job's accusation. How could anyone even insinuate that the Almighty was unjust? His very creative power argues against this. Elihu seeks to prove the authenticity and strength of the theory of retribution by using its very principles in a somewhat circular manner. Sovereignty could only belong to the one who has preeminent rule over all. This means that such a one is responsible for the order in the universe. How could the author of cosmic order be guilty of any form of disorder? It is clearly out of the question and thus the righteousness of God is vindicated. Another avenue of argument is the theory that power and superiority are the visible manifestations of reward for virtue. The Almighty has this power and superiority in a supereminent manner. This is a proof of divine righteousness.

Job has never doubted the surpassing creative power of God. He too is well versed in the tenets of retribution. However, his experience flies in the face of all of the arguments. He sees himself and his dilemma as a prime example of the irregularity that forces a reexamination of the theory. Once again Elihu is expounding on a point that is not being contested by Job. Only the universal applicability of every detail of the principle is being challenged.

When he moves from the realm of the divine to that of human government, Elihu uses even less reliable examples in an attempt to make his point. He believes that because one occupies a position of prominence and authority it is safe to conclude that one is rewarded or blessed for one's integrity. This argument can hardly convince a man who has witnessed wicked people in positions of governance. Prominence and authority are no guarantee of righteousness. They merely signify power. Job rejects Elihu's argument because it is based on the false premise that prominence is a sign of reward or blessing.

THE OMNISCIENT JUDGE
Job 34:21-37

> [21]"For his eyes are upon the ways of a man,
>   and sees all his steps.

22There is no gloom or deep darkness
   where evildoers may hide themselves.
23For he has not appointed a time for any man
   to go before God in judgment.
24He shatters the mighty without investigation,
   and sets others in their place.
25Thus, knowing their works,
   he overturns them in the night, and
   they are crushed.
26He strikes them for their wickedness
   in the sight of men,
27because they turned aside from following him,
   and had no regard for any of his ways,
28so that they caused the cry of the poor
   to come to him,
   and he heard the cry of the afflicted—
29When he is quiet, who can condemn?
   When he hides his face, who can behold him,
   whether it be a nation or a man?—
30that a godless man should not reign,
   that he should not ensnare the people.
31"For has any one said to God,
   'I have borne chastisement;
   I will not offend any more;
32teach me what I do not see;
   if I have done iniquity, I will do it no more'?
33Will he then make requital to suit you,
   because you reject it?
   For you must choose, and not I;
   therefore declare what you know.
34Men of understanding will say to me,
   and the wise man who hears me will say:
35'Job speaks without knowledge,
   his words are without insight.'
36Would that Job were tried to the end,
   because he answers like wicked men.
37For he adds rebellion to his sin;
   he claps his hands among us,
   and multiplies his words against God."

The first point of departure for a defense of the justice of God was the divine creative power. Elihu now turns to the omniscience of the judge. Since nothing is hidden from God, no one can escape inevitable judgment. Earlier Job had claimed otherwise (cf. 24:13-17). Darkness conceals the wicked, or at least that is what they seem to think. And, according to Job, their sin goes unpunished. Elihu thinks otherwise. God sees all things and will bring judgment at the appropriate time. Job has consistently called for recompense at the time that he, Job, would determine. Although it appears that no appointed time has been set, there will be a reckoning. God is not accountable to any human being, and to clamor for divine accountability is to presume equality with God.

To say that God is all-knowing says nothing about divine justice. Such knowledge could merely give God an advantage over creation and allow for unrestrained divine whimsy. Job has attested to divine omniscience. It is this very power that has enabled God to hound him relentlessly. Elihu is confident of the reliability of his teaching and gives no thought to re-examining his presuppositions. It is this underlying premise that Job is challenging. Until this fundamental tenet is agreed upon there can be no fruitful discussion and no possible resolution.

Elihu concludes his second speech with a statement about admission of guilt and acceptance of chastisement (vv. 31-33). Job is not only criticized for his empty talk but his manner of speech itself is considered deserving of severe chastisement. In spite of all his apparent sensitivity toward and respect for Job, Elihu would have Job "tried to the end", without interruption, without reprieve. The tormented man is deemed unworthy on two counts: he has persisted in attacking God's governance and justice, and he has totally ignored the wisdom and counsel offered him by those who represent the religious tradition. Indeed, Job is a man who has spurned his God and his companions and should be left to his own fate, which is total ruin.

SPEECH TO JOB

EFFECT OF HUMAN CONDUCT ON GOD
Job 35:1-8

35   And Elihu said:
²"Do you think this to be just?
   Do you say, 'It is my right before God,'
³that you ask, 'What advantage have I?
   How am I better off than if I had sinned?'
⁴I will answer you
   and your friends with you.
⁵Look at the heavens, and see;
   and behold the clouds, which are higher than you.
⁶If you have sinned, what do you accomplish against him?
   And if your transgressions are multiplied,
   what do you do to him?
⁷If you are righteous, what do you give to him;
   or what does he receive from your hand?
⁸Your wickedness concerns a man like yourself,
   and your righteousness a son of man.

Turning again to Job, Elihu challenges the allegation that a god-fearing person is no better off in the sight of God than one who scorns divine law and follows the way of wickedness. The charge itself brings into question the order of harmony and justice that is attributed to the creator of the universe. For a second time Elihu refers to Job's declaration of innocence (cf. 34:5a) as well as to his contention that such innocence is profitless (cf. 34:9). He now takes up this challenge in order to refute it. Though Elihu addresses his statement to Job, he intends to show that the other 'friends' have been in error on this point as well (v. 4).

Elihu attempts to use wisdom methodology to the greatest advantage. Calling attention to the magnitude of the heavens, he wishes to remind his listeners of the majesty of the creator. How can a mere creature think that human behavior of any kind would affect the divine sovereign? Sinfulness can do nothing to God (v. 6) nor can righteousness add anything (v. 7). The evil effects of sin are borne by the wicked themselves and by others who must shoulder the burden of this oppression.

If this is true, then why should God be concerned to punish the wrongdoers or allow suffering for disciplinary or pedagogical reasons? Why does the tradition insist that righteousness will be rewarded with peace and prosperity? Why have those around Job scorned him and maintained that his adversity is just recompense? Elihu has indeed introduced a new perspective on the notion of God's transcendence. It may very well be true that human behavior does not disrupt the harmony of the universe nor frustrate divine tranquillity. However, to suggest such a state of affairs throws the prevailing theory of order and retribution into question and merely accentuates the question of Job's situation. Why does he suffer, if not for sin or some other unexplained disorder? Is God totally disinterested in the behavior of human beings or is their conduct out of the realm of divine control? Is Elihu placing emphasis on the teaching which holds that actions contain within themselves the beneficial or destructive powers which are released during the performance of the deed? Even this does not deal with Job's claim to innocence.

A CRY FROM PAIN, NOT PIETY
Job 35:9-16

> 9"Because of the multitude of oppressions
>   people cry out;
>   they call for help because of the arm of the mighty.
> 10But none says, 'Where is God my Maker,
>   who gives songs in the night,
> 11who teaches us more than the beasts of the earth,
>   and makes us wiser than the birds of the air?'
> 12There they cry out, but he does not answer,
>   because of the pride of evil men.
> 13Surely God does not hear an empty cry,
>   nor does the Almighty regard it.

¹⁴How much less when you say that you do not see him,
   that the case is before him, and you are waiting for him!
¹⁵And now, because his anger does not punish,
   and he does not greatly heed transgression,
¹⁶Job opens his mouth in empty talk,
   he multiplies words without knowledge."

The truly righteous cry out for God. Elihu believes that most people wail because of the oppression that they experience. If they were really god-fearing they would search for God rather than for relief. It is for this reason, he claims, that God will not answer their pleading. Their appeal is self-seeking and, therefore, God must correct them even in their pain. If this is the way that God will instruct those of weak faith, how should he treat one like Job who has assumed an adversary role in his relationship with God? Job has demanded that God act when and how Job would determine. The sovereign God will be commanded by no one, nor will he be accused by one whose lot in life indicates his lack of wisdom and righteousness.

The two sections of this argument are in opposition with each other. First, Elihu states that God is not influenced by human conduct. Then he proceeds to justify the divine delay in responding to entreaties for relief in some cases and for vengeance in others. This incongruity illustrates the inadequacy of the instruction and counsel that is being offered to Job. The teaching may be more nuanced than what has been offered previously, but it flows from the identical principles and presuppositions. Therefore, it can hardly throw light on the incomprehensibility of Job's quandary.

THE JUSTICE OF GOD
Job 36:1-23

36   And Elihu continued and said:
²"Bear with me a little, and I will show you,
   for I have yet something to say on God's behalf.

³I will fetch my knowledge from afar,
   and ascribe righteousness to my Maker.
⁴For truly my words are not false;
   one who is perfect in knowledge is with you.
⁵"Behold, God is mighty, and does not despise any;
   he is mighty in strength of understanding.
⁶He does not keep the wicked alive,
   but gives the afflicted their right.
⁷He does not withdraw his eyes from the righteous,
   but with kings upon the throne
   he sets them for ever, and they are exalted.
⁸And if they are bound in fetters
   and caught in the cords of affliction,
⁹then he declares to them their work
   and their transgressions, that they
   are behaving arrogantly.
¹⁰He opens their ears to instruction,
   and commands that they return from iniquity.
¹¹If they hearken and serve him,
   they complete their days in prosperity,
   and their years in pleasantness.
¹²But if they do not hearken, they perish by the sword,
   and die without knowledge.
¹³"The godless in heart cherish anger;
   they do not cry for help when he binds them.
¹⁴They die in youth,
   and their life ends in shame.
¹⁵He delivers the afflicted by their affliction,
   and opens their ear by adversity.
¹⁶He also allured you out of distress
   into a broad place where there was no cramping,
   and what was set on your table was full of fatness.
¹⁷"But you are full of the judgment on the wicked;
   judgment and justice seize you.
¹⁸Beware lest wrath entice you into scoffing;
   and let not the greatness of the ransom turn you aside.
¹⁹Will your cry avail to keep you from distress,
   or all the force of your strength?

20Do not long for the night,
   when peoples are cut off in their place.
21Take heed, do not turn to inquity,
   for this you have chosen rather than affliction.
22Behold, God is exalted in his power;
   who is a teacher like him?
23Who has prescribed for him his way,
   or who can say, 'Thou hast done wrong'?

Elihu continues in his discussion of God. He has tried to demonstrate the meaninglessness of Job's claims and now he turns his attention to God's majesty and justice (vv. 1-4). He reasserts the reliability and indeed the superior nature of his words. Those who listen can be certain of their accuracy.

With three emphatic negatives (vv. 5-7) he disputes Job's denunciation of God. God does not despise the weak; he does not indulge the wicked; he does not ignore the just. Any hardship that befalls one is for the sake of warning or reproof. It is God's intention to raise up those who may have fallen because they strayed from the right path. Yet this can only be accomplished if one acknowledges the error of one's ways. In reality, chastisement is a disciplinary measure ultimately intended for the advancement of people and not for their defeat as Job has alleged. God is impartial in this regard. All must face their just recompense be they lowly or royal, weak or proud. Repentance and reform will be rewarded with prosperity. Failure to reform will result in ruin and darkness.

This point regarding correction seems to be Elihu's major contribution to the debate. Unlike the others, he offers the possibility of a conditional and temporary aspect to the chastisement. It need not be seen as merely retributive punishment. Although rather harsh in itself, in the hand of a caring God suffering can serve to set right what is disordered but yet can be remedied. The encouraging tone of the message is obvious. However, the reality of error and guilt is taken for granted or else the justice of God could indeed be called into question. Elihu portrays God as just but merciful.

It is very difficult to interpret verses 16-23. Because of the obscurity of the Hebrew, the *New American Bible* omits it from the text but includes the Vulgate (Latin) translation in a footnote. In order to provide any kind of reading the text has to be emended, hence the variety of translations. Apparently the addressee of verses 16-20 is prosperious and thus cannot be Job in his present state. If it is intended for him, the imagery calls him to reflect on his former life and his attitudes and conduct at that time. Had he previously perhaps mistaken success and security as immutable evidence of his righteousness? Had he succumbed to the temptation to use his wealth as bribery to ward off what ever was troublesome? If this is an accusation from Elihu, there is nothing in the earlier text to suggest that Job was guilty in this way. Job is portrayed in the Prologue, and later in the Dialogue describes himself, as a generous and trustworthy man of means. He was innocent of any form of oppression, manipulation, or bribery.

Verses 21-23 constitute a warning against turning to evil which will eventually result in affliction such as Job is currently suffering. This affliction serves a pedagogical purpose. By it, God is trying to point out to Job the error of his ways. Learn the lesson that suffering has to teach. Escape from it is impossible and attempt at this results in further frustration.

THE POWER OF THE GOD OF NATURE
Job 36:24-33

24"Remember to extol his work,
 of which men have sung.
25All men have looked on it;
 man beholds it from afar.
26Behold, God is great, and we know him not;
 the number of his years is unsearchable.
27For he draws up the drops of water,
 he distils his mist in rain

28which the skies pour down,
   and drop upon man abundantly.
29Can any one understand the spreading of the clouds,
   the thunderings of his pavilion?
30Behold, he scatters his lightning about him,
   and covers the roots of the sea.
31For by these he judges peoples;
   he gives food in abundance.
32He covers his hands with the lightning,
   and commands it to strike the mark.
33Its crashing declares concerning him,
   who is jealous with anger against iniquity.

This passage begins the last majestic theme of the Elihu speeches and brings the reader to the threshhold of the great revelation of God from the whirlwind. Here the wisdom,and power of God are extolled together, although the primary emphasis is on the power of God revealed through the wonders of the storm. This imagery comes from the very ancient Near Eastern mythology wherein the mightiest god rules over the forces of life and fertility. Because of their agrarian setting, the people believed that the natural occurrences necessary for growth were gifts from this great god. Gradually they came to think of storm activity as a manifestation of this great and powerful deity. Naturally Israel appropriated this theology into her concept of her great and powerful God. Yahweh was considered the unrivaled God of nature and of the storm. He had not only conquered these forces but had actually made them. It was he who determined the waters of the heavens, the rain, the mist and the clouds. The thunder was the sound of his voice resounding through the heavens. He held in his hand all of the heavenly power. If he possesses the wisdom and power to control the cosmic realm, who would dare to question his dominion in the human sphere? This theme is continued to the end of the next chapter.

GOD IN THE THUNDER
Job 37:1-24

37 "At this also my heart trembles,
and leaps out of its place.
2Hearken to the thunder of his voice
and the rumbling that comes from his mouth.
3Under the whole heaven he lets it go,
and his lightning to the corners of the earth.
4After it his voice roars;
he thunders with his majestic voice
and he does not restrain the lightnings
when his voice is heard.
5God thunders wondrously with his voice;
he does great things which we cannot comprehend.
6For to the snow he says, 'Fall on the earth';
and to the shower and the rain, 'Be strong.'
7He seals up the hand of every man,
that all men may know his work.
8Then the beasts go into their lairs,
and remain in their dens.
9From its chamber comes the whirlwind,
and cold from the scattering winds.
10By the breath of God ice is given,
and the broad waters are frozen fast.
11He loads the thick cloud with moisture;
the clouds scatter his lighning.
12They turn round and round by his guidance,
to accomplish all that he commands them
on the face of the habitable world.
13Whether for correction, or for his land,
or for love, he causes it to happen.
14"Hear this, O Job;
stop and consider the wondrous works of God.
15Do you know how God lays his command upon them,
and causes the lightning of his cloud to shine?
16Do you know the balancing of the clouds,
the wondrous works of him who is perfect in
knowledge,

17you whose garments are hot
  when the earth is still because of the south wind?
18Can you, like him, spread out the skies,
  hard as a molten mirror?
19Teach us what we shall say to him;
  we cannot draw up our case because of darkness.
20Shall it be told him that I would speak?
  Did a man ever wish that he would be swallowed up?
21"And now men cannot look on the light
  when it is bright in the skies,
  when the wind has passed and cleared them.
22Out of the north comes golden splendor;
  God is clothed with majesty.
23The Almighty—we cannot find him;
  he is great in power and justice,
  and abundant righteousness he will not violate.
24Therefore men fear him;
  he does not regard any who are wise in their own
conceit."

The praise of the creative power and majesty of God
continues with the concentration on the fury of the thunder.
This picture is reminiscent of Marduk the great storm god of
Mesopotamia who made his presence and vigor known by
roaring through the heavens. There is a slight shift of
emphasis from the earlier passages where the works of
creation were the focus of wonder and awe. Now Elihu seeks
to call attention to the impending theophany of the great
God Yahweh himself (vv. 2-5). This concept is not foreign to
Israel who has long preserved and cherished her memory of
Yahweh's revelation on Mount Sinai amidst thunder and
lightning.
    When God speaks from the celestial throne all obey. The
poet enumerates the water forms of the sky — snow, shower
and rain, clouds, winds and lightning. All are subject to his
call as are the creatures of the earth (vv. 6-11). No one can
comprehend (v. 5) but all must accomplish his will (v. 12).
Elihu concludes this tribute to God with a restatement of his

principal theme. The divine cosmic activity is often meant for human admonishment as well as for the sake of fertility of the land. The motivation behind all of this is God's love for all that has been created.

Job is admonished: "Hear. . . stop and consider. . ." and then is beseiged with questions. The answers are obvious and are designed to force him to acknowledge the wisdom and power of God and his own abominable deficiency in contrast. "Do you know . . .?" "Do you know . . .?" "Can you . . . ?" are really taunts intended to humble him (vv. 15-18). In order to plumb the depths of the mysteries of the skies one would need superhuman, indeed, divine knowledge and authority. Job has inferred that he has exceptional insight. Let him teach the sages who modestly admit their inadequacy before God and, with tongue in cheek, before Job.

All attention is riveted to the north, the direction of the dwelling place of the magnificent God who is preparing to reveal himself. The imagery that embellishes the tradition of the great storm god enhances this description of the theophany or revelation of Yahweh. There was common belief in the Ancient Near Eastern world that a powerful deity resided in the heights of a prominent northern mountain and revealed himself in the midst of the storm. References to this theme can be found in other places of the Hebrew Scriptures (cf. 26:7; Isa 14:13; Ps 48:2). Here the imagery becomes an essential part of the description of the experience and, as will be seen later, a pedagogical tool used by the divine wisdom teacher. Fear and trembling attend a manifestation of this magnitude. Creatures are dumbstruck at the thought of the approach of this mighty god; how much more at the prospect of his judgment.

The first three visitors had chided Job for demanding a divine response. Nevertheless, Elihu announces one. They felt that Job should be satisfied with the direction offered to him through the long standing tradition of the current religion. There was no need for new revelation. All that was required for harmonious living could be found wthin the wisdom of their teaching. Elihu recognizes that the mighty

God is not bound to the present theology and can and will make known his will as he pleases. His concept of God is not as rigid as that of his companions, although he too believes that whatever is to be declared will be in accord with the already established principles of theology. His contribution to the Dialogues prepares the way for a revelation of Yahweh that actually addresses the dilemma of Job.

CHAPTER FIVE
YAHWEH SPEECHES

Job had repeatedly demanded an answer from God, some explanation for the confusion of his life. Again and again his advisors had condemned him for this arrogance and had defended the divine order against Job's attacks. Now, contrary to their expectations God does confront Job. The manner and nature of this encounter is not at all what Job had begged for.

The source of Job's dilemma is the apparent meaninglessness of his sufferings. Given the contemporary and conventional worldview of universal order and moral retribution, three should be some form of wrongdoing at the basis of his trouble. Job claims that there is not, while the others insist that there must be. This is the irregularity for which Job demands an explanation that only God can give. Surprisingly, the speeches of Yahweh never mention the suffering much less the alleged sinfulness of Job. Neither does God address any of the questions or challenges of the tormented man. This has led to many different interpretations of the discourses and, therefore, possible solutions to the dilemma of Job and the theological meaning of the book.

The present commentary will attempt to show that contrary to what some hold God does not ignore the basic concern of Job but treats it at its core. The manner in which this is done is consistent with the technique of the wisdom teacher who, rather than replying directly to Job's unrelenting pleadings, leads him to new insights by means of careful questioning.

The literary form and content of the Speeches are reminiscent of an Ancient Near Eastern pattern known as onomasticon. These were lists of names of things that had similar characteristics and were probably early attempts at classification of natural phenomena. They demonstrate the universal human desire to understand the universe and have survived as a pre-scientific effort to preserve this understanding. To suggest a similarity between this ancient literary form and the Yahweh Speeches does not imply that the Joban texts are dependent upon such a model. It merely indicates that lists of cosmological, meteorological or other natural phenomena were not unique in the ancient world. Further, the use of nature as a means of instructing is a well established characteristic of the wisdom tradition and is used extensively throughout the Book of Job itself. The manner of questioning is also in accord with the pedagogical style of the wisdom teacher. There is a sardonic tone to the queries put to Job which is similar to the satirical questioning that persisted in the wisdom schools.

The manner in which this literary form is used in the Book of Job and the very reason that it is used at all are very significant. In addressing Job, Yahweh elaborates upon each item in the scientific list noting the unique characteristics of each marvel and challenging Job's knowledge of and power over it. Assuming the role of the teacher, Yahweh utilizes the didactic method of interrogation. Because the situation is polemical rather than merely instructional, the rhetorical questions set to Job are ironic in nature. Job is forced to acknowledge his limitations. This indirect procedure leads him to new anthropological insights and a different theological position.

The two speeches of Yahweh follow a pattern of interrogation-declaration-interrogation followed by a short reply from Job. These chapters have been considered some of the most beautiful nature poetry of the Ancient Near East. The principal theme permeating this section is the purposefulness of the creator. There is a masterful governing structure within the universe that far transcends human comprehension or control.

THE FIRST SPEECH

THE MARVELS OF CREATIVE POWER
Job 38:1-11

> **38** Then the Lord answered Job out of the whirlwind:
> ²"Who is this that darkens counsel by
>   words without knowledge?
> ³Gird up your loins like a man,
>   I will question you, and you shall declare to me.
> ⁴"Where were you when I laid the foundation of the
>   earth?
>   Tell me, if you have understanding.
> ⁵Who determined its measurements—
>   surely you know!
>   Or who stretched the line upon it?
> ⁶On what were its bases sunk,
>   or who laid its cornerstone,
> ⁷when the morning stars sang together,
>   and all the sons of God shouted for joy?
> ⁸"Or who shut in the sea with doors,
>   when it burst forth from the womb;
> ⁹when I made clouds its garment,
>   and thick darkness its swaddling band,
> ¹⁰and prescribed bounds for it,
>   and set bars and doors,
> ¹¹and said, 'Thus far shall you come, and no farther,
>   and here shall your proud waves be stayed'?

At last the Lord breaks the cosmic silence and thunders through the heavens. Meteorological occurrences often accompanied a theophany or experience of God as mentioned above (cf. pg. 174). The question put to Job in verse 2 may be derived from the idea that the ancient god consulted a heavenly council whose wisdom was sought at the time of creation. The role of the 'First Human' in this regard has already been treated (cf. pp. 92-93). Although he never claimed it for himself, Job has been accused of presuming such an exalted role. Is the Lord implying that Job's demand for understanding is really an arrogation of wisdom that far exceeds human ability? Has Job's contention exposed his pride? Does the interrogation that follows (vv. 4-11) suggest that Yahweh would bring Job to an admission of his own inadequacy by challenging him to behavior befitting a *strong man* but not a primordial companion?

A second possible explanation of Yahweh's question is also related to the theme of creation although the emphasis is slightly different. Counsel refers to the purpose or scheme of God in the creation, control and maintenance of the universe. Job has admitted that this counsel is God's, yet throughout the Dialogues he has questioned the wisdom and justice of divine control and maintenance. He is now called by God to stand up to this questioning. He is commanded to prepare himself for this strenuous and difficult undertaking and to respond as a *strong man*. He had pleaded for a confrontation; now he is challenged to a contest. It is not a dispute about Job's morality but one of much greater proportions. It is Job's experiential knowledge that is challenged. Only one who was present at creation can comprehend the extend of the universe and the intricacies of its operation.

The image of verse 3 is of a *strong man* of valor prepared for a trial. Elihu had used the same word to speak of Job (cf. 34:7) but within a description that is debasing and condemnatory. There is no trace of any taunting in the challenge of Yahweh. Job has called for a hearing and encounter with the divine; his plea has been heard and his demand is being met. He is now ordered to rise to the occasion. Although previously the man had clamored for a clarification from

God, instead Yahweh will require answers from Job. This is not merely a show of strength with the mighty God turning the tables on the weak human creature. The setting for the encounter is quite different than what Job had envisioned. He had consistently employed language and imagery from the world of the court room. He was seeking vindication and believed that it would be granted as the result of some kind of trial. Contrariwise, Yahweh ignores the juridical dimension of the struggle, never mentioning sin or punishment and refusing to condemn or exonerate Job. The real issue is deeper and Job must be led to more profound insights in this regard. Thus, the role of divine teacher is indispensable for the resolution of the dilemma and the message of the book, and the setting is pedagogical rather than judicial.

Job is repeatedly questioned about the creation of the world (vv. 4-7). There is no doubt about who did the creating for it is very clearly stated that Yahweh laid the foundations. Job is quizzed as to his whereabouts while it was happening. He is interrogated further about his knowledge of this foundation. The questions are steeped in gentle mockery for Yahweh is really not looking for answers. God knows where Job was, but is determined that Job acknowledge his finite condition. The questions seek to demonstrate to Job the limitations of his creaturehood. They preclude even the slightest arrogant response. The stars of morning and the sons of God, who in the ancient world were lesser gods but have been relegated by Israel to the realm of celestial creatures, provided primordial rejoicing. Where was Job? This poetic imagery is consistent with other passages within the Israelite tradition (cf. Pss 24:2; 89:11; 102:25; 104:5; Isa 48:13; 51:3; etc.). Yahweh is the skillful architect of the universe, responsible for its structure and symmetry. The author of the Speeches is artistically sketching a portrait of a magnificently balanced universe.

Power over the waters below as well as those above was the prerogative of the mighty and victorious conqueror of chaos. Verses 8-11 describe Yahweh's control of the sea (cf. Ps 104:6-9). The text does not say that Yahweh created the sea, nor does it identify the womb from which it sprang. There is no evidence that the womb is the earth. This may be an allusion to a mythological tradition. There is no thought of a struggle between Yahweh and the sea. From the moment it comes forth from the womb it is under the uncompromising divine control. Pictured as the vanquisher of chaos, Yahweh controls not only by his direct activity but also by his word (v. 11). There is a tone of challenge in this description. Can Job match the creative and regulative power of God? Is he even able to understand it? The answers to these questions are obviously negative.

These few verses lay the foundation for Yahweh's response to Job. The perplexed man has called into question the activity of God in regulating human affairs. He believes that if he is not vindicated, it is either because of divine caprice and injustice or because of Yahweh's powerlessness against the forces of disorder. God first has Job acknowledge the divine wisdom (vv. 4-7) and power (vv. 8-11) manifested in creation. The next step will be to show the steadfast nature of this control.

EXTRAORDINARY MANAGEMENT OF THE UNIVERSE
Job 38:12-38

> [12]"Have you commanded the morning
>   since your days began,
>   and caused the dawn to know its place,
> [13]that it might take hold of the skirts of the earth,
>   and the wicked be shaken out of it?
> [14]It is changed like clay under the seal,
>   and it is dyed like a garment.
> [15]From the wicked their light is withheld,
>   and their uplifted arm is broken.
> [16]"Have you entered into the springs of the sea,
>   or walked in the recesses of the deep?
> [17]Have the gates of death been revealed to you,
>   or have you seen the gates of deep darkness?

¹⁸Have you comprehended the expanse of the earth?
　　Declare, if you know all this.
¹⁹"Where is the way to the dwelling of light,
　　and where is the place of darkness,
²⁰that you may take it to its territory
　　and that you may discern the paths to its home?
²¹You know, for you were born then,
　　and the number of your days is great!
²²"Have you entered the storehouses of the snow,
　　or have you seen the storehouses of the hail,
²³which I have reserved for the time of trouble,
　　for the day of battle and war?
²⁴What is the way to the place where the light is
　　distributed,
　　or where the east wind is scattered upon the earth?
²⁵"Who has cleft a channel for the torrents of rain,
　　and a way for the thunderbolt,
²⁶to bring rain on a land where no man is,
　　on the desert in which there is no man;
²⁷to satisfy the waste and desolate land,
　　and to make the ground put forth grass?
²⁸"Has the rain a father,
　　or who has begotten the drops of dew?
²⁹From whose womb did the ice come forth,
　　and who has given birth to the hoarfrost of heaven?
³⁰The waters become hard like stone,
　　and the face of the deep is frozen.
³¹"Can you bind the chains of the Pleiades,
　　or loose the cords of Orion?
³²Can you lead forth the Mazzaroth in their season,
　　or can you guide the Bear with its children?
³³Do you know the ordinances of the heavens?
　　Can you establish their rule on the earth?
³⁴"Can you lift up your voice to the clouds,
　　that a flood of waters may cover you?
³⁵Can you send forth lightnings, that they may go
　　and say to you, 'Here we are'?
³⁶Who has put wisdom in the clouds,
　　or given understanding to the mists?

37Who can number the clouds by wisdom?
  Or who can tilt the waterskins of the heavens,
38when the dust runs into a mass
  and the clods cleave fast together?

Having subdued chaos and determined the structure of the universe, Yahweh continues to exert control over every aspect of this masterpiece whether it touches upon the sphere of human concerns or not. The constant return of morning and the effect of the light of day are the subjects of verses 12-15. Job is asked only one question. Has he ever had any control over the morning and its light? This refers not only to the first daylight of creation but to the dawn of any and every day. Light is instrumental in giving form and color to the earth (v. 14) and it exposes the wicked and their evil (vv. 13, 15), thereby functioning both physically and ethically. If Job has control over it he has power in both of these spheres. The questioning is intended to force Job to admit that only God commands the light and its activities and has dominion over both the material and the moral orders. Job is powerless and unfit for such command.

Job is further asked about his knowledge of the profundity and extent of the cosmos (vv. 16-18). What does he know of the depths of the sea and of the earth? *Sea* and *deep* refer to the primordial waters of chaos over which only the conquering god has control. What does Job know of the gates of death which were thought to be at the entrance of Sheol? The kingdom of death was situated in the depths of the earth, at the bottom the the abyss. This section ends with a challenge similar to the one found in verses 4b and 5b. Job's supposed superhuman wisdom surely encompasses such information. The imperative verb requires a response from Job on the condition that he is able to respond, which he is not.

In his initial lament (3:3-10) Job had called for total disruption of celestial order by consigning not only the night but also the day to the gloom and deep darkness of chaos. Both light and darkness have their respective places. Does

Job know the *way* to these dwelling places? Does he understand the plan that has been ordained for them (vv. 19-20)? The gibe of verse 21 recalls a similar taunt of Eliphaz (15:7-8). There the sage refers to the 'First Human' in the same way that Wisdom is spoken of in Proverbs 8. Being present at creation this 'First Human' would have extraordinary wisdom. Job should be able to answer Yahweh's questions for he was this primordial creature, or at least his behavior implies that he acts as if he were. Yahweh is mocking Job, gently pointing out the serious implications of his demands.

Control over the elements of nature and their proper functioning is the gist of the further querying by God. While it is true that these elements directly affect women and men (vv. 22-24; 28-30; 34-38), God's concern embraces more than humankind. There are areas on the earth where there are no humans, yet Yahweh manages the land (vv. 25-27). Job has a very myopic view of divine control. His cosmos is anthropocentric; Yahweh's is not. Job's narrowness prevents him from seeing more than himself and his concerns. This is a rather important point and will be treated in more detail later.

Mention of storehouses wherein the waters above are preserved until it pleases God to release them is additional evidence of divine organization and management, as is the question regarding "the *way* to the place where the light is distributed. . . where the east wind is scattered upon the earth". In the ancient myth, it was the storm god who was finally able to vanquish the unruly waters and thereby bring all forms of precipitation under his sway. Much of the imagery of this section of the discourse reflects similar ideas, with Job being quizzed about the origin of the phenomena or his power over it.

Besides the meteorological elements there are cosmic movements beyond Job's comprehension (vv. 31-33). He has little if any knowledge of their influence over the earth, much less power to regulate them. Once again the existence of an underlying pattern in creation is suggested even if the human mind cannot grasp its scope.

The creation, control and maintenance of the world are beyond Job. He is in fact without understanding of it. It is by means of ironic questions rather than harsh accusations that Yahweh makes this very clear. Job does not possess primordial wisdom, nor does he share in the power inherent in such wisdom. The humble realization of his limitations should prevent him from assuming the role of the exalted 'First Human'. It may be argued that Job never makes such a presumption, but he does demand a deference which surpasses that to which he is entitled. This assertion implies a failure to recognize certain fundamental human limitations.

DOMINION OVER WILD BEASTS
Job 38:39-39:12

> 39"Can you hunt the prey for the lion,
>   or satisfy the appetite of the young lions,
> 40when they crouch in their dens,
>   or lie in wait in their covert?
> 41Who provides for the raven its prey,
>   when its young ones cry to God,
>   and wander about for lack of food?

> **39** "Do you know when the mountain goats bring forth?
>   Do you observe the calving of the hinds?
> 2Can you number the months that they fulfil,
>   and do you know the time when they
>   bring forth,
> 3when they crouch, bring forth their offspring,
>   and are delivered of their young?
> 4Their young ones become strong, they
>   grow up in the open;
>   they go forth, and do not return to them.
> 5"Who has let the wild ass go free?
>   Who has loosed the bonds of the swift ass,
> 6to whom I have given the steppe for his home,
>   and the salt land for his dwelling place?

> ⁷He scorns the tumult of the city;
>   he hears not the shouts of the driver.
> ⁸He ranges the mountains as his pasture,
>   and he searches after every green thing.
> ⁹"Is the wild ox willing to serve you?
>   Will he spend the night at your crib?
> ¹⁰Can you bind him in the furrow with ropes,
>   or will he harrow the valleys after you?
> ¹¹Will you depend on him because his strength is great,
>   and will you leave to him your labor?
> ¹²Do you have faith in him that he will return,
>   and bring your grain to your threshing floor?

Job's attention is now directed to the world of animals, specifically those outside the realm of ordinary human experience. Questions put to him challenge his power over or knowledge about the habits of these creatures. The lion (vv. 39-41) is not only of little use to humans but is actually a threat to their safety. They, like the ravens, are predators and have no need of human assistance in order to survive. In fact, domestication would hamper their activity and probably lead to their extinction.

The habits of many animals are beyond the sphere of human observation and Job would need extraordinary wisdom to understand them. Animals of the wilderness such as the mountain goat, wild ass and wild ox carry on the necessary functions of life without human aid and far from the habitation of men and women. Their haunts are the high cliffs (39:1-4), the barren steppe (vv. 5-8), and the desolate marshes (vv. 9-12). These animals fiercely resist any attempts at subjugation and avoid places of human settlement. Their freedom belongs to their very nature and their instinct seems to prevent them from compromising it. An honest Job would have to admit that such creatures are out of his reach of control and are mysterious to him as well. They seem to possess a kind of innate wisdom which enables them to survive and to flourish.

CREATURES WITH UNIQUE CHARACTERISTICS
Job 39:13-30

¹³"The wings of the ostrich wave proudly;
  but are they the pinions and plumage of love?
¹⁴For she leaves her eggs to the earth,
  and lets them be warmed on the ground,
¹⁵forgetting that a foot may crush them,
  and that the wild beast may trample them.
¹⁶She deals cruelly with her young, as if
  they were not hers;
    though her labor be in vain, yet she
      has no fear;
¹⁷because God has made her forget wisdom,
  and given her no share in understanding.
¹⁸When she rouses herself to flee,
  she laughs at the horse and his rider.
¹⁹"Do you give the horse his might?
  Do you clothe his neck with strength?
²⁰Do you make him leap like the locust?
  His majestic snorting is terrible.
²¹He paws in the valley, and exults in his strength;
  he goes out to meet the weapons.
²²He laughs at fear, and is not dismayed;
  he does not turn back from the sword.
²³Upon him rattle the quiver,
  the flashing spear and the javelin.
²⁴With fierceness and rage he swallows the ground;
  he cannot stand still at the sound of the trumpet.
²⁵When the trumpet sounds, he says 'Aha!'
  He smells the battle from afar,
    the thunder of the captains, and the shouting.
²⁶"Is it by your wisdom that the hawk soars,
  and spreads his wings toward the south?
²⁷Is it at your command that the eagle mounts up
  and makes his nest on high?
²⁸On the rock he dwells and makes his home
  in the fastness of the rocky crag.

^{29}Thence he spies out the prey;
  his eyes behold it afar off.
^{30}His young ones suck up blood;
  and where the slain are, there is he."

Up to this point all of the considerations have been put to Job in the form of questions. The section dealing with the ostrich (vv. 13-18) is in declarative form. This, as well as the fact that the description is not found in all of the ancient manuscripts, has presented a problem for some scholars. They omit it from their analysis judging it as a later intrusion into the original text. It does add an interesting dimension to the present examination, however. The description of this cruel and foolish bird can be contrasted with the wisdom and solicitude observed in the hawk and the eagle (vv. 26-30). The latter birds, like the wild animals mentioned above, are totally independent of human support, possessing instincts which enable them to thrive far from human society. The ostrich, on the other hand, judged by human standards of care and nurturing, endangers her offspring and the very existence of her species. In spite of this, by reason of some mysterious providence the ostrich continues to endure. The animals of the natural world are not only marvelous in their vitality but in the uniqueness of their diversity as well.

Consideration of the unparalleled speed of the ostrich leads to the description of the war horse (vv. 19-25). Although there is the possibility of human mastery here, the emphasis of the analysis is on the high-spiritedness of the beast. There seems to be a fearlessness in this animal that belies the caution and survival instinct that was obvious in the other animals mentioned. This characteristic contributes but another nuance to the catalog of animal marvels.

The diversity and complexity of inherent laws of behavior and perpetuation merely hint at the magnitude of the cosmic plan and the provident attention given to minute details. Different categories of creatures, both inanimate and animate, comprise a chain of interdependence whose scope baffles the mind. Important as they may be, human beings make up but one classification in this intricate network. The irony of the rhetorical questions put to Job underscores his creaturely limitations. There is a considerable amount of animal behavior of which Job is ignorant and over which he has no rule. His is not the sole dominion over all the earth nor over all of the living things of the earth. This section of the discourse also illustrates the attentiveness that Yahweh has toward creation. Job was aware of this concern in his own earlier life but must now admit that a similar providence looks after creatures that are totally out of his sphere of interest or influence. The scope of Yahweh's reign and solicitude is not limited to the narrow confines of Job's world. It is broader than his anthropocentric frame of reference and cannot be judged by his meager fallible criteria.

CHALLENGE AND REPLY
Job 40:1-5

> **40** And the Lord said to Job:
> 2"Shall a faultfinder contend with the Almighty?
>   He who argues with God, let him
>   answer it."
> 3Then Job answered the Lord:
> 4"Behold, I am of small account; what
>   shall I answer thee?
>   I lay my hand on my mouth.
> 5I have spoken once, and I will not answer;
>   twice, but I will proceed no further."

The Lord closes the first speech with a challenge similar to the one with which the discourse began. Job has been extremely critical of God's management of the moral order and has even intimated that, if consulted, the rest of creation would substantiate his claims. He has also been so brazen as to demand a confrontation with the Almighty on his, Job's, terms. Now Job is challenged to answer not charges but questions.

What can Job say? He does not have the wisdom necessary to understand the world as the Lord has suggested, nor can he claim mastery over all of its operations. The magnitude of the universe forces Job to admit his inferiority. The ascending numeration, ". . . once . . . twice . . . " (v.5) is a technique within the wisdom tradition which underscores the importance of what follows. Job's attitude is one of submission before a reality far greater than he. His response is humble silence.

THE SECOND SPEECH

THE EXECUTION OF JUSTICE
Job 40:6-14

> 6Then the Lord answered Job out of the whirlwind:
> 7"Gird up your loins like a man;
>   I will question you, and you declare to me.
> 8Will you even put me in the wrong?
>   Will you condemn me that you may be justified?
> 9Have you an arm like God,
>   and can you thunder with a voice like his?
> 10"Deck yourself with majesty and dignity;
>   clothe yourself with glory and splendor.
> 11Pour forth the overflowings of your anger,
>   and look on every one that is proud,
>   and abase him.
> 12Look on every one that is proud, and bring him low;
>   and tread down the wicked where they stand.
> 13Hide them all in the dust together;
>   bind their faces in the world below.
> 14Then will I also acknowledge to you,
>   that your own right hand can give you victory.

The introductory formula of the second speech of Yahweh (vv. 7-14) is almost identical with that of the first (cf. 38:3). The challenge is repeated and enlarged. Job has accused God of injustice (cf. 9:20, 22) in an apparent attempt to justify himself. Could it be that God has been remiss in the exercise of divine authority, failing to hold in check the forces that continually threaten the order of the universe? Or, worse than that, is Yahweh a God of whim and inconsistency, swayed by malevolent or personal fancy? For the first time Yahweh speaks directly to this charge. Verse 9 once again juxtaposes the two major aspects of any description of the deity, justice and power.

The 'arm of God' had the figurative meaning of strength and became a technical way of speaking of the military might of God (cf. Pss 77:15; 89:13). Thunder also refers to the majesty of God (cf. 26:14; 37:2-5). Job is pressed to manifest the same awe-inspiring command. Yahweh continues the challenge using technical language from yet another tradition. *Majesty* and *dignity* appear in reference to God (cf. Pss 96:6; 111:3; 145:5) and also in reference to the king (cf. Pss 21:5; 45:3-4). Psalm 104:1 is especially significant here, for it praises God who is clothed in honor and majesty. The same verb *clothe* appears in the psalm as in this verse in Job. With the power and might of God (v. 9) and clothed in royal majesty (v. 10), Job should be able to rule with the justice he claims is lacking in God's reign. When Job can accomplish this, God will praise him.

Actually, Job has made no explicit claim to superhuman prominence. It is his erroneous conception of human ability to grasp the hidden meaning of all the essentials of life that has led him to this point of unrealistic expectation. He would need the wisdom and power of God to truly comprehend life and judge all things rightly. Job has not yet accomplished this and, therefore, Yahweh sets out to teach him.

THE BEAST BEHEMOTH
Job 40:15-24

> [15]"Behold, Behemoth,
>   which I made as I made you;
>   he eats grass like an ox.
> [16]Behold, his strength in his loins,
>   and his power in the muscles of his belly.

17He makes his tail stiff like a cedar;
   the sinews of his thighs are knit together.
18His bones are tubes of bronze,
   his limbs like bars of iron.
19"He is the first of the works of God;
   let him who made him bring near his sword!
20For the mountains yield food for him
   where all the wild beasts play.
21Under the lotus plants he lies,
   in the covert of the reeds and in the marsh.
22For his shade the lotus trees cover him;
   the willows of the brook surround him.
23Behold, if the river is turbulent he is not frightened;
   he is confident though Jordan rushes against his
   mouth.
24Can one take him with hooks,
   or pierce his nose with a snare?

The descriptions of Behemoth and Leviathan (40:15-41:26) have been given various scholarly interpretations. Certain features of this section immediately set it off from the rest of Yahweh's discourses on various animals. Each unit is considerably longer than any of the other animal descriptions, much of the material is in declarative rather than interrogative form as was the case with most of the other characterizations, and the focus is on the physical dimensions of the monsters and not on their habits and dispositions. For these reasons some have rejected the authenticity of this section of the Speeches. The picture of each animal contains both zoological and mythological features. Consequently, some scholars have maintained that these are descriptions of real creatures while others hold that they are of mythical beasts. While it cannot be denied that Israel knew of and was influenced by contemporary Ancient Near Eastern mythological folklore, it seems inappropriate to consider mythic nuances as more than literary allusions used by the author. By divesting these animals of all legendary features and portraying them as ponderous but restrained creatures of Yahweh, the author may well be minimizing the significance of these popular primeval beasts and enhancing the prominence of God.

Behemoth may find its mythological origins in one of the two monsters of chaos of an ancient religion. One beast was identified with the sea while the second, Behemoth, was consigned to the wilderness. In the intertestamental books of IV Esdras and the Apocalypse of Baruch these two beasts are named as the fish to be eaten at the great messianic banquet which will celebrate God's final victory over the forces of chaos and evil.

Although the name Behemoth is the plural form for beast or cattle, the picture sketched is more like that of the hippopotamus. Regardless of the immensity of this creature, there is no question as to its origin. It is a handiwork of God like Job himself (v. 15) and is dependent upon grass for food as were the oxen that Job possessed during his days of prosperity (cf. 1:3). Whatever this description implies, Behemoth was not independent of God nor a threat to God's power. Verse 19a, though cryptic, states the same idea.

His relationship to the rest of creation and, therefore, to Job is quite another matter. His mammoth proportions rival all other beasts that have been cited in the Speeches and nature itself seems to cater to its living habits. That he is called "the first of the works of God" can be interpreted in two ways. This might be reminiscent of a former mythological concept (cf. Prov 8:22 where wisdom was called the first of God's works and witnesses to the subsequent creation activity), or it may be a reference to his priority by reason of size. Regardless of the interpretation chosen, Job is no match for this animal nor can he presume to exercise authority over it. While there are no ironic questions put to Job in this passage, one is implied in verse 24. This animal is fierce and the companion of other wild beasts (v. 20). Who is brave and cunning enough to capture it? Surely not Job.

THE MYTHICAL MONSTER OF THE SEA
Job 41:1-11

> **41** "Can you draw out Leviathan with a fishhook,
>   or press down his tongue with a cord?
> ²Can you put a rope in his nose,
>   or pierce his jaw with a hook?
> ³Will he make many supplications to you?
>   Will he speak to you soft words?
> ⁴Will he make a covenant with you to take him for your
>   servant for ever?
> ⁵Will you play with him as with a bird,
>   or will you put him on leash for your maidens?
> ⁶Will traders bargain over him?
>   Will they divide him up among the merchants?
> ⁷Can you fill his skin with harpoons,
>   or his head with fishing spears?
> ⁸Lay hands on him;
>   think of the battle; you will not do it again?
> ⁹Behold, the hope of a man is disappointed;
>   he is laid low even at the sign of him.
> ¹⁰No one is so fierce that he dares to stir him up.
>   Who then is he that can stand before me?
> ¹¹Who has given to me, that I should repay him?
>   Whatever is under the whole heaven is mine.

Compared to the sections devoted to the other animals, the description of Leviathan is disproportionately long. Whether it is a representation of one animal (vv. 1-34) or of two (vv. 1-11 and vv. 12-34) is not certain. The first part of the chapter is mainly interrogative in form and mythological in imagery, whereas the second is descriptive and sets forth the picture of a crocodile.

In early Canaanite myths of Leviathan was the primordial monster of the chaotic waters of the sea. He is described in one of the myths as a serpent with seven heads. A passage almost identical to this ancient Ugaritic poem is found in Isaiah 27:1 and the same image is pictured in Psalm 74:12-

14. The mythical battle between this personification of disorder and destruction and the superior god of order and creation has already been described (cf. pg. 132f). The inclusion in the Yahweh Speeches of a section on Leviathan is indispensable to the argument of the author.

None of the myths of the ancient world tells of the ultimate destruction of chaos. Instead, the god who is equal to the battle and able to conquer this enemy can only restrain it. Constant and perpetual vigilance over this captive threat is vital for the continued safety and harmony of the universe. Job had accused Yahweh of having lost this control claiming that his own inexplicable predicament was evidence of this. Now Yahweh portrays Leviathan as a ferocious menace but nonetheless a creature like the crocodile. Can Job snare and repress him? Can he cajole him as he would a domesticated pet? Can he train him and lead him around as a showpiece? In effect, Yahweh has been able to do this. While the animal may pose a threat to Job he certainly does not jeopardize God in any way. If the physical crocodile öffers such a challenge to a man, how could Job even dream of pitting himself against the mythological monster that this watery creature suggests?

The interrogative section ends with a note of argumentation (41:10b-11) similar to the passage with which this discourse began (cf. 40:8-9). Here as there, the power of God is offered as a substantiation for his righteousness. If Yahweh has bridled the monster of chaos, then divine control is exercised in each and every realm of creation, be it mythological, material or moral. No human has the capacity to confront Leviathan; who then can challenge the monster's captor? God is beholden to no one, and has no equal to question divine governance.

PHYSICAL FEATURES OF THE MONSTER
Job 41:12-34

> [12]"I will not keep silence concerning his limbs,
> or mighty strength, or his goodly frame.

¹³Who can strip off his outer garment?
  Who can penetrate his double coat of mail?
¹⁴Who can open the doors of his face
  Round about his teeth is terror.
¹⁵His back is made of rows of shields,
  shut up closely as with a seal.
¹⁶One is so near to another
  that no air can come between them.
¹⁷They are joined one to another;
  they clasp each other and cannot be separated.
¹⁸His sneezings flash forth light,
  and his eyes are like the eyelids of the dawn.
¹⁹Out of his mouth go flaming torches;
  sparks of fire leap forth.
²⁰Out of his nostrils comes forth smoke,
  as from a boiling pot and burning rushes.
²¹His breath kindles coals,
  and a flame comes forth from his mouth.
²²In his neck abides strength,
  and terror dances before him.
²³The folds of his flesh cleave together,
  firmly cast upon him and immovable.
²⁴His heart is hard as a stone,
  hard as the nether millstone.
²⁵When he raises himself up the mighty are afraid;
  at the crashing they are beside themselves.
²⁶Though the sword reaches him, it does not avail;
  nor the spear, the dart, or the javelin.
²⁷He counts iron as straw,
  and bronze as rotten wood.
²⁸The arrow cannot make him flee;
  for him slingstones are turned to stubble.
²⁹Clubs are counted as stubble;
  he laughs at the rattle of javelins.
³⁰His underparts are like sharp potsherds;
  he spreads himself like a threshing sledge on the mire.
³¹He makes the deep boil like a pot;
  he makes the sea like a pot of ointment.

> ³²Behind him he leaves a shining wake;
>   one would think the deep to be hoary.
> ³³Upon earth there is not his like,
>   a creature without fear.
> ³⁴He beholds everything that is high;
>   he is king over all the sons of pride."

The beast possesses an outer covering that can be described as impenetrable armor. Both his eyes and his nostrils give off flashing and terrifying light that adds to the menacing nature of this creature of God and enemy of humankind. His extraordinary strength is rivaled only by his stoutheartedness. But then, whom should we fear? Who is there that can match his fearsomeness? While the text of verse 25 reads *mighty,* the Hebrew word means *gods.* This may be an allusion to the fear of the ancient gods of Canaan who cowered at the thought of the mythological sea monster. Only the brave young warrior-god spurned the safety of the divine court and ventured out to battle with this adversary. It is really the dominance of God that holds the monster at bay while all others continue to tremble at the thought of him. No weapon can inflict injury nor does the thought of physical harm worry him. The beast not only fills others with indescribable terror but is impervious to it himself. What can Job say or do in the face of Leviathan?

The *sea* (v. 31b) and the *deep* (v. 32a) are the poet's way of speaking of the waters of chaos. The reference here could be to the ease with which the mythic monster moves within them, or it could be a demythologized description of the wake of the frolicking crocodile. Whichever interpretation is preferred, the animal is pictured at home in the treacherous water, unparalleled in his stalwartness, supreme in his ferocity.

This speech ends devoid of challenge or ironic interrogation. It terminates abruptly and does not return to the themes of divine power or righteousness and Job's powerlessness. Such a conclusion does not preclude understanding this section as the preceding sections have been seen.

Behemoth and Leviathan are creatures of Yahweh that are beyond Job's realm of experience and influence. The careful attention that has been paid to the smallest detail of their habitat and of their physical makeup indicates the ingeniousness of the creator as well as the continuity of divine solicitude in their regard. This is another illustration of the extensiveness of God's creative and providential rule. While Job seems to want to limit divine governance to those areas that can be comprehended by the human mind, Yahweh refuses to be so confined.

What have the Yahweh Speeches intended to accomplish? Was the display of cosmic wonders meant to dazzle Job with the magnitude of creative ability; or the parade of rare animals aimed at confounding him with their grace and agility or awesome dimensions? Is God merely concerned with forcing a confession of weakness and pride from this already beaten-down man? Will this show of unquestioned superiority be enough to quell Job's turmoil, end his supplications, and satisfy his demand for an explanation? A closer look at the design of the questioning will disclose the profound probing of the fundamental issues of the dilemma.

Each of the questions or statements points to some dimension of wisdom and/or power. Detail upon detail unites to produce an accumulative effect. More and more the point becomes clear. As the height and breadth of Yahweh's dominion is revealed, the inadequacy and inferiority of Job becomes glaring. The intent of the author is to highlight the former and not the latter aspect of the reality. This is intended to be a manifestation of God and not a humiliation of Job. It is only because of his previous inflated anthropological expectation that it seemed necessary to thrust Job upon a stage where he is unqualified to perform. No human being can be expected to cope with the wonders with which Job has been challenged.

As for Yahweh, several salient points become clear. Beginning with Behemoth and Leviathan, Yahweh's ability to subdue and restrain them demonstrates more than merely superhuman power. These monsters of chaos have been relegated to the simple grasses of the wilderness and the river currents. They have been singled out for examination so that Job can be assured of Yahweh's irrevocable victory over the forces of disorder and the unrelenting vigilance with which these powers are guarded. There should be no doubt in Job's mind as to the identity of the uncontested master of the universe.

Having established this, one can make a further point about the manner in which Yahweh deals with supposed enemies. There is no suggestion of retaliation nor of vindictiveness. Instead, the creatures are praised for their remarkable traits and provided for in their natural habitats. They may be dangerous and repulsive to humans but they obviously have a place in the broader scheme of God's creation. What is revealed is divine solicitude rather than the vengeance and lawless caprice that Job alleged.

The providence of God is further illustrated in the way in which the animals of the wild possess the instincts necessary to survive and to perpetuate their kind. The mysterious habits of these creatures are evidence of the unseen care of a God who has created and continues to sustain what humans cannot even imagine. The marvels of life and death all have their seasons. There is a rhythm in nature that may demand the diminution of some things in order to preserve the overall balance and harmony. Contrary to some erroneous views, the world was not created for the sake of humankind but for the sake of God. Human beings may well be privileged creatures, but they are creatures nonetheless. They comprise but one group of the totality. By cataloging the unfamiliar animals, God seems to be placing great stress on this point.

One can draw the following conclusions from the theophany. Disorder has been vanquished by the Almighty and has been committed to divine supervision and control which is benevolent and extends to every possible corner of creation. This means that the God of Nature is also the God of History, reigning over and concerned about the lives of women and men. If the patterns of nature are often beyond the horizon of human comprehension, so too are the workings of history. The human mind, in all of its brilliance and depth, is still finite and unqualified to encompass the workings of a limitless God.

Job had insisted that the injustice of his situation is proof of the triumph of chaos. Yahweh has responded by directing Job's attention to the celestial and meteorological order as well as the demythologization of the primordial monsters. Job had accused God of whimsy and abandonment. Yahweh produces examples of sustenance and protection. Job demanded answers to his questions. Yahweh has plumbed the depths of the question and awaits Job's response.

CHAPTER SIX
RESOLUTION AND
IMPLICATIONS

The final chapter of this examination of the Book of Job will include Job's response to the second speech of Yahweh, the prose Epilogue and some reflections on the message of the book. The second reply contains the last words that Job utters and reveals the man's final state of mind. The opposing tensions of his life appear to be reconciled and the development of the book is brought to a conclusion. On several levels this chapter is aptly entitled RESOLUTION.

SECOND REPLY AND LAST WORDS
Job 42:1-6

> **42** Then Job answered the Lord:
> ²"I know that thou canst do all things,
>   and that no purpose of thine can be thwarted.
> ³'Who is this that hides counsel without knowledge?'
>   Therefore I have uttered what I did not understand,
>   things too wonderful for me, which I did not know.
> ⁴'Hear, and I will speak;
>   I will question you, and you declare to me.'
> ⁵I had heard of thee by the hearing of the ear,
>   but now my eye sees thee;

⁶therefore I despise myself,
and repent in dust and ashes."

The poetic exchange of the book ends with Job's reply wherein he once again acknowledges the power of God (v. 2) and his own lack of understanding of the marvels of this power (v. 3; cf. 9:10). Job seems to repeat almost verbatim the challenges of Yahweh (v. 3a; cf. 38:2 and 4b; cf. 38:3), and then, admitting his inadequacy, answers them.

What had Job uttered that surpassed his understanding? Was it something about himself or was it something about God? He had resolutely insisted upon his integrity. Surely this is not what is meant, for Job's own life experience would have given him the necessary confidence to declare himself righteous. What had he said about God that was not true? He had never disputed divine power and majesty. Instead, he had claimed that it was this advantage that had been directed against him. Was this perhaps his error? Job could not know, as the reader does, that this is exactly what had happened. God is indeed responsible for Job's reversal of fortune (cf. 1:12 and 2:6). He is ignorant of the wager between the Lord and the satan and so Job could very well be reconsidering his charge of divine irresponsibility or his suggestion that God has been overtaken by forces of disorder.

The Yahweh Speeches have demonstrated that, contrary to Job's accusation, chaos does not reign, God does. And, although it has not been entirely destroyed, it remains securely under the supervision and control of the great cosmic conqueror, Yahweh. Job had indeed spoken of matters that he did not understand. The universal and supreme dominion of Yahweh is too wonderful for him to comprehend. Even though Yahweh is responsible for allowing Job's afflictions to occur, it was never without qualification. Evil was restrained and the testing was held in check.

Job had known of God by hearing the teaching of the wisdom school (v. 5), the testimony of the ancients or the words of the sages (cf. 8:8; 15:18). He now possesses knowledge of his own, knowledge that is his as a result of his encounter with God. He does not repent of sinfulness but of foolish speech (v. 6). Dust and ashes may either refer to the place of rejection and humiliation wherein he sat (cf. 2:8) or to his lowly condition as a mortal human being presuming to speak to the Lord (cf. Gen 18:27). While the first interpretation is not excluded, the second is preferred. It is fitting that Job acknowledge his mortal state and the limitation that this implies. He has already done this implicitly (v. 3) and here repeats his admission in figurative language. The major trend of the Yahweh Speeches seems to substantiate this understanding.

Anthropological insinuations in the Yahweh Speeches are concerned with the status of Job as a creature and the manner and degree of respect that is his due as a consequence of his nature. This attitude is expressed indirectly by means of the ironic interrogation. The questions expose Job's restricted knowledge of and power over the cosmos. It is arrogant of him to press for deference that is not his right. The satiric allusion to the 'First Human' tradition suggests Yahweh's rejection of any such arrogation on the part of Job.

Delineation of the limits of human sovereignty does not contradict the theme of human superiority over and dominion of the animal as found in the creation account of Genesis 1 (cf. Gen 1:26; 28; 9:2) and a similar theme in Psalm 8 (cf. vv. 6-9). The difference between these traditions is not so much one of contradiction as one of distinction. Job has failed to recognize certain human limits and what he demands is inappropriate. As a result of the chiding of Yahweh, the confines of Job's scope of influence are clearly drawn.

Job never intends to usurp divinity nor is he accused of this. His anthropological presuppositions, however, are false and so God sets out to correct them using exaggeration and irony. Throughout the Speeches one note resounds again and again, and Job has heard it. Yahweh is God and Job is not. The splendor of creation transcends Job's comprehension and he can only stand in awe and wonder. The purpose of the theophany was not to silence Job, but to reassure him of divine cosmic control and to inspire him to confidence. Job's questions may not have been answered nor his demands met, but his fears have been dissipated and his trust in God restored.

EPILOGUE
Job 42:7-10

> [7]After the Lord had spoken these words to Job, the Lord said to Eliphaz the Temanite: "My wrath is kindled against you and against your two friends; for you have not spoken of me what is right, as my servant Job has. [8]Now therefore take seven bulls and seven rams, and go to my servant Job, and offer up for yourselves a burnt offering; and my servant Job shall pray for you, for I will accept his prayer not to deal with you according to your folly; for you have not spoken of me what is right, as my servant Job has." [9]So Eliphaz the Temanite and Bildad the Shuhite and Zophar the Naamathite went and did what the Lord had told them; and the Lord accepted Job's prayer.
>
> [10]And the Lord restored the fortunes of Job, when he had prayed for his friends; and the Lord gave Job twice as much as he had before.

It is generally held that this passage did not belong to the original folktale. It, like its counterpart in the Prologue (cf. 2:11-13), is an addition that links the prose framework to the poetic Dialogue. These are the only places in the prose sections where the three visitors are mentioned. The author deemed it necessary to introduce them before the first speech (cf. 4:1) and to dismiss them after Job is vindicated.

Job had never asked for the return of his health nor the restoration of his goods but for vindication. Although he was unaware of it, his righteousness had been acclaimed before the satan in the Prologue. It is now applauded before his counsellors (v. 7). Surprisingly, the sages with their traditional theory of retribution are chided by the very God whose justice they had championed. They are accused of error while Job's point of view is correct. What could they have possibly said that would kindle God's wrath against them? Where were they wrong and Job right?

According to the theory of retribution, Job's hardships in life are directly linked to some wickedness on his part. All of the antagonists of this argument have held perseveringly to this position. Job, on the other hand, has obstinately rejected one of the premises leading to this conclusion. He is *not* guilty. Job knows this; Yahweh knows this; and the reader knows this.

The omnipotent God is responsible for harmony in the universe. No one questions this. A particular world view is a way of understanding this harmony. No one questions this. The dilemma of the book lies in the irreconcilability of the experience of harmony and the theory or understanding of it. Job's visitors repudiate the authenticity of his experience, uphold the integrity of God and divine harmony, and insist upon the universality of retribution. Refusing to relinquish his claim of righteousness, Job attacks the omnipotence of God and the harmony of the universe. The Yahweh Speeches have clearly exposed the error of this indictment and Job has humbly conceded. Correct about himself, he is now corrected about Yahweh. Both he and his counsellors were mistaken about the conventional world view, but God's anger is not flaming because of this misconception in itself. Job trusted the validity of human experience even when it did not appear to conform to standard assumptions, while the others remained unwilling to accord credibility to the unfamiliar. Job's unwillingness to distort reality may have forced him to the erroneous conclusion of indicting God, but he is closer to truth than are the others with their empty platitudes. The outrageousness of their perspective is highlighted when one recalls that it is precisely human experience that constitutes the basis of this theory. Before one can begin to formulate any theory of experience, accurate observation and evaluation of it is essential. Unwillingness to examine or endorse what appears to be unorthodox disqualifies these men from the exalted ranks of the trustees of wisdom. They are pronounced guilty of serious error and reparation must be made. Ironic as it may appear, the very man they have condemned as villainous is the one called upon to intercede for them.

Yahweh again refers to Job as "my servant" (vv. 7-8) whose righteousness is further recognized when he becomes the agent of justification for the others as he had been in the past (cf. 1:5). Both the Prologue and the Epilogue firmly establish the integrity of Job. This characterization is more than a simple prose description or a resumption of the style of the folkloric framework. If the vindication of verse 7 is genuine, then Job never really lost the integrity that was his from the beginning. He merely lost his reputation. He has no need to be reinstated before God but only before others. Acknowledgement of his integrity demands a reinterpretation of the inflexible theory of retribution. The possibility of virtue alongside and in the midst of suffering forces a new dimension to one's world view.

The Yahweh Speeches contain no clear solution to the quandary of Job. He is called upon to trust in the love and care of a God whose actions are not always intelligible to him. Job proves himself equal to the challenge, admitting his limitations and repenting his presumption. This attitude was the desired outcome of the theophany and, along with Job's indefatigable authenticity, the source of the pleasure that Yahweh takes in him.

RESTORATION
Job 42:11-17

> 11Then came to him all his brothers and sisters and all who had known him before, and ate bread with him in his house; and they showed him sympathy and comforted him for all the evil that the Lord had brought upon him; and each of them gave him a piece of money and a ring of gold. 12And the Lord blessed the latter days of Job more

than his beginning; and he had fourteen thousand sheep, six thousand camels, a thousand yoke of oxen, and a thousand she-asses. [13]He had also seven sons and three daughters. [14]And he called the name of the first Jemimah; and the name of the second Keziah; and the name of the third Kerenhappuch. [15]And in all the land there were no women so fair as Job's daughters; and their father gave them inheritance among their brothers. [16]And after this Job lived a hundred and forty years, and saw his sons, and son's sons, four generations. [17]And Job died, an old man, and full of days.

Once Job is vindicated and his reputation is restored all of his fair weather relatives and friends come to rejoice with him. He is compensated for all of his losses by double payment as was the rule when an individual had been unjustly dispossessed. Some manuscripts state that he had twice as many sons as well. This might explain why, although the number of daughters remained the same, their status was elevated. Rather than double the sum of possible dowries and inflate Job's future losses, the author has taken pains to describe the daughters in a manner that enhances their attractiveness, a real boon to a father concerned about their marriagibility. Besides enjoying hereditary rights (v. 15), the maidens possess stereotypical feminine charms as indicated by their names: 'Dove', the symbol of beauty; 'Perfume' and 'Eye Paint'. After having double his previous life span, Job dies in the fullness of days. This is a perfect ending for a perfect man.

The return and increase of Job's fortunes have caused certain theological problems. The restoration seems to substantiate rather than question the theory of retribution. Such difficulties dim when the entire work is viewed as a complete literary entity. While certain isolated elements of the work may have originated at different times and possess literary value of their own, it is the overall text that communicates the final message. Viewing the Epilogue from this perspective urges the interpreter to incorporate it into any serious examination of the total composition.

Most narratives have a basically simple structure: status quo, crisis, and resolution. An ordinary situation is disrupted or threatened and the principals of the narrative strive to overcome this peril. They are either successful or unsuccessful. By the substitution of the theme that has been the focus of this commentary the pattern becomes: 'order-disorder-order'. The Book of Job follows just such a pattern on several levels. The most obvious of these is the story line. The uprightness of the man's character, the contentment of his life, and the triumph of his achievements are succintly but meticulously recounted in the Prologue. This section has undeniable significance in its own right. Judged as one of the most concise technical descriptions of the ideal righteous one, it enjoys a unique prominence within the wisdom tradition. Its prominence is not lost with its incorporation into this compostion, but enhances the work of which it is now a part by painstakingly portraying Job as a man undeserving of the affliction about to befall him.

Job is suddenly inundated by tragedy from every side. In itself this is not really the crisis facing him but its occasion. The ominous threat is to his faith in God. Given his view of a harmonious universe under the control of an omnipotent deity, and a just social order as an intricate part of this universe, will Job remain steadfast in the face of inexplicable desolation? The major part of the book is devoted to this struggle and to various attempts at its resolution. Job insists that only God can intervene and rectify the injustice of the situation. The four men who have come to advise him perceive the crisis quite differently. They contest Job's point of view, regard his insolence as the real threat, and believe that only confession of guilt and a change of heart will be able to reestablish the harmony in Job's life. The third possibility for resolution is offered by Yahweh. Job is encouraged to cling to his faith in God's power and trust in God's care regardless of the apparent incongruity of his predicament. The only viable counter measure for the throes of a crisis of faith is blind faith. Job triumphs over what appear to be insurmountable obstacles and acquiesces to the promptings of Yahweh. Thereby Job opens the door to a redefinition of the order in the universe.

A second expression of the pattern 'order-disorder-order' is found in the literary form itself. The prose Prologue is an example of a tightly constructed linear development of the story. Technical expressions abound: the description of Job as the righteous man (cf. 1:1; 8; 2:3) possessing all things in numbers of perfect balance (cf. 1:2-3); and his designation by Yahweh as "my servant" (cf. 1:8; 2:3). There are also various stylistic features: the alternation of scenes on earth and in heaven; identical introductions into the court of the Lord (cf. 1:6-8 and 2:1-3); the repetition of the phrase " 'and I alone have escaped to tell you.' while he was yet speaking there came another and said," (cf. 1:15-19). All of this contributes to the picture of a deliberately refined narrative.

The Dialogue offers quite a different picture. Although patterns of Hebrew poetry are observed, the images created seem to produce a collage effect rather than a finely detailed portrait. The themes of one speech are not picked up by the following character and at times the responses seem to be meaningless when compared with what preceded them. There is seldom if ever an introduction or conclusion to a speech. The speakers are merely identified and then plunge immediately into their address. The arguments are repeated almost to the point of monotony and the impasse reached often leaves the reader with the impression that this is a series of monologues rather than dialogues.

The Epilogue resumes the regular movement of the narrative. It provides the necessary transition from the poetic section as the Prologue had done earlier and brings the story line to conclusion. It repeats some of the technical expressions of the Prologue: "my servant Job" (cf. 42:7-8); prosperity in perfect balance (cf. 43:12-13). It accords the narrative the traditional ending — "And they lived happily ever after."

The third and most significant dimension of this 'order-disorder-order' pattern touches the theological implications

of Job's restoration. Does the reestablished harmony undermine the new insights into retribution brought to birth by
the resolution of the dilemma? If Job is merely being
rewarded for his faithfulness then serious doubt can be cast
upon the motives of Yahweh in allowing him to be tested in
the first place.

In the Prologue the structure of order is easy to understand. Even after each series of trials Job remains loyal and
humbly submissive (cf. 1:21-22 and 2:10), accepting unquestioningly what is meted out to him. It will take the soul-
searching probings of the Dialogue to illustrate the extent
and effects of the collapse of the patterns of comprehension.
The visitors represent the status quo while Job is torn
between this traditional explanation which now appears
radically deficient and the reality of his experience. It is the
theory of world order that is at stake. Job's capitulation (cf.
42:2-6) resolves his real dilemma and this resolution is con-
firmed by God himself (cf. 42:7b). Job moves onto an
entirely different plain, a new level of faith. From the van-
tage point of this height he perceives the harmony within the
cosmos as a mystery to be esteemed rather than as a theory
to be mastered. He has emerged from his trauma a tranquil
man. The external circumstances of his life are of little
relevance. He no longer views them as explicit evidence of
the quality of his relationship with God. Admitting his
inability to fathom the mysteries of cosmic order, he
believes that righteousness can exist alongside and in the
midst of tribulation. There can indeed be innocent suffering
and, while he may never be able to comprehend it, he knows
that he will be able to endure it with an unshakeable faith in
God's universal providence and personal solicitude.

IMPLICATIONS FOR TODAY

The drama of Job has touched the hearts of women and
men down through the ages to the present time. It has never
lost its appeal because of the universality of the issues

addressed. Although humankind has not basically changed, the world in which it finds itself and which it has helped to create presents new challenges for each generation. If a society's religious tradition is to remain vital and creative, it must be able to speak to the contemporary world in the language of the time. Its message must be capable of being interpreted without being compromised. As stated in the Introduction (cf. pg. 23), it is not possible to treat all of the concerns of the book in a commentary of this nature. The following are reflections that flow from those issues that have been considered here.

The underlying motif of the book is ORDER, cosmic and experiential. At the heart of Job's dilemma is the collapse of his world of meaning brought on by the incomprehensible events of his life. This is not a unique experience for Job alone but one that he shares with every thinking human being. The simple process of growth and maturation demands that world views be constructed and revised or changed constantly throughout one's life. This usually occurs gradually and with little or no distress, but there are many normal situations that can result in unusual trauma and there are experiences that can wrench one from the securities of life and terrify one with the prospect of annihilation. A certain amount of understanding seems essential for human stability. When the framework of this understanding crumbles and life ceases to make sense, people often thrash around for some means of survival or, too often, despair of any solution and give up.

No one is protected from personal misfortunes such as sudden and tragic death, human exploitation or betrayal, unexpected collapse of business or career, or from disasters such as flooding or other ravages of nature. The horrors of war, or of ethnic, racial, sexual, or other social discrimination or brutality victimize countless women and men and defy all standards of justice and harmony. Is it any wonder that scores of people attempt to escape the apparent meaninglessness of existence? The gravity of these situations and the demand to remedy the evils and help bear the burdens of the afflicted are not to be minimized. However, these human miseries often lead to an even greater tragedy —the denial of any meaning to life. This is the great temptation that faces Job and it is to this trial that the book speaks.

When one's authentic and profound life experience and the generally accepted way of understanding life are in conflict, an individual seldom embraces an external standard which opposes one's own practical knowledge. The impasse between the visitors and Job reflects just such a conflict. It is more than foolhardy; it is unconscionable to tell a victim of exploitation or violence that he or she is always in some way responsible for what has happened. Even when there is some degree of culpability, the extent of the evil endured frequently far exceeds the seriousness of the human error. How does one explain crime, social injustice or war from a retributive frame of reference? The author of the Book of Job has done a masterful job of exposing the inadequacy of a rigid theory of retribution. The men who had come to assist Job with their wisdom only compound his hardship with their disregard of his many afflictions, their insensitivity to his intellectual dilemma, and their offensiveness in offering empty counsel and harsh judgment. They would have him deny what he knows to be true and accept the conventional teaching which they espouse rather than listen to his protestations and admit their inability to offer him a more suitable explanation. They are right about one thing, however. The religious tradition need not be scorned nor discarded. The truth contained within it, if it is indeed truth, must be rediscovered, embraced and allowed to speak to the present situation. They err in refusing to admit that the expression of truth is wanting and needs to change and evolve.

A similar situation faces society today. Not only sinfulness and inhumanity but the pace of life, the burst of technology with its frightening implications, human accomplishments that seem to proliferate by leaps and bounds can all rip away a false security of certainty and order and catapult the vulnerable human creature into a world of rapid change and ambiguity. The theories and answers of the past are frequently inadequate and new structures of meaning must be devised. The guardians of tradition cannot merely perpetuate the perceptions and articulations of the past. In their devotion to truth they must allow the development of its understanding and expression or they will end up as antiquarians collecting treasures of the past rather than sages possessing wisdom for the present and the future.

What message is the author propounding by presenting Job as he does? From the outset Job is an upright man whose virtue is attested to by God. When calamity befalls him it is completely unrelated to his own doing. This initial portrayal of Job as an innocent sufferer either undermines any inflexible belief in retribution or casts doubt on the management and justice of God. These are the options available to Job as the Dialogue opens. There is one thing that Job never doubts and that is his own integrity. Nor will he compromise human dignity and admit to something that he knows is false. It makes no difference that he is opposed by as cherished a treasure as his religious tradition. He will not relinquish his forthrightness nor minimize the veracity of his stand. Such a position is difficult to take when one is assured of understanding and support from others. To assume it alone, in opposition to religious custom and belief, with no buttress but the assurance of one's own life is indeed a courageous act. It also runs the danger of alienating one from the rest of reality.

Men and women of conscience have often been brought to this point of decision. Many have had to stand in opposition to the religious, political or social groups which they love and of which they are a part. Denounced as rebels and apostates, they have chosen to side with reality as experienced rather than as traditionally interpreted and have unwittingly become the real champions of truth.

There is, however, a serious flaw in Job's argument. Immersed in misfortune of which he is innocent, Job points an accusing finger at God and falls into the same trap as did his inept counselors. While they uphold strict retribution and thus reject the authenticity of Job's claims, he clings to the same theory and charges God with folly of injustice. It is only through the insights gained from the theophany that Job can see the deficiency of this world view and reconcile his dilemma.

Many times when people are caught in similar predicaments, they too accuse God of injustice. They wonder how a just God could allow the inhumanity that seems to run rampant across the face of the earth. They watch defenseless victims stricken by unbridled evil and feel compelled to deny the existence of a loving God. As in the case of Job, traditional explanations are hollow, familiar advice is flat, and customary devotion is saccharine. The temptation is to declare God a hoax and life absurd or cruel.

In such desperate situations intellectual discussions are seldom effective because the operations of the universe are beyond human comprehension. Anyone who blames God still believes in God's existence and so it is this faith rather than concepts of logic that must be strengthened and developed. Job is a perfect example of a person whose previous religious ideas had to be broken in order that a more vibrant and mature faith could emerge. Unlike the traditionalists who remained imprisoned in their theories, Job availed himself of the new insights received and risked the uncertainties of an evolving world view. It is the combination of honesty, humility and openness that is praised by the Lord.

Several meaningful insights can be drawn from reflection on Yahweh's attitude toward Job. He does not directly defend himself against Job's charge of injustice. Perhaps this is because the accusation is more an erroneous conclusion than an outright rebellion. Since Job was certain of his own guiltlessness and was an adherent of the orthodox world view, he had no other alternative but to be skeptical about God's integrity. Innocent suffering is neither denied nor explained. Instead, the discussion is moved to an entirely different plane and the fundamental issue of cosmic sovereignty is addressed. The force of God's interrogation elicits awe and submission and Job stands quietly before a panorama that has burst the confines of his narrow perspective. Neither prosperity nor affliction matters in the face of such wonders. If this is true on the cosmic plane, it is all the more so on the human plane. Contrary to a widely held misconception, happiness and success are not demonstrable rewards for righteous living nor are grief and failure concomitant reprisals. Wealth may well be the fruit of wise management, but it can also stem from greed and graft. Likewise, there are too many examples of decent men and women and helpless children suffering indignities. One implication of the Yahweh Speeches clearly illustrates the serious error of an inflexible theory of retribution. Misfortune can indeed befall the righteous. Suffering is not the sure sign of alienation from God.

A second point concerns anthropological presuppositions. Yahweh may have denounced any grandiose notion of human prominence but did not undermine the authentic dignity of Job. In fact, whenever Job is called to a superhuman feat he comes to see his own inadequacy. This is not an affront but an honest appreciation of true human potential. It includes admitting limitations as as well as praising abilities.

Confidence in his own integrity was Job's only mainstay throughout his turmoil. When all else seemed to have deserted him or to have turned against him, he continued to trust his human powers of discernment and judgment and he insisted that others accord him the hearing and justice that were his due. Here is a man who will not relinquish his self-respect nor sense of right regardless of the odds against him. He may be crushed by adversity but his spirit is undaunted. The other men read this as insolence and blasphemy, but Yahweh never accused Job of either. He calls upon Job to stand as a man of valor before the divine teacher (cf. pp. 182 & 193) and there is no trace of insult in God's speech to Job. Job survives his encounter with God without having to demean himself nor disavow his sense of dignity. He admits that his perception has been wrong but that admission is not self-deprecating. Had he succumbed to the pressure of the others and renounced his point of view, there would have been no breakthrough to a new insight. Job would have had to live with mediocre compromise rather than stark honesty, with false humility rather than human dignity, and with empty teaching rather than challenging truth. His vindication by Yahweh affirms him in his stand and justifies his perspective.

Genuine and forthright human accomplishments are to be valued and trusted as long as they are not an act of defiance in the face of God. In the normal course of human life, one cannot always determine whether progress is advantageous or defiant. This was true in the case of Job and it is true today. The only safeguards available are profound commitment to the sovereignty of God, honesty in testing limits, and humble acknowledgement of finite creaturehood.

Several questions were posed at the beginning of this study. "What is the origin of the universe and what holds it together?" "What is the meaning of suffering?" "What role does God play in life as humans experience it?" The biblical tradition, specifically the Book of Job, offers direction and insights for coming to grips with these questions. Ultimately, each person must face them, struggle with them, and somehow resolve them.

ADDITIONAL READING

COMMENTARIES

Dhorme, E. *A Commentary of the Book of Job.* London: Nelson, 1967.

Gordis, Robert. *The Book of God and Man.* Chicago: University of Chicago Press, 1965.

——————— *The Book of Job: Commenatry.* New York: Jewish Theological Seminary of America, 1978.

Habel, Norman C. *The Book of Job.* Cambridge Bible Commentary London; New York: Cambridge University Press, 1975.

Pope, Marvin. *Job.* Garden City, New York: Doubleday, 1973.

Rowley, H.H. *Job.* London:Nelson, 1970.

STUDIES

Cox, Dermot, O.F.M. *The Triumph of Impotence. Job and the Tradition of the Absurd.* Rome: Gregorian University Press, 1978.

Crenshaw, James L. *Old Testament Wisdom, An Introduction.* Atlanta: John Knox Press, 1981.

Ewing, Ward B. *Job: A Vision of God.* New York: Seabury Crossroad Books, 1976, pp. 100-125.

Gordis, Robert. *Poets, Prophets and Sages.* Bloomington: University of Indiana Press, 1971, pp. 280-324.

Job, John. *Job Speaks to Us Today.* Atlanta: John Knox Press, 1980.

Patrick, Dale. *Arguing With God.* St. Louis: The Bethany Press, 1977.

Polzin, Robert and Robertson, David, eds. *Semeia* #7. Missoula, Montana: University of Montana Press, 1977.

Rad, Gerhard von. *Wisdom in Israel.* Nashville: Abingdon;London: SCM, 1972.

Robertson, David. *The Old Testament and the Literary Critic*. Philadelphia: Fortress Press, 1977.

Westermann, Claus. *The Structure of the Book of Job*. Philadelphia: Fortress, 1981.

ECCLESIASTES

INTRODUCTION

The Book of Qoheleth, better known to most as the Book of Ecclesiastes, does not enjoy the universal renown that belongs to the Book of Job, but there are several themes found within it that are familiar to many people today. Proverbs like "You can't take it with you" or "There's nothing new under the sun" might well epitomize some of the thinking of this provocative work. In a more contemporary vein, the song "Turn, Turn, Turn" was inspired by the poem about time that is found in Chapter Three. All of this points to the relevant message that unfolds as one listens to "the Preacher". The meaning of the names given to the book, as well as the designation "the Preacher", will be treated later (cf. 230).

Qoheleth, like Job, belongs to the wisdom tradition of ancient Israel. The text itself will show that he is well versed in the conventional theory of retribution although, again like Job, he challenges its validity. The earlier INTRODUCTION in this volume (cf. pp. 15-19) set forth a brief description of ancient Israel's world view. Qoheleth's instruction must be understood within this same context. While it may be skeptical of certain tenets of sapiential teaching, this challenge originates from within the tradition itself and not from some foreign opposition. Qoheleth's new and rather unorthodox perspective illustrates the direction taken by later post-exilic wisdom speculation.

The book has the literary characteristics of a Royal Testament, a common form of the Ancient Near Eastern world. It is written in the first person and purports to be advice out of the accumulated wisdom of a sage's experience of life. Such works as *Instruction of Ptahhotep, Instruction of King Amenemhet, Instruction for King Merikere,* as well as *Teaching of Amenemope,* to name but a few, have come down to us from Ancient Egypt. There is no dialogue in Qoheleth for there is but one person in the entire book and that is the speaker. Consequently, there will be no comparison of world views and no need to wonder which is the true message of the author and what is being challenged, for the author is advancing the views that Qoheleth holds.

In addition to the major literary genre of the book there are several traditional wisdom forms employed by the author. These include proverbial quotations, contrasting proverbs, rhetorical questions, as well as the customary religious vocabulary. The mode of expression is determined by the ideas put forward and enhances the overall impact of the book. This will be explained as the commentary progresses.

There are several unresolved literary questions in the interpretation of Qoheleth. They have to do with the integrity of authorship, dating and provenance, and composition and structure of the book. As was the case with Job, the concern of this commentary is with the final product. Therefore, the origin of each unit is not as important here as is its incorporation into the final composition. While the author of the book most likely composed several of the maxims, there are also a good many that he cites for the purpose of discussion. Finally, the book concludes with an Epilogue composed by another hand.

The language of the book resembles the kind of Hebrew that is very late in the biblical period and almost exclusively literary in usage. It also contains several Aramaic words which lead scholars to date the book around the Third Century B.C.E. (Before the Common Era), when Aramaic was becoming the spoken language of the Ancient Near Eastern world and Hebrew was slipping into desuetude.

There is a great diversity of opinion concerning the structure of the book. Some feel that it is without organization, a collection of independent wisdom pieces. Others divide the book into two parts: Qoheleth's observation of life, and the conclusions that he draws. The present commentary belongs with those who recognize a deliberate structure. This will become clearer in the course of this examination.

The diversity of opinion about structure mentioned above is minimal when compared to the wide range of opinion regarding the meaning of the book. Qoheleth has been described as a skeptic or cynic and also as a pragmatist. His view of life has been called anything from pessimistic, fatalistic or nihilistic to realistic. His religious perspective has been considered variously as heterodox, heretical, amoral or profoundly Israelite. Recognized as disillusioned with the structures of society, he is accused of lacking the enthusiasm of a reformer and the vision of a mystic. This has led some to perceive him as a frustrated man resigned to the injustice and meaninglessness of life, intent upon making the most of any fleeting pleasures in the spirit of Epicureanism.

This broad gamut of viewpoints results from widely diverging perspectives employed in interpreting the major themes of the book. Basic to all of the ideas is a recognition of the inadequacy of the theory of retribution, a theme that occupied the attention of the author of Job as well. Coupled with this are the inevitability and universality of death and the sense of futility it often accords life. Death is not the only reality that challenges life's purposefulness. Since the search for wisdom is endless, the acquisition of goods can be experienced as empty, and the direction taken by life is out of human hands. Such themes are prevalent in the literature of societies that are experiencing great upheaval. Ancient Egypt's *The Song of the Harper* reflects a lack of trust in the pursuits of life and encourages enjoyment of pleasures while there is time, for death ends everything. Because of the dilemma that he faced, Job asked "What is the meaning of suffering?" Qoheleth looks at human endeavor in general and asks an even more encompassing and perhaps more profound question: "What is the meaning of life?"

CHAPTER ONE
OBSERVATION OF LIFE

If there is one idea that characterizes this section of Qoheleth it is VANITY. "Vanity of vanities" (1:2). This is the evaluation that is repeatedly given after each short discourse on some aspect of life. It is found only in the first part of the book and can be used to determine its inner structure.

THE PROFITLESSNESS OF TOIL
Qoheleth 1:1-11

1 The words of the Preacher, the son
of David, king in Jerusalem.
²Vanity of vanities, says the Preacher,
vanity of vanities! All is vanity.
³What does man gain by all the toil
at which he toils under the sun?
⁴A generation goes, and a generation comes,
but the earth remains for ever.
⁵The sun rises and the sun goes down,
it hastens to the place where it rises.
⁶The wind blows to the south,
and goes round to the north;
round and round goes the wind,
and on its circuits the wind returns.

[7]All streams run to the sea,
   but the sea is not full;
   to the place where the streams flow,
   there they flow again.
[8]All things are full of weariness;
   a man cannot utter it;
   the eye is not satisfied with seeing,
   nor the ear filled with hearing.
[9]What has been is what will be,
   and what has been done is what will be done;
   and there is nothing new under the sun.
[10]Is there a thing of which it is said,
   "See, this is new"?
   It has been already,
   in the ages before us.
[11]There is no remembrance of former things,
   nor will there by any remembrance
   of later things yet to happen
   among those who come after.

The superscription in verse 1 describes rather than identifies the speaker in the book. The exact meaning of Qoheleth is still debated, but the form of the word suggests that it is probably not a name. A derivative of the Hebrew word *qahal* or *assembly,* it refers to one who calls forth or presides over a meeting, perhaps for the purpose of teaching. The Greek word used to translate *qahal* is *ekklesia,* which referred to the citizens' assembly in Greece. The feminine ending of Qoheleth (*eth*) can be traced to the practice of using feminine participles to designate functionaries. This functionary within the *qahal* is called Qoheleth. In the Greek, the functionary within the *ekklesia* is called Ecclesiastes, or "Preacher". The man is further identified as the son of David, the king of Israel. There can be no doubt that the reference is to Solomon, who has been esteemed in popular devotion as the wise man par excellence. There was a tradition that Solomon was not only versed in human wisdom (cf. 1 Kgs 3:16-28) but had encyclopedic knowledge as well (cf. 1 Kgs 4:29-34). The sage in this book depicts himself in a similar fashion. What better way to assume the sapiential authority of Solomon than to ascribe to oneself royal designations. From the outset the teaching will be authenticated even though it will prove to be unorthodox.

Verses 2-11 consist of a poetic construction that deplores the profitlessness of toil. It begins with the characteristic phrase "Vanity of Vanities". (The book begins and ends in the same way, cf. 12:8). The Hebrew word *hebel,* most often translated as 'vanity' is also rendered as 'vapor' or 'thin air', and when used descriptively connotes pointlessness or futility. Just what is it that receives such a dismal assessment? Human toil! The word *amal* or *toil* appears twice in verse 3, leaving no doubt in any mind as to the subject under discussion, *amal* is elsewhere translated 'trouble' (cf. 5:17; Job 3:10; 7:3; Ps 73:5; etc.) and, therefore, connotes great effort or difficulty. Qoheleth is saying that human toil is trouble and he asks, "What profit or gain is there in such toil?" The Hebrew word *yitron* or *gain* comes from a commercial milieu and implies that there is a dividend involved. Most people will endure significant difficulty (*amal*) if they can be guaranteed some gain (*yitron*) for their labor. The more materialistic they are, however, the less apt they are to put forth energy when the rewards are not substantial. Remembering the basic premise of retribution — 'wise conduct will be rewarded' — recompense is probably the real reason for most labor. While there may be some like Job whose faithfulness to virtue is disinterested, very few people will accept unquestioningly the deprivation of the fruits of their labor. Qoheleth doubts whether the trouble experienced in human toil is worth the possible rewards. The phrase, "under the sun", appears frequently within the Egyptian instruction genre and exclusively within this biblical book. It is a figurative way of speaking of the place where the human drama unfolds. Life must be lived here on earth and all hopes must be realized here as well. The question may appear simple but the implications are profound. In spite of all of the effort exerted in human strivings, what comes of it? Is the reward worth the labor? Is there even a sure reward.

One of the most common techniques of the sage was looking at nature for insights that might be applied to life. Qoheleth employs this device as he turns to the movements of the earth (v. 4), the sun (v. 5), the wind (v. 6), and the sea (v. 7). The characteristic that they have in common and upon which he wishes to capitalize is their regularity. The earth does not change, it seems constant. The sun rises and sets and rises and sets in the same pattern day after day. Although the wind appears at times to be irregular, it follows certain paths that, upon observation, can be predicted. Even the sea, though constantly fed, is never full. The regularity in nature is also monotonous and appears devoid of any kind of progress. What advantage does the earth have in being changeless? What does the sun accomplish by rising and setting if it must repeat the cycle again and again with no variation and no advance? What profit comes from the wind's constant flow if it never arrives at any destination? To what avail do the streams nourish an insatiable sea? Learn from nature! Human striving for gain is nothing but wearisome labor that must be repeated and repeated with no promise of conclusion and no assurance of gratification (v. 8).

One might be tempted to think that things do change and that there is hope for improvement. It is only because of the fleetingness of life and the lack of a sense of history that such a position can be held. Human life is basically the same regardless of the society or generation into which one is born. The cycles of life repeat and the experiences are similar. Earth-shaking events do occur, but they seldom disrupt the fundamental rhythms of existence. "There is nothing new under the sun." A new generation rarely remembers the lessons learned by its predecessors. Hence it is unprepared for the inevitable consequences of their actions. Nature repeats itself and so does history. And what is the point of it all? Nothing seems to have permanent significance.

THE QUEST
Qoheleth 1:12-18

¹²I the Preacher have been king over Israel in Jerusalem. ¹³And I applied my mind to seek and to search out by wisdom all that is done under heaven; it is an unhappy business that God has given to the sons of men to be busy with. ¹⁴I have seen everything that is done under the sun; and behold, all is vanity and a striving after wind.

¹⁵What is crooked cannot be made straight,
  and what is lacking cannot be numbered.

¹⁶I said to myself, "I have acquired great wisdom, surpassing all who were over Jerusalem before me; and my mind has had great experience of wisdom and knowledge." ¹⁷And I applied my mind to know wisdom and to know madness and folly. I perceived that this also is but a striving after wind.

¹⁸For in much wisdom is much vexation,
  and he who increases knowledge increases sorrow.

The section begins with a royal declaration, common in the Ancient Near Eastern world, wherein Qoheleth describes himself as the wise king. This appropriation of sapiential authority only occurs in the first two chapters of the book. Here the author avails himself of the traditions surrounding that king's wisdom and wealth. Ancient Near Eastern societies universally held that the monarch possessed extraordinary and even superhuman wisdom bestowed upon him by the gods. With the Solominic involvement in and appropriation of such royal theology, the Israelite king was credited with exceptional human insight and divinely allotted wisdom (2 Sam 14:17, 20). The tradition emphasized, however, that this was as a reward for Solomon's devotion to Yahweh (cf. 1 Kgs 3:3-15). Assuming this identity, Qoheleth describes himself with the wisdom, wealth, power and freedom necessary if one is to test life's pursuits.

The word *seek* implies a probing for depth, while *search* connotes investigation from all angles. Qoheleth set out to discover the depths and the breadth of all of human endeavor. Having the necessary wisdom and insight, he was better equipped than anyone else to embark on this quest which is a tedious venture imposed on all (v. 13). What conclusion has he come to as a result of his scrutiny? "All is vanity and a striving after the wind." The meaning of vanity has already been discussed (cf. p. 231) and the continuous activity of the wind has been described (cf. p. 232). Qoheleth claims that all of human striving is profitless and unending pursuit of emptiness. He then turns to recognized wisdom in order to strengthen his point (v. 16). In addition to expressing shortcomings, the proverb suggests rigid determinism as well. Things are as they are and nothing can change them.

While this proverb is accurate in many respects, there is much that it does not take into consideration. Improvements can sometimes be made. Also, limitations that are irremedial often help to bring into focus the positive aspects of the situation. Limits not only highlight finitude but also set the boundaries within which advantage can be enjoyed.

Using his wisdom Qoheleth searched for meaning (v. 13). Here he speaks of directing his wisdom to knowledge of wisdom itself. He is not speaking of some speculative exercise. The word *to know* means to experience intimately not merely to ruminate in one's head. Wisdom is not understood as a body of principles or dogma but as an experiential search for truth. Using the wisdom and knowledge that he has already gained, Qoheleth launched out in an attempt to know wisdom by experiencing its opposite. The outcome of this experience was the same as of his previous scrutiny (v. 14), "a striving after wind." He closes his second statement as he had the first, with a proverb that captures the burden of his endeavor. Neither insight nor practical knowledge can assure one of happiness. The opposite seems to be true. The more one achieves wisdom the more one realizes its inadequacy. And what is the point of it all?

IN SEARCH OF PLEASURE
Qoheleth 2:1-11

2 I said to myself, "Come now, I will make a test of pleasure; enjoy yourself." But behold, this also was vanity. ²I said of laughter, "It is mad," and of pleasure, "What use is it?" ³I searched with my mind how to cheer my body with wine—my mind still guiding me with wisdom—and how to lay hold on folly, till I might see what was good for the sons of men to do under heaven during the few days of their life. ⁴I made great works; I built houses and planted vineyards for myself; ⁵I made myself gardens and parks, and planted in them all kinds of fruit trees. ⁶I made myself pools from which to water the forest of growing trees. ⁷I brought male and female slaves, and had slaves who were born in my house; I had also great possessions of herds and flocks, more than any who had been before me in Jerusalem. ⁸I also gathered for myself silver and gold and the treasure of kings and provinces; I got singers, both men and women, and many concubines, man's delight.

⁹So I became great and surpassed all who were before me in Jerusalem; also my wisdom remained with me. ¹⁰And whatever my eyes desired I did not keep from them; I kept my heart from no pleasure, for my heart found pleasure in all my toil, and this was my reward for all my toil. ¹¹Then I considered all that my hands had done and the toil I had spent in doing it, and behold, all was vanity and a striving after wind, and there was nothing to be gained under the sun.

In his search for ultimate fulfillment, Qoheleth tested the extent to which pleasure can give satisfaction but found disappointment here as well. Neither prosperity nor self-gratification brought lasting contentment (vv. 1-2). He becomes more specific in relating his accomplishments. He admits that he indulged himself and flirted with folly in order to challenge the constricting limitations of conventional values. How is one to be sure of the validity and worth of society's mores unless they are tested? Such an experiment might be judged foolish, but Qoheleth claims that he was not foolhardy but continued to be guided by wisdom (v. 3). His purpose was to discover which goals should be pursued during the short span of time that is allotted to human beings. It is folly to chase after something that will only leave one empty and frustrated.

Significant human accomplishments are listed (vv. 4-8). Here again Qoheleth credits himself with feats similar to those of Solomon (cf. 1 Kgs 10). Architectural masterpieces with vineyards as embellishments, and horticultural delights with refreshing pools, all bespeak affluence and elegance. Countless women and men strive relentlessly to achieve such opulence. Qoheleth was able to realize their dreams in his own lifetime.

Others prefer a multiplicity of possessions. Herds and flocks and even ownership of men and women are considered an enhancement of their importance and power. When prestige is a primary value people will struggle feverishly to acquire and retain chattels. It would appear that Qoheleth's social standing included great possessions as well as material wealth. He did not have to secure them. Nor was he deprived of the amusements, both entertaining and stimulating, that wealth can provide. All of these pleasures, coveted by many people, were at Qoheleth's command. He had the means to satisfy any human desire and he did not restrain himself.

He summarizes his accomplishments by claiming an unparalleled renown as well as a moderation in his pursuit of pleasure (v. 9). He had denied himself nothing and admits that he truly enjoyed what he had done. Verse 10b contains a statement of great consequence for understanding Qoheleth. So far he had asked about the gain that can be had from toil (cf. 1:3), from seeking and searching (cf. 1:13), from knowing (cf. 1:17). He has consistently arrived at the same conclusion. There is no lasting gain, no tangible dividend. Here he identifies a possible reward. It is in the actual toil, in the doing, in the enjoying and not in any anticipated gain.

Looking back over all of his accomplishments and comparing them with the energy that had been expended in order to achieve them, he does not think that the gain was worth the effort. Such striving is profitless and an unending pursuit of emptiness.

IN SEARCH OF WISDOM
Qoheleth 2:12-17

> [12]So I turned to consider wisdom and madness and folly; for what can the man do who comes after the king? Only what he has already done. [13]Then I saw that wisdom excels folly as light excels darkness. [14]The wise man has his eyes in his head, but the fool walks in darkness; and yet I perceived that one fate comes to all of them. [15]Then I said to myself, "What befalls the fool will befall me also; why then have I been so very wise?" And I said to myself that this also is vanity. [16]For of the wise man as of the fool there is no enduring remembrance, seeing that in the days to come all will have been long forgotten. How the wise man dies just like the fool! [17]So I hated life, because what is done under the sun was grievous to me; for all is vanity and a striving after wind.

Having stripped pleasure of any pretentious claims, Qoheleth turns to consider wisdom as the final goal of human effort. The second part of verse 12 is difficult to understand. Perhaps it means that possessing royal wisdom and wealth and searching for meaning, Qoheleth had plumbed the depths of human experience in a way that no one can imitate much less excel. Another interpretation identifies the man who follows the king as his successor. Regardless of the meaning preferred, the end of the verse clearly states that another can merely arrive at the insights already gained.

Verses 13 and 14 express conventional wisdom. The abstract nature of the statements indicates that the thoughts contained within them have long since been lifted from the

scene of human experience and elevated into the realm of
general principle. Wisdom is compared to light and the
vision that results from it, while folly is regarded as darkness
fraught with danger and destruction. The second proverb
repeats the idea and the comparison but the verse ends on a
negative note. Regardless of one's life style, death is the
ultimate fate of all. The intent of the proverbs was to illustrate the advantage wisdom and the wise have over folly and
the fools. In reality the advantage is only temporary and,
therefore, questionable. In fact, the fool who disregards the
conventions of life may really have an edge over the one who
conforms at the cost of enjoyment. This is the first of many
times when Qoheleth will concentrate his attention on the
specter of death. Since Israel did not entertain the prospect
of afterlife, death was the grim reality that deprived everyone of the proceeds of wise living. If wisdom is merely a
device for assuring worldly success or prosperity and if
death snatches these treasures from one's hands, then it is
pointless to pursue such wisdom. Besides, who will
remember the effort one has put forward? Who will even
care whether one is wise or foolish? The future generations
will probably not benefit from the insights and knowledge
of the past. This sounds terribly cynical unless one
remembers that, although closely dependent upon each
other, practical knowledge and traditional wisdom are not
the same. Immediate experience results in the practical
wisdom of knowing what is right in a particular situation.
As this becomes appropriate to more situations, the knowledge generalizes and the wisdom can become part of the
tradition of the society. While one generation passes its
tradition to the next, immediate experience determines
whether or not the wisdom continues to be meaningful. In
this way, each generation must learn anew the validity of its
common wisdom. The teaching of the past may be forgotten
until it is experienced in a new way. One fact, however
remains undisputed. The wise die just as the fools do. Wisdom has no advantage in this regard. Experience shows this
to be true. To deny it is foolish.

This realization unsettled the seemingly impersonal Qoheleth and he cried out against life. He hated it with a loathing that included physical illness. It is disappointing enough to discover that the prize of human striving is not worth the effort. Now it appears that even the greatest, wisdom itself, does not really outclass folly after all. The effort exerted to achieve it is not only excessive; it is wasted. Life with all its promises and enticements has insulted humankind by instilling false hopes of achievement in the hearts of women and men and then dashing these hopes against the rocks of death. Qoheleth is overcome by the grievousness of this tragic and universal disillusionment and passes judgment on the search for wisdom. It is profitless and an unending pursuit of emptiness.

TOIL THAT BENEFITS ANOTHER
Qoheleth 2:18-26

[18]I hated all my toil in which I had toiled under the sun, seeing that I must leave it to the man who will come after me; [19]and who knows whether he will be a wise man or a fool? Yet he will be master of all for which I toiled and used my wisdom under the sun. This also is vanity. [20]So I turned about and gave my heart up to despair over all the toil of my labors under the sun, [21]because sometimes a man who has toiled with wisdom and knowledge and skill must leave all to be enjoyed by a man who did not toil for it. This also is vanity and great evil. [22]What has a man from all the toil and strain with which he toils beneath the sun? [23]For all his days are full of pain, and his work is a vexation; even in the night his mind does not rest. This also is vanity.

[24]There is nothing better for a man than that he should eat and drink and find enjoyment in his toil. This also, I saw, is from the hand of God; [25]for apart from him who can eat or who can have enjoyment? [26]For to the man who pleases him God gives wisdom and knowledge and joy;

but to the sinner he gives the work of gathering and
heaping, only to give to one who pleases God. This also is
vanity and a striving after wind.

Qoheleth resumes his musings on toil and the profits that
accrue from it. He reacts here as he had toward life itself,
i.e., with violent hatred. A careful reading of verse 18 reveals
that it is not the toil itself but its fruits that must be left to
another. It is not clear whether Qoheleth's loathing is
directed toward work or its results. Verse 19 would lead one
to think that it is the latter. He is still struggling with the
consequences of death. Having been successful and prosperous during life, he must relinquish all that he has attained
and leave it to one who has done nothing to deserve it. How
can this be reconciled with a theory of just recompense?
Gone from his immediate consciousness is the early Israelite
concept of corporate personality where the blessings of one
are enjoyed by the entire community. Qoheleth is caught in
the wasteland between the demise of one point of view and
the birth of another. He finds no comfort in the thought of
heirs relishing in his accomplishments, nor is he consoled by
the promise of a future life where his wisdom will be
rewarded. His frustration is compounded by the prospect of
some fool inheriting the fruits of his wisdom and labor. This
is the ultimate incongruity and brings into question any
kind of order or justice. It all seems pointless. What did
Qoheleth do? He gave up expecting to find order and he
resigned himself to the irrationalities of life and the arbitrary consequences of death. What he awaited as his reward
will be handed over to another. This is not only pointless but
a grave evil as well (v. 21). What then can one expect from
labor and effort if there is no certainty of delighting in well
earned rewards? It is vanity, pointlessness, to strive day and
night in spite of obstacles when in the end the benefits are
snatched from one's grasp.

The theme mentioned in verse 10b is expanded in verses
24 and 25. Qoheleth would look for enjoyment in the
performance rather than in the outcome of human under-

takings. The acts of eating and drinking are perfect examples of his thought. Their enjoyment is in the act itself and not in some product. Men and women should find fulfillment in living and should not judge the worth of a thing by the quality of some possible gain. The pleasure that accompanies human activity is part of the natural order and comes from the hand of God.

Verse 26 is variously interpreted. Some commentators consider it an addition intended to uphold the retributive doctrine and thereby neutralize the apparent hedonistic tenor of the previous verses. Others believe that the one who really pleases God is the one who enters fully into human life and the enjoyment of its simple pleasures. This person attains practical wisdom, experiential knowledge, and uncomplicated enjoyment.

The way in which the author used the word *sinner* calls for a brief explanation. Coventional wisdom stated that the sinner will be deprived of enjoyment. Qoheleth reverses the thought and maintains that the one who rejects enjoyment in favor of reward is the sinner. Actually, the author seldom uses the word *sinner* in a moral context. He prefers the word *wicked* (cf. 7:15; 8:10; 9:2) when he is contrasting the righteous with the evil. The verse under consideration makes a comparison between those upon whom are bestowed wisdom and knowledge and the one who misses the mark (the literal translation of *sinner*). The one who ignores natural pleasure in the pursuit of more tangible ends will be sentenced to the task of amassing goods only to relinquish them in favor of whomever God chooses. Enjoyment is not in itself adequate but it is a practical goal that one receives from the hand of God. It cannot be guaranteed and to strive for it condemns one to the same frustrating predicament as described above. It is pointless and an unending pursuit of emptiness.

PREDETERMINED TIMES
Qoheleth 3:1-15.

> **3** For everything there is a season, and time for every matter under heaven:
> [2]a time to be born, and a time to die;
>   a time to plant, and a time to pluck up what is planted;
> [3]a time to kill, and a time to heal;
>   a time to break down, and a time to build up;
> [4]a time to weep, and a time to laugh;
>   a time to mourn, and a time to dance;
> [5]a time to cast away stones, and a time
>   to gather stones together;
>   a time to embrace, and a time to refrain
>   from embracing;
> [6]a time to seek, and a time to lose;
>   a time to keep and a time to cast away;
> [7]a time to rend, and a time to sew;
>   a time to keep silence, and a time to speak;
> [8]a time to love, and a time to hate;
>   a time of war, and a time for peace.
> [9]What gain has the worker from his toil?
>
> [10]I have seen the business that God has given to the sons of men to be busy with. [11]He has made everything beautiful in its time; also he has put eternity into man's mind, yet so that he cannot find out what God has done from the beginning to the end. [12]I know that there is nothing better for them than to be happy and enjoy themselves as long as they live; [13]also that it is God's gift to man that every one should eat and drink and take pleasure in all his toil. [14]I know that whatever God does endures for ever; nothing can be added to it, nor anything taken from it; God has made it so, in order that men should fear before him. [15]That which is, already has been; that which is to be, already has been; and God seeks what has been driven away.

The section with which this chapter begins is probably the most familiar piece of the entire book. The more popular understanding interprets it in a positive even inspiring vein. The broader context of the unit discloses its hard almost cynical edge. The poem found in verses 1-9 can be best understood when read in conjunction with the reflections that follow in verses 10-15.

The words *season* and *time* (v. 1) create the tone of what follows. Seasons are fixed, predetermined and inexorable. Observation of nature and the resulting ability to recognize and chart its rhythms were central preoccupations of the sages. The unyielding regularity which they perceived prompted them to collect significant data, arrange it in bodies of knowledge (-ologies, i.e., astrology, biology, etc.), and reason to conclusions about human behavior from these principles. One must remember that the ancients believed in the interdependence of the cosmic, physical and moral orders. If a rigid regularity or an undeniable relationship was observed in one of these orders, its governing principles were presumed to be operative in the others. Regular seasons are part of the natural order and each has its appointed *time* or occurrence. Qoheleth takes this framework and applies it to the events of human life which, he declares, each has its own appointed *time* or occurrence. The form of verses 2-8 is two-fold consisting of a poetic structure which will be examined shortly, and a less known form called onomasticon. This form, a listing of similar objects, appeared in the Yahweh Speeches of the Book of Job (cf. p. 180). The similarity within the onomasticon may be apparent to the modern reader such as is the case in a cataloging of plants and animals, or it may be allusive as when the things listed actually belong to different species but have one characteristic in common. The common element in the passage under consideration is *time* or historical occurrence. Each item in the poem is an event of human life.

Each verse contains two antithetic pairs which are usually somehow related to each other. The antithesis within each pair can be understood in two different ways. According to one way of interpreting it, juxtaposing the extremes of something can be taken as a poetic way of expressing a totality. It creates an inclusion of not only the two poles but of everything in between as well. Examples include: 'the knowledge of good and evil' meaning universal knowledge (cf. Gen 2:9; 17); 'bone and flesh' referring to the entire body (cf. Gen 2:23) as does the contemporary phrase 'flesh and blood'. Another way of interpreting the antithesis is in terms of relativity. This may be the author's way of insisting that there are no absolutes. Probably both interpretations are at play here. What better way to underscore the notion that all things are dependent upon external circumstances and not upon fixed principles than by employing the poetic device of inclusion? The artistry of the poet and the force of the message begin to unfold. There is an inevitability in the regularity of human events that is nonetheless relative. The circumstances of life determine which activity is appropriate. One must be constantly attuned to life for there is no guarantee of accuracy in one's choice of action. What is right at one time may lead to disaster at another.

A final note on structure. There is internal parallelism in each verse with the exception of verse 8. The parallelism takes this form. When the first line of the verse mentions a favorable event followed by mention of an unfavorable event, the second line of that verse repeats the pattern. Verse 2 is a good example:

> a time to be born, and a time to die;
> a time to plant, and a time to pluck up what is planted;

The same pattern is followed when the first mention is of something unpleasant. Verse 8 is an exception, probably because the author wished to end on the positive note of *peace* rather than its opposite *war*.

Verse 2 establishes the limits of life within which every other thing occurs. From the outset one is stuck by the human inability to decide. The determinations of birth and death are out of one's hands. The remaining activities do call for decision on the part of men and women and they demand discerning wisdom. Timing is of the essence! The poem ends on a note that is becoming characteristic of Qoheleth. The rhetorical question calls for a negative answer. What gain? There is none! The similarities between the intent of this poem and that of the earlier one on toil (cf. 1:2-11) are striking. In both instances Qoheleth calls attention to the regularity evident in nature in order to comment on the corresponding regularity in the human sphere, thus revealing his classical wisdom technique. Both times he underscores the negative aspects of this regularity. In the first instance he bemoans its monotony and fruitless character. In the second he is concerned with its predetermined and inflexible nature. He poses the same question in each poem. What gain is there in human striving? (cf. 1:3; 3:9). The answer to the first question is "weariness" (cf. 1:8). The answer to the second is found in the following reflections on the nature of reality.

Verse 10 reiterates the observation of 1:13b. The task of living is not easy. Qoheleth explains why in verse 11. This verse may be the most difficult one of the book because of the questions surrounding the translation and interpretation of the Hebrew word *olam*. The present version translates it as *eternity* while others prefer *world, future,* or *ignorance.* God is pictured as the creator who has produced a masterpiece in creation and has instilled in the human creature the desire to comprehend this universe. It is this inner urging that is at the heart of the wisdom movement. Humans want to know, to understand, even to control the world. However — and here is the pinch — God has also put *olam* in the human mind. If this means *ignorance,* it is clear that the desire to know and the ability to do so are in constant conflict. The result is frustration and the pessimism of which Qoheleth is often accused. If the word is better translated as comprehension of the *world* or information about its *future* course, such wisdom is a divine prerogative. Human longing for it will produce a dilemma comparable to the one already described. To understand the word in its usual sense, *eternity,* allows for a rich interpretation of the verse. Qoheleth has described the world as fixed and closed, yet there is an urgency within the human heart to burst the confines of restrictive determinism and delight in the splendors of freedom and mystery. Rather than to the inflexible seasons of appointed times or occurrences, men and women are drawn to the boundlessness of eternity. However, God may have graced humankind with limitless desire, but not with the means to satisfy it. The human race is finite and must learn to live in peace within the confines of finitude.

The tragedy of Qoheleth's instruction reappears (vv. 12-13). After describing the impracticality or impossibility of some aspect of human striving, he turns to that dimension of life which is often overlooked in times of feverish activity. It is one which is always within one's reach and may well be the key to true fulfillment and contentment (cf. 2:24-26). Happiness and enjoyment can be experienced in the very act of living, i.e., in eating, in drinking, in the work itself rather than in the amassed treasures that one may hope to produce by it. This pleasure is a gift from God and must be received as such. One cannot calculate it nor manipulate it as might be possible in a business transaction. Life is not a business transaction and to expect a strict *quid pro quo* return can only end in disappointment.

Qoheleth acknowledges the superiority of the creator and the impossibility of altering creation in any way. The reason given for God's resistance to modification or variation in the universe resembles an ancient concept, 'the jealousy of the gods'. It is present in earlier Israelite theology (". . . and now, lest he put forth his hand and take also of the tree of life, and eat, and live forever" (cf. Gen 3:22b) and could very well be reflected here. Thus Qoheleth explains God's concern to keep humans from achieving extraordinary wisdom lest they pose a threat to the divine sovereignty. The unit ends with a reiteration of the theme found in 1:19. There is nothing new under the sun, only a recurrence of what had been ordained from the beginning (v. 15).

IS THERE A MORAL ORDER?
Qoheleth 3:16-22

> [16]Moreover I saw under the sun that in the place of justice, even there was wickedness, and in the place of righteousness, even there was wickedness. [17]I said in my heart, God will judge the righteous and the wicked, for he has appointed a time for every matter, and for every work. [18]I said in my heart with regard to the sons of men that God is testing them to show them that they are but beasts. [19]For the fate of the sons of men and the fate of beasts is the same; as one dies, so dies the other. They all have the same breath, and man has no advantage over the beasts; for all is vanity. [20]All go to one place; all are from the dust, and all turn to dust again. [21]Who knows whether the spirit of man goes upward and the spirit of the beast goes down to the earth? [22]So I saw that there is nothing better than that a man should enjoy his work, for that is his lot; who can bring him to see what will be after him?

Qoheleth claims that the bankruptcy of justice is a clearly visible fact (v. 16). He is not merely questioning the adequacy of the theory of retribution, but even challenging the very fabric of the moral order. Previously his meticulous examination uncovered the ostensible futility of life. Now he doubts its equity and fundamental rightness. The verse gives no indication as to the source of this wickedness. Is it of human origin? Is it cosmic? Throughout the book Qoheleth has used the phrase "under the sun" to speak of the realm of human experience. One can safely assume that it is within the same context that the question of justice should be examined. The meaning of verse 17 is somewhat obscure. It begins with the traditional position on retribution which appears in direct contradiction with the data of verse 16. Is this a pious addition of another writer or is Qoheleth stating the axiom in order to refute it? The text is not clear and the remainder of the verse only complicates it further. The phrase, 'a time for every matter', repeats the theme of 3:1ff.

Just as every human event has its appointed time, so does the judgment of God. The *Revised Standard Version* translation dispenses with the last word of the Hebrew text of verse 17. It has been rendered elsewhere as an adverb of place, *there*, as well as an adverb of time, *then*. In either case it would refer to another bar of justice where the inequity referred to in verse 16 is rectified. Wickedness is "under the sun" (v. 16), but is judgment? Human activity takes place "under the sun", but is God limited to this arena? Remembering that Israel does not yet have a doctrine of afterlife, to what is Qoheleth referring? Is he thinking of Sheol, that shadowy realm of the dead (cf. p. 63)? Is that where judgment will take place? Such a view seems out of place in Qoheleth whose notion of retribution insists that wickedness be conquered in this world and that righteousness will ultimately reign supreme.

Qoheleth underscores the instability of any doctrine of universal justice by introducing once again the specter of death (vv. 19-21). As described earlier (cf. 2:14ff) this great leveler is no respecter of persons, but strips both the wise and the foolish of their possessions. Here humankind is reduced to the level of the beasts for whom justice is of no concern. Qoheleth seems to say that God refrains from carrying out justice in order to demonstrate the improverishment of human standards. Death is the final stroke, returning humans and beasts to their common origin, the dust from which they were formed (vv. 19-21, cf. Gen 2:7; 19; 3:19; 6:17; Pss 49:12; 20; 104:29). This reality, which is substantiated by the experience of life itself, is enough to divest one of any pretentious sense of superiority. To presume otherwise is foolish. The idea that the human spirit might go upward is not to be viewed as a hint at resurrection. It may reflect the ancient Mesopotamian astral religion which believed that the human spirit was a spark of the divine and destined to return to the deity after death. Qoheleth does not affirm this, but he does not deny it either. His answer is that of the agnostic. Who knows?

If the human spirit does rise, who can say that the beast's

does not rise as well? It is only by insightful observation that the sage comes to wisdom and, while it is possible to document the perishability of the bodies of both human and beast, there is no way of knowing the destiny of the spirits. If one cannot be sure that the human spirit has a more respectable destiny, then the struggles of life are indeed vanity. Later Christian interpreters have suggested that Qoheleth is entertaining the possibility of a different fate for the human spirit than that of the beast. Such a position is not in keeping with the general tone of the book which is skeptical of any kind of compensation (cf. 8:10-17; 9:1-6; 12:7).

For a third time Qoheleth counsels enjoyment (cf. 2:24ff; 3:12-13). To wait in anticipation of something greater than the actual doing is absurd because the future is uncertain. Only one thing is sure — death, and that certainly offers no advantage.

THE EVIL OF OPPRESSION
QOHELETH 4:1-6

4 Again I saw all the oppressions that are practiced under the sun. And behold, the tears of the oppressed, and they had no one to comfort them! On the side of their oppressors there was power, and there was no one to comfort them. ²And I thought the dead who are already dead more fortunate than the living who are still alive; ³but better than both is he who has not yet been, and has not seen the evil deeds that are done under the sun.

⁴Then I saw that all toil and all skill in work come from a man's envy of his neighbor. This also is vanity and a striving after wind.

⁵The fool folds his hands, and eats his own flesh.

⁶Better is a handful of quietness than two hands full of toil and a striving after wind.

The first few verses pick up two themes of the preceding chapter, injustice and death. After reporting the discovery of evil in the place of righteousness (cf. 3:16) Qoheleth becomes more specific and even impassioned. Oppression is inhumanity against the vulnerable who are not only helpless but often abandoned in their greatest need. When one is at the mercy of powerful and ruthless forces even death appears in a different light. Qoheleth sounds very much like Job when he lamented his life and looked to death as a more desirable option (cf. Job 3). Considering Qoheleth's abhorrence of death, this statement is rather curious. Has he softened his aversion, or was he overstating his case against death in the first place? More than likely, Qoheleth is so appalled with the thought of oppression that any relief is to be preferred. When one remembers that his primary concern is life and the total and joyful living of it, his disdain of anything that might hamper or prevent gratification and contentment is easily understood. Verse 3 clearly shows that he is not a lover of death. According to him, the fortunate person is the one who has not had to cope with injustice. Qoheleth does not wish, as had Job, that such a person never be born. The word *yet* is significant, for it bespeaks a birth in the future.

Although verse 4 does not mention oppression or injustice, it does deplore the tension between people which results in competition. In this situation, as in so many others already considered, people seem to be driven by standards outside of themselves. This is the vanity of which Qoheleth speaks. It is pointless and an unending pursuit of emptiness.

The unit concludes with two proverbs which seem to be independent of each other as well as of the rest of the section. Actually, this is an example of contrasting proverbs. Qoheleth often quotes a maxim that has captured a bit of conventional wisdom only to follow it with contradictory facts. He uses this technique to neutralize the former and to emphasize the latter. The wisdom tradition laid great stress on industry and anyone who challenged this work ethic was cast in a very unfavorable light. Qoheleth did not encourage indolence when he repeatedly criticized the value placed on work. He was contrasting meaningless effort with what was meaningful. He is the champion of quiet contentment and satisfaction, which is far better than the frenzied activity which is really a pursuit of emptiness.

THE SOLITARY LIFE
Qoheleth 4:7-16

> 7Again, I saw vanity under the sun: 8a person who has no one, either son or brother, yet there is no end to all his toil, and his eyes are never satisfied with riches, so that he never asks, "For whom am I toiling and depriving myself of pleasure?" This also is vanity and an unhappy business.
>
> 9Two are better than one, because they have a good reward for their toil. 10For if they fall, one will lift up his fellow; but woe to him who is alone when he falls and has not another to lift him up. 11Again, if two lie together, they are warm; but how can one be warm along? 12And though a man might prevail against one who is alone, two will withstand him. A threefold cord is not quickly broken.
>
> 13Better is a poor and wise youth than an old and foolish king, who will no longer take advice, 14even though he had gone from prison to the throne or in his own kingdom had been born poor. 15I saw all the living who move about under the sun, as well as that youth, who was to stand in his place; 16there was no end of all the people; he was over all of them. Yet those who come later will not rejoice in him. Surely this also is vanity and striving after wind.

This is a series of descriptions pointing to the effect human endeavors may have on others. The first paints a picture quite different from the one found in 2:18-21. There Qoheleth is upset because the fruits of labor must be left to successors. Here the absence of heirs is viewed as a deprivation. The person depicted in verses 7 and 8 has not only disregarded the satisfaction inherent in labor itself, but is consumed by a voracious appetite which sacrifices all pleas-

ure in search of its goals. And for what purpose? Death will
not be kinder to the rich and with no heir one's wealth will
go to strangers. This is pointless.

The "better. . . than" comparison was frequently used by
the wisdom teachers and introduces the proverb in verse 9 as
well as the comparison in verse 13. To all appearances,
Qoheleth censures the solitary life because community was
highly regarded in Israel. This proverb is slightly out of step
with the major direction of his thinking, however. He seems
to advocate working together because of the increase of
production that is bound to result from joining forces. If the
proverb was standing alone it would be easy to agree with
those commentators who believe that Qoheleth is quoting
an aphorism of traditional wisdom only to disagree with it.
The explanation of verse 10 casts doubt on that interpretation for the profits of mutual support are clearly stated. A
second proverb in verse 11 substantiates this. Qoheleth is
affirming the value of collaboration and solidarity.

The final sketch is a 'rags to riches' tale. One of the
principal responsibilities of the wisdom school was to prepare young men for leadership both within the society itself
and on the broader international scene. Obviously, a lower
class youth had little opportunity for such training. Israel's
tradition abounded with stories of exceptional young men
who rose from obscure beginnings to the highest positions
in the land. The list includes such prominent figures as
Moses, Joseph, and the great king David. This is not to
suggest that Qoheleth had any one of these men in mind and
was recounting the events of their ascent to power, but
merely to indicate the popularity and frequency of the
theme.

Although the length of years was almost always equated
with sagacity, the king described here (v. 13) has closed
himself to counsel and lacks the necessary qualifications for
ruling. Again Qoheleth stresses the need for collaboration.
There is also a nuance of the idea of succession here. The
youth is obviously not the natural heir of the king and yet
the throne becomes his. This is reminiscent of the proverb in

verses 7 and 8 as well as of Qoheleth's concern in 2:18-21. Although the circumstances are quite different in each of the three cases, the common theme remains. One must eventually relinquish worldly goods and achievements which then become the possession of another. The earliest mention highlights the foolishness in placing all one's emphasis on acquisition which cannot be lasting. The second instance depicts a greedy man who denies himself to no avail. In this final case the principal focus is twofold: the importance of societal cooperation and the primacy of wisdom over foolishness.

The final verses of the section contribute to the difficulty of understanding the entire unit. After picturing the youth as wise and successful, Qoheleth goes on to state that this will not last. Eventually the people will cease being happy with him. His path will follow that of the old king for his good fortune is not permanent either. Scholars have been perplexed by these examples. Is Qoheleth really praising the values that are advanced in these descriptions or is he stating them only to criticize? However one is to interpret this material, it must be read against the backdrop of Qoheleth's dominant themes. No human success has permanence and all human endeavor that loses sight of this is vanity. The values to be espoused and to be cherished are those that give meaning to life as it is being lived. Everything else is profitless and an unending pursuit of emptiness.

AUTHENTIC PIETY
Qoheleth 5:1-7

> **5** Guard your steps when you go to the house of God; to draw near to listen is better than to offer the sacrifice of fools; for they do not know that they are doing evil. ²Be not rash with your mouth, nor let your heart be hasty to utter a word before God, for God is in heaven, and you upon earth; therefore let your words be few.
>
> ³For a dream comes with much business, and a fool's voice with many words.

> ⁴When you vow a vow to God, do not delay paying it;
> for he has no pleasure in fools. Pay what you vow. ⁵It is
> better that you should not vow than that you should vow
> and not pay. ⁶Let not your mouth lead you into sin, and
> do not say before the messenger that it was a mistake;
> why should God be angry at your voice, and destroy the
> work of your hands?
> ⁷For when dreams increase, empty words grow many:
> but do you fear God.

This is one of the rare instances in the wisdom literature
where attention is given to explicit religious practice. The
commentary will show that Qoheleth is not really exhorting
one to piety as much as to faithfulness to one's responsibility. While it may not be accurate to call him devout, it is just
as incorrect to accuse him of being irreligious as some
commentators have. The wisdom movement was interested
in the secular world and not in the realm of religious observ-
ance. This is not a repudiation of religion but an example of
interest in and appreciation of another dimension of reality.

Qoheleth urges caution when approaching the temple. He
also reiterates the sentiment found in earlier tradition, "To
obey is better than sacrifice" (1 Sam 15:22). Although the
text reads *listen*, the Hebrew word has a stronger meaning
than the English translation. This is the word with which the
great Hebrew prayer *Shema* begins. "Hear, O Israel!" It is a
call to active listening, listening that is both hearing and
obeying. This explains why the text quoted from the Book
of Samuel exhorts one to obedience and not meely to listening. What is wrong with the sacrifice of the fools? What is it
about their sacrificing which makes them foolish? Is it that
they do not approach the temple reverently? Do they lack
the caution that Qoheleth advises? The prophets of Israel
were always railing against halfhearted or carelessly performed worship (cf. Hos 9:4; 10:4; Isa 1:10-15). Being a man
attuned to social conventions, Qoheleth is concerned that
things be done properly in every area of life. This interpretation may make him sound very pragmatic with no religious
feeling. This need not be true. In the first place, no religious

sentiment is expressed. Secondly, pragmatism does not cancel out devotion.

Qoheleth also warns against the tendency to multiply words when at prayer (vv. 2-3). Many people believe that 'more is better', a principle that Qoheleth regularly refutes. When this idea is carried into religious practice, devotion is often heaped upon devotion at the expense of wholehearted involvement. This propensity in people is further evidence of their consuming desire to produce and to accumulate.

Ancient Israel took seriously the practice of making promises and pronouncing vows. Qoheleth's admonition (vv. 4-6) shows that he was well versed in the tradition (cf. Deut 23:21-23). The *messenger* is probably the temple official who had come to collect what has been promised. There was a monetary or material payment to be made. To fail to meet it was to risk divine punishment. The message is the same throughout the unit. Do what you say you are going to do! Carry out your responsibilities?

Many commentators believe that verse 7a is out of place. It is a repetition of verse 3 and it does not appear to have any connection with the thought that precedes it. (Because of a different versification in the Hebrew text, these verses are 6a and 2 respectively.) It has often been amended to render it a suitable summary of the entire unit. Whichever interpretation is adopted, the second half of the verse remains the concluding statement. Qoheleth's counsel is the classical exhortation of the Yahwistic wisdom tradition. Fear God! Although it is not in keeping with the observations and reflections that constitute the bulk of the book, it is in perfect harmony with the unit under discussion and the most appropriate advice to give after criticizing halfhearted devotion.

THE VANITY OF WEALTH
Qoheleth 5:8-20

> [8] If you see in a province the poor oppressed and justice and right violently taken away, do not be amazed at the

matter; for the high official is watched by a higher, and there are yet higher ones over them. [9]But in all, a king is an advantage to a land with cultivated fields.

[10]He who loves money will not be satisfied with money; nor he who loves wealth, with gain: this also is vanity. [11]When goods increase, they increase who eat them; and what gain has their owner but to see them with his eyes? [12]Sweet is the sleep of a laborer, whether he eats little or much; but the surfeit of the rich will not let him sleep. [13]There is a grievous evil which I have seen under the sun: riches were kept by their owner to his hurt, [14]and those riches were lost in a bad venture; and he is father of a son, but he has nothing in his hand. [15]As he came from his mother's womb he shall go again, naked as he came, and shall take nothing for his toil, which he may carry away in his hand. [16]This also is a grievous evil: just as he came, so shall he go; and what gain has he that he toiled for the wind, [17]and spend all his days in darkness and grief, in much vexation and sickness and resentment?

[18]Behold, what I have seen to be good and to be fitting is to eat and drink and find enjoyment in all the toil with which one toils under the sun the few days of his life which God has given him, for this is his lot. [19]Every man also to whom God has given wealth and possessions and power to enjoy them, and to accept his lot and find enjoyment in his toil—this is the gift of God. [20]For he will not much remember the days of his life because God keeps him occupied with joy in his heart.

Qoheleth returns to one of his major themes, wealth's inability to ensure lasting happiness. He begins by giving examples of the grasping nature of greed and the insecurity that possessions really afford. The first group under his piercing eye is the public office holders. The hierarchy that exists in government provides ample opportunity for those on the lower levels of society to be victimized by those above them. Each stratum has its own overseer who is subsequently overseen by another. The evil of this corruption is doubly heinous for it is the responsibility of public officials to safeguard the rights of others. When they not only fail in this sacred duty but are themselves exploiting those entrusted to them, justice is a mockery and oppression is the order of the day. Qoheleth may sound cynical when he says, "Don't be surprised when this happens." Actually, he is realistic about the evil propensities in the human heart and knows that before one can cope with life one must admit its realities, good or bad.

Verse 9 is another perplexing line. The Hebrew allows for different translations and interpretations. Following the present version, one might read it as an expression of a 'lesser of two evils' attitude. In spite of the corruption that can make its way into a corporate structure, the organization is far better than anarchy.

Greed rears its head in the private domain as well as in the public arena. The multiplication of goods does not guarantee happiness, as the three examples testify. Those with rapacious appetites are never satisfied (v. 10). They seem possessed by the possessions and always want more. Even if they could find pleasure in the wealth their drive prevents it. In addition to this, the more wealth and possessions one has the greater is the retinue necessary for management (v. 11). This can become an enormous expense. It is true to say — It costs money to have money! Finally, wealth often leads to an opulent life style which includes gluttonous habits. This is seen in many societies where fortunes are spent to reduce what overindulgence has created. The rich mentioned in verse 12 are not suffering from insomnia because of worry and tension but because of overeating. The comparison with the common laborer makes this clear. In each of these instances wealth has become more of a burden than the blessing it was thought to be.

Here again Qoheleth speaks of inheritance (vv. 13-18). This time it is of a lost legacy. A man is described as working strenuously and diligently in order to amass a fortune. It was "to his hurt" that he failed to enjoy life as it came to him and all for the sake of riches (v. 17). Qoheleth's position on such a situation is quite clear. But this man's predicament is a "grievous evil". He loses his fortune during his own lifetime. Qoheleth regretted being forced at death to leave his goods to a successor. If this must be done, then at least let it be to a relative with common sense. The man in this example is prevented from doing even this. He had turned his back on happiness in order to attain empty wealth and then even that fell through his fingers. He suffered personal loss and his son was deprived of an inheritance. The adage in verse 15 brings to mind the scene of Job after he had been stripped of all of his possessions (cf. Job 1:21). The attitudes of the two men are quite different. The Job of the Prologue is depicted as content with whatever comes to him from the hand of God. He has the disposition that Qoheleth is urging, while the mood of the man in this sketch is painted in somber colors. When one places a tremendous emphasis on what can be attained, loss of fortune can be a devastating experience.

The chapter ends with Qoheleth's positive admonition. Be content with what life offers, eating, drinking and finding enjoyment in one's work. There is reward in simple living (cf. 2:10; 3:22). Qoheleth elaborates. He does not really scorn wealth but the vain search for it. If one has acquired riches, let them be seen as coming from the hand of God and intended for enjoyment. When one is living a full and happy life the passage of time is not feared as a thief snatching away opportunities for productivity. This is a very important point to remember lest one miss the subtlety of Qoheleth's judgment. He is not opposed to work nor does he disdain its honest achievements. He objects to raising human accomplishment to the honor of the primary or exclusive objective in life. He adovcates that men and women should find pleasure in what they are doing and if they are fortunate enough to have become prosperious, they should enjoy this gift as well.

WEALTH WITHOUT ENJOYMENT
Qoheleth 6:1-9

> **6** There is an evil which I have seen under the sun, and it lies heavy upon men: ²a man to whom God gives wealth, possessions, and honor, so that he lacks nothing of all that he desires, yet God does not give him power to enjoy them, but a stranger enjoys them; this is vanity; it is a sore affliction. ³If a man begets a hundred children, and lives many years, so that the days of his years are many, but he does not enjoy life's good things, and also has no burial, I say that an untimely birth is better off than he. ⁴For it comes into vanity and goes into darkness, and in darkness its name is covered; ⁵moreover it has not seen the sun or known anything; yet it finds rest rather than he. ⁶Even though he should live a thousand years twice told, yet enjoy no good—do not all go to the one place?
>
> ⁷All the toil of man is for his mouth, yet his appetite is not satisfied. ⁸For what advantage has the wise man over the fool? And what does the poor man have who knows how to conduct himself before the living? ⁹Better is the sight of the eyes than the wandering of desire; this also is vanity and a striving after wind.

The last chapter closed with an exhortation to delight in whatever success and prosperity one acquires. This final observation of the first part of the book looks at the opposite situation. Often circumstances do not allow this enjoyment. Reputation and wealth come from God, but so does the ability to savor them. Some have one gift but not the other. Qoheleth has observed that often a person has a great capacity for happiness and pleasure but lacks possessions that might enhance this contentment. At times like those described here, one is inundated with the goods of this world and the esteem of others but finds no pleasure in these. The first type of person can be satisfied with life itself, while the second finds satisfaction in nothing and is to be pitied rather than envied.

When one has labored long and hard to gather a fortune only to hand it over to strangers (cf. 4:8), or when, in spite of having descendants, one cannot take delight in them or in anything else, the gift of prosperity weighs heavily on the human heart. The work ethic and the corresponding *quid pro quo* mentality are repudiated by Qoheleth. Life guarantees nothing, not wealth nor success, not blessing nor enjoyment. All things come from the hand of God who is bound by no rules or regulations. Qoheleth not only denounces retribution, but he challenges any type of determinism that attempts to confine God. Both Qoheleth and Job are confronted with the freedom of God and the limits of human freedom. God can either give the power to enjoy or can withhold it, for God is supreme.

Once again Qoheleth employs an image also used by Job. While lamenting his birth, Job thought it better to be stillborn and protected from the hardships of life than to have to endure what he did (cf. Job 3:16). Qoheleth thinks that life's frustrations are often so great as to bring one to the same conclusion. A stillborn would not have to face the light of day and grapple with its disappointments. Instead it would enjoy unending rest. The longer a person lives with unfulfilled desires the more attractive early death becomes.

Verses 7-9 are proverbial summaries of much of Qoheleth's teaching. Verse 7 calls attention to the threadmill on which many people spend their lives. It goes nowhere but brings them back to the beginning only to repeat the cycle. They live to feed their appetites which are never sated and become more demanding as they are nourished. This situation resembles the endless paths of the sun and the wind (cf. 1:5-6). The impartiality of death clearly demonstrates that the wise have no advantage over the fools (cf. 2:15). Even though one of the pious poor may be wise in the way of living this does not guarantee a share in the wealth of the world. It is far better to take pleasure in what one has than to be continually yearning for more. Trying to gratify insatiable human desire is profitless and an unending pursuit of emptiness.

CHAPTER TWO
CONCLUSIONS DRAWN

INABILITY TO KNOW
QOHELETH 6:10-12

[10]Whatever has come to be has already been named, and it is known what man is, and that he is not able to dispute with one stronger than he. [11]The more words, the more vanity, and what is man the better? [12]For who knows what is good for man while he lives the few days of his vain life, which he passes like a shadow? For who can tell man what will be after him under the sun?

Several themes that have already been developed converge in these few verses. Some scholars include this section with that which precedes because it seems to summarize Qoheleth's thought. Others look upon it as an introduction to what follows. In the first part of the book, Qoheleth seems to conclude his comments with the same dominant theme, i.e., the vanity of most human striving. Because 6:9 ended on this note, the present commentary agrees with those who view this section as more of an introduction than a summary. This position does not deny the combination of earlier themes.

In the ancient world naming was a most significant function. It was considered part of the very act of creating or making. In the creation narrative of the Yahwist, the superiority of the human creature was established by the act of naming the animal world (cf. Gen 2:19-20). Qoheleth touches on this as he insists upon the determinism in the world. Things have been created and set. To think that there is a possibility of altering this arrangement is an indication of foolishness. No human being can contend with the one who has ordained the present order. Qoheleth acknowledges this whereas Job would not. Instead, Job cried out for the opportunity of bringing God to court and of disputing there with the deity. The reason for this difference between the men is quite clear. Job was in the throes of despair and made his demands as a last resort. What had he to lose with his foolhardiness? Qoheleth, on the other hand, is more an observer of the situation and is drawing conclusions from his reflections and not from his immediate experience.

If human knowledege is inadequate in the search for the meaning of the universe, then persistent discussion and argumentation is meaningless and can accomplish nothing (v. 11). Life is fleeting (cf. Job 7:7; 8:9; 9:25; etc.) and to spend time in empty pursuits is pointless. And yet, deep within every human heart is the burning desire to know what is truly good and beneficial and what life will hold in the future. These are the very secrets kept from human reach. No wonder so many people despair of ever discovering meaning in life.

THE GOOD LIFE
Qoheleth 7:1-14

> 7   A good name is better than precious ointment;
>   and the day of death, than the day of birth.
> ²It is better to go to the house of mourning
>   than to go to the house of feasting;
>   for this is the end of all men,
>   and the living will lay it to heart.

[3]Sorrow is better than laughter,
   for by sadness of countenance the heart is made glad.
[4]The heart of the wise is in the house of mourning;
   but the heart of fools is in the house of mirth.
[5]It is better for a man to hear the rebuke of the wise
   than to hear the song of fools.
[6]For as the crackling of thorns under a pot,
   so is the laughter of the fools;
   this also is vanity.
[7]Surely oppression makes the wise man foolish,
   and a bribe corrupts the mind.
[8]Better is the end of a thing than its beginning;
   and the patient in spirit is better than the proud in
spirit.
[9]Be not quick to anger,
   for anger lodges in the bosom of fools.
[10]Say not, "Why were the former days better than these?"
   For it is not from wisdom that you ask this.
[11]Wisdom is good with an inheritance,
   an advantage to those who see the sun.
[12]For the protection of wisdom is like the protection of
money;
   and the advantage of knowledge is that wisdom
   preserves the life of him who has it.
[13]Consider the work of God;
   who can make straight what he has made crooked?
[14]In the day of prosperity be joyful,
   and in the day of adversity consider God
   has made the one as well as the other, so
   that man may not find out anything that
   will be after him.

This poetic assortment of proverbs has caused interpreters considerable difficulty. Qoheleth's usual style of observation followed by comment is set aside here and elsewhere
throughout the remainder of the book in favor of a typical
listing of various and often unrelated proverbial sayings. Is
this an indication of the author's use of already existing

maxims, or has another hand inserted this traditional material? There is no easy answer to this question. Its solution
does not, however, alter the message of the final composition. The end product provides proverbial sections which
contribute to the total work and which express ideas
deemed necessary for an understanding of the meaning of
the book.

There are seven proverbs that articulate the comparative
value of some aspect of life (vv. 1; 2; 3; 5; 8; 11). Many of
them are followed by explanatory material. The tone is
quite negative, not unlike the rest of Qoheleth's evaluation
of life. The first six verses state the advantage of sorrow and
adversity over contentment while the remaining verses describe the possibility of corruption even among the wise.

Hebrew poetry, and consequently proverbial statements,
delight in the use of puns. Examples of this technique are
found in verses 1 and 6 where there is a play on the Hebrew
words *shem* and *shemen* (*name* and *ointment*), as well as on
the words *sirim* and *sir* (*thorns* and *pot*). A final stylistic
point concerns verse 6c. The appearance of one of Qoheleth's favorite phrases has led some scholars to divide the
section at this point, for the author has used this phrase
repeatedly for just such division.

The importance of a good name (v. 1) is well documented
in ancient literature. This importance was twofold. In the
first place, since the name embodied the personality of the
individual, a good name or a good reputation was closely
associated with the very essence of the person. Secondly, the
fulness of life that was referred to by the use of the word
'shalom' included well-being, longevity as well as a good
reputation. It is easy to understand why this should be
preferred over precious ointment which itself has considerable value. The second half of the verse contains the real
point which Qoheleth wishes to make. The day of death with
all of its finality is better than the day of birth replete with
promise. The saying is somber. For a man who has exhorted
his hearers to grasp hold of the present but fleeting joys of
life, this statement is rather startling. Is this a reversal of

perspective? Or is this, perhaps, evidence of the hand of another author? Qoheleth has shown himself a realist throughout the earlier chapters of the book and has not changed here. True, the day of birth is filled with hopes and promises, but one must look at them with open eyes. It is far better to judge the value of a life at its end rather than at its beginning when there is nothing substantial to evaluate. Qoheleth does not favor death over life, but reality over dreams. Dreams are like ointment that is rich and luxurious but of no substance. The day of birth may be full of dreams but the day of death will reveal the full reality of one's life.

Verses 2-4 direct the reader's attention to Qoheleth's assessment of sorrow. The key for understanding his position is found in the second half of verse 2. Death is the fate of all. This reality puts everything else in the proper perspective. One who refuses to consider the inevitability of death and chooses instead a life of feasting and frivolity is a fool. A passage like this should put to rest any thought of Qoheleth's encouraging a life of hedonistic irresponsibility. It is far better to remember one's last end when deciding upon one's course in life.

A second point to consider here is the human wisdom and insight that can come only by living through the sorrow that is the lot of every man and woman. Certain life experiences tend to mellow the naive, giving them the mind and heart of maturity.

Verses 5 and 6 should be seen as a unit. If one is seeking honesty and truth, it is far better to listen to the wise even when their words are harsh and filled with reproach than to attend to the empty flattery or superficiality of the fool who may make much noise but little sense (v. 6).

The verse ends, "this also is vanity." To what does the author refer? Is this judgment directed only toward what immediately precedes it or to all of verses 1-6? In the earlier part of the book, whenever this phrase was used it was a sweeping statement which covered the entire unit. It should be so understood here as well. If that be the case, it appears that Qoheleth is urging his listeners to choose the harder road in each situation mentioned. This is contrary to his previous advice. Is he vacillating in his position? If one remembers that Qoheleth believes that everything has its time and place and that this allows for not only diversity but contradiction, this section can be seen as a tempering of his admonination to appreciate the pleasures of life. One of the salient points of Qoheleth's teaching is his insistence on the absence of absolutes. Everything, enjoyment as well as morality, is relative. To expect to find a rule that tolerates no exception is vain. Though it may appear to be preordained, life is not static.

Qoheleth turns to a situation similar to that found in the Book of Job. The theory of retribution held that the wise would enjoy life and know contentment rather than distress. Job shows that a wise and righteous person can be afflicted. Qoheleth entertains the same possibility as Job. He even goes further, stating that oppression will turn the wise away from wisdom and toward wickedness instead (vv. 7-10). Nothing is certain or permanent, not even wisdom. It is foolish to place undue confidence in anything. Once again he points to the end which will tell the true worth of a thing. Promises and dreams are important and often serve as a motivation to great things, but only the final product is deserving of serious evaluation. To rely on wisdom is to open oneself to the temptation of arrogance, which is doubly foolish considering its uncertainty. Pride and anger reside in the heart of the fool. Only such a one would complain after having forfeited this most sought after prize. A wise person would admit that the ensuing straits were warranted. But then a wise person would not capitulate under duress.

In the early chapters of the book, Qoheleth described himself in the guise of the great Solomon. He has wisdom and the wealth necessary to make it effective (cf. 1:12; 2:4-8). Qoheleth has been very clear in his condemnation of excessive trust in money and yet here (v. 12a) he seems to change his view. His comparison of the benefits of wisdom with those of wealth is not a critique. This is clear from verse 12b where he speaks of advantage. It is a statement like this that persuades some that Qoheleth is quoting traditional teaching in order to refute it. This may be the case, but who would deny that it is far better to have both wisdom and wealth? The wise person would not squander the money but would know how to us it for noble ends. Qoheleth is merely stating an indisputable fact. It is as advantageous to possess wisdom as it is to have wealth, but it is far better to have both. However, neither is a guarantee to happiness nor can either be considered a permanent possession.

The last poetic line (v. 13) reiterates the idea of determinism. No one can alter the order ordained by God. Even if from a human perspective this order appears to be crooked or irregular, humans are unable to change the work of God (cf. 1:15). Qoheleth ends this series of proverbs (v. 14) with the advice he has offered time and again. Accept what life metes out and enjoy what you can as you can. Both prosperity and adversity come from the hand of God and their meaning lies beyond human comprehension. The implications of this line are rather significant. Qoheleth admits what Job had stated (cf. Job 1:21b). Both weal and woe come from God. Job does not question God's reasons nor the appropriateness of the situation but praises God instead. Qoheleth, on the other hand, reflects on this situation and draws a conclusion that flies in the face of a strict retributive doctrine. According to that theory one's behavior determines the future. Qoheleth is claiming that God decides the future and he does so in a way which precludes the possibility of human prediction and even more, of certainty. Does God send prosperity and advesity indiscriminately in order to confuse? This might appear to be the case from the point of view of one who attempts to chart the course of fate. But the question would not even enter the mind of one who accepts life as it comes and makes the most of it without trying to fit everything into the confines of retribution. Admittedly, v. 14 is very difficult to understand and allows for a diversity of interpretations. The one offered here, although it differs slightly from many others, can be derived from the Hebrew text and is in harmony with the overall thought of Qoheleth.

THE GOLDEN MEAN
Qoheleth 7:15-24

> [15]In my vain life I have seen everything; there is a righteous man who perishes in his righteousness, and there is a wicked man who prolongs his life in his evildoing. [16]Be not righteous overmuch, and do not make yourself overwise; why should you destroy yourself? [17]Be not wicked overmuch, neither be a fool; why should you die before your time? [18]It is good that you should take hold of this, and from that withhold not your hand; for he who fears God shall come forth from them all.
>
> [19]Wisdom gives strength to the wise man more than ten rulers that are in a city.
>
> [20]Surely there is not a righteous man on earth who does good and never sins.
>
> [21]Do not give heed to all the things that men say, lest you hear your servant cursing you; [22]your heart knows that many times you have yourself cursed others.
>
> [23]All this I have tested by wisdom; I said, "I will be wise"; but it was far from me. [24]That which is, is far off, and deep, very deep; who can find it out?

Qoheleth has depicted himself as an observer of life. He restates this and proceeds to explain what he has seen. Experience has shown him that the good are not always rewarded nor are the evil punished. This observation contradicts the theory of retribution and leads him to question the wisdom of carrying righteousness to extremes. Verses 16 and 17 have caused quite a bit of consternation for they seem to foster a compromising of principles. Can one be too righteous? Is he speaking of an inflated concept of self-righteousness? Or do his admonitions flow from a realization that happiness cannot be assured by any kind of behavior? Is he suggesting that it is far better to live a balanced life than to pursue anything to excess, even virtue? One can do harm by pursuing extemes on either side. Nothing is sure. Nothing is absolute. He urges a balanced life and the fear of God. If this is to be achieved at the price of some stringent principles, then practical wisdom counsels compromise. This may sound jarring to the devout, but it is in keeping with the pragmatism of Qoheleth.

Verses 19-22 contain three apparently unrelated bits of wisdom. A closer look reveals that the first two contradict each other. As noted earlier (cf. p. 226). Qoheleth often quotes contrasting proverbs in order to refute the first by means of the second. Traditional wisdom would embrace the first saying but experience shows the second to be true. Perhaps Qoheleth has brought these teachings together at this point in order to relate them to the preceding section. There is no point in wearing oneself out in the pursuit of perfection (v. 16) because no one has succeeded in achieving it. Even the righteous sin (v. 20). Qoheleth does not advocate sinning, but challenges the reasonableness of exertion if it is excessive.

The final bit of advice is always timely. One should not be overly concerned with what others think for their opinions may be negative and piercing and the hearer may be personally offended.

Verses 23 and 24 are often considered the introduction to what follows. This is not the view held in this commentary. Since one of the major themes of the second part of the book is the inability to understand the working of God, and since Qoheleth seems to conclude some of his observations with a statement of a major theme, these verses are considered the conclusion of what has gone before. Qoheleth is speaking here of two different kinds of wisdom. He used his insight to test his observations. This very process increased his practical wisdom, but when he looks for meaning he is searching for ultimate wisdom which belongs to God alone (cf. Job 28:12-13; 20; 23). One cannot fathom the mind of God.

NO ONE IS TRUSTWORTHY
Qoheleth 7:25-29

> [25]I turned my mind to know and to search out and to seek wisdom and the sum of things, and to know the wickedness of folly and the foolishness which is madness. [26]And I found more bitter than death the woman whose heart is snares and nets, and whose hands are fetters; he who pleases God escapes her, but the sinner is taken by her. [27]Behold, this is what I found, says the Preacher, adding one thing to another to find the sum, [28]which my mind has sought repeatedly, but I have not found. One man among a thousand I found, but a woman among all these I have not found. [29]Behold, this alone I found, that God made man upright, but they have sought out many devices.

In the pursuit of wisdom, Qoheleth plumbed the depths of every thing and every experience. His investigation of human nature convinced him that neither women nor men could be trusted. He does not have a very high opinion of women. In fact, his evaluation will probably be offensive to every woman be she feminist or not. It is clear that Qoheleth was very attracted to women. He had been taken in by what he calls "snares and nets" and had known the touch of a woman's hand. The fact that he judges his encounters to be worse than death says more about the extent of his entanglements and the subsequent disappointments he experienced than about the feminine nature.

His opinion of men is little better. One in a thousand is righteous. This is a terrible indictment of the entire human race. Is Qoheleth so pessimistic or has he come to a realistic view of fallible human nature? Had he previously expected perfection of others and been disillusioned? Whatever the case may be, he acknowledges that evil finds its origin in human beings. They have "sought out" wickedness, they were not predestined to it.

COURT PROTOCOL
Qoheleth 8:1-9

8 Who is like the wise man?
and who knows the interpretation of a thing?
A man's wisdom makes his face shine,
and the hardness of his countenance is changed.
²Keep the king's command, and because of your sacred
oath be not dismayed; ³go from his presence, do not delay
when the matter is unpleasant, for he does whatever he
pleases. ⁴For the word of the king is supreme, and who
may say to him, "What are you doing?" ⁵He who obeys a
command will meet no harm, and the mind of a wise man
will know the time and way. ⁶For every matter has its time
and way, although man's trouble lies heavy upon him.
⁷For he does not know what is to be, for who can tell him
how it will be? ⁸No man has power to retain the spirit, or
authority over the day of death; there is no discharge
from war, nor will wickedness deliver those who are given
to it. ⁹All this I observed while applying my mind to all
that is done under the sun, while man lords it over man to
his hurt.

This section is a fine example of the advice given to those
who aspired to a place of prominence in the court. It should
be noted at this point that while the wisdom movement was
universal in scope and fundamental in orientation, as it took
on more and more organization and specialization it made
its home in the upper classes of society. The maxims that
began as advice for successful living became part of the
instruction offered to those who wished to make their way in
the world, primarily in the court or in diplomatic service.
Contentment in life, the goal of folk wisdom, was replaced
by the coveted favor of those in authority. Discretion was
valued over straightforwardness and pragmatism over sim-
plicity. The admonitions in this section reflect Qoheleth's
familiarity with and adherence to a utilitarian code of
conduct.

The scene is the court and the wise person is the one who

knows how to behave in the presence of the king regardless of the royal disposition or capriciousness. Such a person is shrewd, appearing gracious and pleasant rather than bold or obdurate (v. 1). The royal word was law and was to be obeyed despite its lack of rectitude. To dispute its merits or to show any sign of faltering in its execution was an act of daring and was ill-befitting a successful diplomat (vv. 2-4). The ruler might be fickle and quick to reverse a royal decree. Those at court had to anticipate inconstancy and be adept at discerning the proper time and manner of action (vv. 5-6). The wisdom teachers were not concerned with morality in itself. Their perspective was pragmatic and they were committed to assuring success. There was no advantage to be gained in disregarding the will of the sovereign even when its morality was questionable. Swift punishment for disobedience was certain while reward for conformity could be expected. But then, not even this was guaranteed since the monarch often changed the rules at a moment's notice. If one was to survive the court experience all of these machinations had to be mastered.

This may be an extreme example but it is indicative of the ambiguity of life. No one knows what the future will bring. Even when acceptable patterns of conduct had been followed there is no assurance of success or happiness. One must be prepared to change the course of action that has been chosen. There is no guarantee in anything. Death, the final threat to security, roams unimpeded, plucking women and men at random. There is no escape and there are no substitutions. All alike are subject to its arbitrary selection. Qoheleth has come to these conclusions as a result of his observation of life. He notes that so much of life is cut of human control and no one has the power to pierce the veil of mystery that surrounds it.

THE INADEQUACY OF RETRIBUTION
Qoheleth 8:10-17

> [10]Then I saw the wicked buried; they used to go in and out of the holy place, and were praised in the city where

they had done such things. This also is vanity. ¹¹Because sentence against an evil deed is not executed speedily, the heart of the sons of men is fully set to do evil. ¹²Though a sinner does evil a hundred times and prolongs his life, yet I know that it will be well with those who fear God, because they fear before him; ¹³but it will not be well with the wicked, neither will he prolong his days like a shadow, because he does not fear before God.

¹⁴There is a vanity which takes place on earth, that there are righteous men to whom it happens according to the deeds of the wicked, and there are wicked men to whom it happens according to the deeds of the righteous. I said that this also is vanity. ¹⁵And I commend enjoyment, for man has no good thing under the sun but to eat and drink and enjoy himself, for this will go with him in his toil through the days of life which God gives him under the sun.

¹⁶When I applied my mind to know wisdom, and to see the business that is done on earth, how neither day nor night one's eyes see sleep; ¹⁷then I saw all the work of God, that man cannot find out the work that is done under the sun. However much man may toil in seeking, he will not find it out; even though a wise man claims to know, he cannot find it out.

Qoheleth is appalled at the injustice in the world. The sinner is honored in the very place where wickedness is perpetrated. Under such circumstances, how can one put any confidence in a theory of retribution? That the wicked go unpunished is serious enough, but that they are shown respect makes a travesty of justice. Qoheleth insists that the prospect of severe reprisal can act as a deterrent, but punishment must be meted out to the guilty with dispatch or it loses its effectiveness and others will not be averted from evil (v. 11).

This denunciation of the retribution theory is followed immediately by an acknowledgement of its validity. Here is another case of the juxtaposition of contrasting views. Unlike an earlier example of this technique (cf. 7:19-20), here the statement from experience appears first and the traditional viewpoint follows. The problem of interpretation that this poses is solved by verse 14 where Qoheleth states quite clearly that the theory is not universally authoritative. The strength of the saying can be seen in the manner in which it is phrased. He begins and ends with the claim, "This is vanity."

As he had done so often before, Qoheleth commends enjoyment of life (v. 15). Striving for wisdom, striving for wealth, or striving for justice all end in frustration. The only thing one can be sure of is that which the present moment offers. And so Qoheleth exhorts his hearers to enjoy what is within their reach and not to allow their desires to wander into regions that can only bring disillusionment. Qoheleth has searched out every experience and every expectation and has discovered that the meaning of the world and of life cannot be discovered. One cannot comprehend life. One must simply live it.

COMMON FATE
Qoheleth 9:1-6

> **9** But all this I laid to heart, examining it all, how the righteous and the wise and their deeds are in the hand of God; whether it is love or hate man does not know. Everything before them is vanity, ²since one fate comes to all, to the righteous and the wicked, to the good and the evil, to the clean and the unclean, to him who sacrifices and him who does not sacrifice. As is the good man, so is the sinner; and he who swears is as he who shuns an oath. ³This is an evil in all that is done under the sun, that one fate comes to all; also the hearts of men are full of evil, and madness is in their hearts while they live, and after that they go to the dead. ⁴But he who is joined with all the living has hope, for a living dog is better than a dead lion. ⁵For the living know that they will die, but the dead know nothing, and they have no more reward; but the memory of them is lost. ⁶Their love and their hate and their envy

have already perished, and they have no more for ever any share in all that is done under the sun.

The theme of the previous chapter is continued here. All people face a common fate regardless of the moral quality of their lives. Righteous living assures them of nothing for God determines human destiny and no one knows the mind of God. A strict adherence to the theory of retribution would force God's hand and allow for some insight into the future, but such is not the case. To adopt a mode of living in order to be assured of happiness, whether this be a life of righteousness or of easy crime, is a foolish venture. Death will come upon all with no distinction. Realization of this fact has brought many to the brink of despair. Life is seen as meaningless and, therefore, any kind of disciplined living is absurd. If morality is treated in the same way as is immorality, then why deny oneself (v. 3)?

Although Qoheleth may seriously question the retributive value of virtue there is no doubt about his esteem for life itself. Regardless of the circumstances within which one finds oneself, life is to be prized above all else. Two animals are compared in order to underscore this fact. The dog was a despised creature and the designation 'dog' was often used to stigmatize undesirable members of society, while the lion was universally respected as regal and awe-inspiring. In his insistence on the indisputable value of life, Qoheleth claims that it is far better to be alive under any circumstances than to be dead though respected. The living can at least enjoy what they have, while everything has ceased for the dead and they are even soon forgotten. There is a play on the Hebrew words *sakar* and *zeker, reward* and *memory* respectively. The ancients never thought that they would live forever, but they looked for some semblance of permanence in the perpetuation of their memory. Qoheleth is debunking even this hope. One also things of the state of existence in Sheol. Throughout much of Israel's literature this shadowy place is referred to again and again. Is it a place of happiness or misery? This reference in Qoheleth should suggest that those in Sheol engage in no human activity. It is more a place of darkness, silence, and suspension. The inhabitants know nothing and are somehow less than human. There is no hope after death and, therefore, meaning must be sought in what is existential. One must find whatever possible value in life here and now. If feverish effort can assure nothing then such endeavor is vain. Only living itself can offer happiness.

ENJOY LIFE
Qoheleth 9:7-10

> [7]Go, eat your bread with enjoyment, and drink your wine with a merry heart; for God has already approved what you do.
> [8]Let your garments be always white; let not oil be lacking on your head.
> [9]Enjoy life with the wife whom you love, all the days of your vain life which he has given you under the sun, because that is your portion in life and in your toil at which you toil under the sun. [10]Whatever your hand finds to do, do it with your might; for there is no work or thought or knowledge or wisdom in Sheol, to which you are going.

Qoheleth returns to his favorite conclusion. The only way to live is with enjoyment of the pleasures within one's reach. The reason that one is able to savor the sweetness of life is that God has so planned it (cf. 2:24-25). Gratification and contentment are intrinsic to human existence and should be relished whenever possible. Qoheleth does not believe that asceticism should be valued for its own sake. Quite the contrary. There will be opportunity enough for trouble and suffering. God wills that men and women appreciate the good things of life, enjoy them and each other, and enter into what they can with zest and enthusiasm. Death and Sheol are introduced but from a different perspective. Previously they instilled a sense of finality and pointlessness.

Here Qoheleth uses them to inspire a sense of urgency. Nothing can be accomplished after death and so life should be enjoyed while it is possible. This seems to have been a common theme throughout the Ancient Near East for it is found in the literary works of both Egypt and Babylon. Humans who were in search of immortality were admonished to seek fulness of life which was attainable rather than the coveted but inaccessible prize of life without end.

THE LIMITATIONS OF WISDOM
Qoheleth 9:11-18

[11]Again I saw that under the sun the race is not to the swift, nor the battle to the strong, nor bread to the wise, nor riches to the intelligent, nor favor to the men of skill; but time and chance happen to them all. [12]For man does not know his time. Like fish which are taken in an evil net, and like birds which are caught in a snare, so the sons of men are snared at an evil time, when it suddenly falls upon them.

[13]I have also seen this example of wisdom under the sun, and it seems great to me. [14]There was a little city with few men in it; and a great king came against it and besieged it, building great siegeworks against it. [15]But there was found in it a poor wise man, and he by his wisdom delivered the city. Yet no one remembered that poor man. [16]But I say that wisdom is better than might, though the poor man's wisdom is despised, and his words are not heeded.

[17]The words of the wise heard in quiet are better than the shouting of a ruler among fools. [18]Wisdom is better than weapons of war, but one sinner destroys much good.

Qoheleth points out the folly of trusting in ability or skill. Wisdom did not apply narrowly to only intellectual proficiency but included dexterity and expertise in practical arts as well, and so these are valid examples of the inability of wisdom to ensure success. He chooses cases from four different areas of life: athletics, the military, industry and economics. The content of the verse suggests that the *time* and the *chance* are disadvantageous. Often the wrong time and bad luck contribute to failure when everything seemed to indicate that success was imminent. Men and women often feel caught in the cogs of some mysterious mechanism over which they have no control. They seem snared like animals of prey and victims of fortuity.

Another deplorable instance of the failure of wisdom is found in the tale about the poor man whose wisdom saved the city. His counsel was effective but he was soon forgotten by those who benefited from it. Qoheleth had already praised the effectiveness of wisdom which is accompanied by wealth (cf. 2:4-8; 7:12). Here he shows how people will exploit wisdom without really appreciating its true worth. The chapter ends with two short proverbs extolling this worth. The world puts great stock in its rulers and in its wars. Qoheleth speaks as a genuine sage who prefers wisdom, even when it is relatively silent and unknown, to official teaching which though flamboyant is empty babbling. His story has illustrated that wisdom is more forceful than weapons of war but he closes the chapter on a sober note. A fool can undermine the good that could have been accomplished by prudential decisions.

PRACTICAL WISDOM
Qoheleth 10:1-20

> **10** Dead flies make the perfumer's
>   ointment give off an evil odor;
>   so a little folly outweights wisdom and honor.
> ²A wise man's heart inclines him toward the right,
>   but a fool's heart toward the left.
> ³Even when the fool walks on the road, he lacks sense,
>   and he says to everyone that he is a fool.
> ⁴If the anger of the ruler rises against you,
>   do not leave your place,
>   for deference will make amends for great offenses.

⁵There is an evil which I have seen under the sun, as it were an error proceeding from the ruler: ⁶folly is set in many high places, and the rich sit in a low place. ⁷I have seen slaves on horses, and princes walking on foot like slaves.

⁸He who digs a pit will fall into it;
    and a serpent will bite him who breaks through a wall.
⁹He who quarries stones is hurt by them;
    and he who splits logs is endangered by them.
¹⁰If the iron is blunt, and one does not whet the edge,
    he must put forth more strength;
    but wisdom helps one to succeed.
¹¹If the serpent bites before it is charmed,
    there is no advantage in a charmer.
¹²The words of a wise man's mouth win him favor,
    but the lips of a fool consume him.
¹³The beginning of the words of his mouth is foolishness,
    and the end of his talk is wicked madness.
¹⁴A fool multiplies words,
    though no man knows what is to be,
    and who can tell him what will be after him?
¹⁵The toil of a fool wearies him,
    so that he does not know the way to the city.
¹⁶Woe to you, O land, when your king is a child,
    and your princes feast in the morning!
¹⁷Happy are you, O land, when your
    king is the son of free men,
    and your princes feast at the proper time,
    for strength, and not for drunkenness!
¹⁸Through sloth the roof sinks in,
    and through indolence the house leaks.
¹⁹Bread is made for laughter,
    and wine gladdens life,
    and money answers everything.
²⁰Even in your thought, do not curse the king,
    nor in your bedchamber curse the rich;
    for a bird of the air will carry your voice,
    or some winged creature tell the matter.

Most commentaries include verse 1 with the preceding material. It is a poetic example of the wisdom statement of 9:18b, which illustrates how much harm one sinner can accomplish. This underscores the ease with which evil is perpetrated as compared to the time and effort necessary to effect good. Wisdom and honor can only be attained after long and arduous labor while folly can swoope down suddenly and with no warning destroy everything in its wake. Wisdom is not only elusive; it is fleeting as well.

The entire chapter is a collection of loosely associated proverbs which encourage practical virtues but warn against depending too heavily upon the reliability of wisdom. Experience demonstrates the fickleness of life and the incomprehensibility of its working. Interpreters have found this chapter perplexing. The style is not at all consistent with the earlier part of the book, nor is the point of view of the author clear. In the foregoing chapters, Qoheleth appeared to be rather skeptical of the conventional teaching. Here the maxims are faithful to the traditional wisdom. This had led many to adopt the theory of composite authorship. Most agree that verses 4-7; 14b; 16-17; and 20 belong to the original Qoheleth, while the rest originated in the wisdom school and reflect conventional teaching. The proverbs are usually in parallel construction indicating the refinement associated with extensively reworked material. Even though Qoheleth challenges the customary viewpoints, it must be remembered that he is a teacher of wisdom and this means that he is steeped in the tradition. While he may be a skeptic, he is not an iconoclast and attachment to conservative proverbial teaching is not incompatible with questioning.

The universal and perennial search for wisdom may be futile after all. Of what good is it if, after one achieves the desired goal, wisdom is either lost or ineffective? The 'way' of life is a favorite wisdom theme. Both the wise and the foolish embark on the road, one turning to the right and the other to the left. Life will expose the fools for what they are, for their conduct or their speech will betray them.

Qoheleth gives more advice concerning protocol at court

(v. 4, cf. 8:2-5). He cautions against an abrupt resignation because of the irascibility of the ruler. Absolute potentates are not always rational and often treat their subjects with little if any regard. Those schooled in wisdom will exercise great control rather than indulge themselves in an emotional outburst. They will bide their time, endure a certain amount of indignity, and retain their places at court.

Verses 5-7 direct one's attention to another aspect of the court. Qoheleth's upper-class bias is revealed in his distress over the instability of society. The wisdom tradition supported the status quo and those schooled within the movement were taught to uphold the structures of society and life that were operative. Qoheleth has witnessed social disruption and he lays the blame for this evil at the feet of witless rulers who have often elevated fools to places of prominence in the government. If this is not bad enough, he has seen situations of total social reversal. The lower classes have assumed the life style of the rich who have been reduced to the level of slaves. Qoheleth's resentment is not merely the anger of a deposed upper-class person. It proceeds from the realization of disorder within society and, therefore, of life in general. Remembering Israel's concept of an ordered universe, rigid adherence to the status quo, regardless of how distasteful it may appear to contemporary society, was viewed as a requisite for survival. Qoheleth is merely being faithful to the world view of his day.

Contrary to what some commentators have held, neither this passage nor the reference in 9:14-15 can be used to determine the date of the book. Rather than view them as details of specific historical events, they should be seen as descriptions of the type of social disorder which erupted quite frequently in various kingdoms and which could be used by a writer to illustrate a point.

Further evidence of the unpredicability of life is found in verses 8-11 which depict six accidents that befall the unsuspecting. Skill or ability cannot protect one in these situations. In fact, they may well be the cause of the mishap. The serpent has often been used to symbolize the impending threat of retribution. These proverbs illustrate the presence of chance and ill-fortune in the lives of each human being. Verse 10b seems somewhat out of place in this interpretation. Scholars are not in agreement as to its meaning. If the intent of the verse is to show the error in attempting such a task without a sharpened instrument, then the conclusion of the verse will seem to urge forethought and preparation prior to the undertaking.

The proper selection and use of words as well as the timing of speech or the appreciation of silence were all characteristics of the wise person. The fool, on the contrary, was ignorant in all of these matters. Verse 12 is a perfect example of antithetic parallelism. The first half of the verse expresses one side of a truth while the second half completes it by describing its opposite. The wise win favor by their speech while the fools are their own undoing. The next three verses elaborate on the misfortune of the fool who was not so much dull as evil. Verse 13b points to this interpretation. The fool was the one who would not listen to others and who ignored religious instruction. Qoheleth has already counseled against talking to excess (cf. 6:11). He reiterates the importance of prudence in speech by accusing the fool of failing in this respect. His description of this type of person is very harsh. Ignorance of the way to the city is the same as not knowing enough to come in out of the rain. Qoheleth has no patience with such a person. Verse 14 ends with one of the dominant themes of the second section of the book, i.e., the shrouded nature of the future.

The end of the chapter brings the reader back to the scene of the court. Two different kinds of rule are contrasted. Some kings lack mature judgment and their courtiers live dissolute lives doing harm to the realm rather than serving it. The second rule is conducted by leaders whose retinue is loyal to the king and faithful to proper decorum. These two proverbs (vv. 16-17) are expressed in a typical wisdom form, i.e., "Woe... Happy..." Once again Qoheleth expresses his social bias. He admitted that a poor but wise youth is better than an old foolish king (cf. 4:13), but his preference is for legitimate leadership. A wise king will not allow the land to be neglected in any way (v. 17). This would weaken the defenses and leave the realm vulnerable and open to any kind of attack. Instead, wise management will result in prosperity, a classical position of conventional wisdom. The final bit of advice is to do with guarding one's true assessment of authority. Even the slightest hint of criticism must be stifled lest it be known by the one concerned and reprisal be meted out. To the end Qoheleth is a master of pragmatic sagacity.

THE NEED TO ACT
Qoheleth 11:1-6

> **11** Cast your bread upon the waters,
>   for you will find it after many days.
> ²Give a portion to seven, or even to eight,
>   for you know not what evil may happen on earth.
> ³If the clouds are full of rain,
>   they empty themselves on the earth;
>   and if a tree falls to the south or to the north,
>   in the place where the tree falls, there it will lie.
> ⁴He who observes the wind will not sow;
>   and he who regards the clouds will not reap.
> ⁵As you do not know how the spirit comes to the bones in the womb of a woman with child, so you do not know the work of God who makes everything.
> ⁶In the morning sow your seed, and at evening withhold not your hand; for you do not know which will prosper, this or that, or whether both alike will be good.

The last advice that Qoheleth offers before the conclusion of the book is a positive attitude toward action. Throughout this work he has stressed the uncertainty of results and the foolishness of undue expectation. As stated earlier, the present interpretation does not view Qoheleth as a cynic or a fatalist but as a realist. His challenge has been hurled against the sturdy wall of inherent determinism. His attacks have been piercing and unrelenting, for this was seen as the only way that the inflexibility and inadequacy of the prevailing world view could be exposed. Now, lest one thinks that he advocates inertia in the face of the ambiguity of life, he urges decision-making and action even when one's foreknowledge is incomplete.

The proverb in verse 1 has been variously interpreted as an exhortation to liberality, to judicious commerce, or to agricultural practice. Qoheleth does not counsel charity in any other place in the book and so it is unlikely that he is doing so here. His pragmatic approach to life can be seen in the attention given to the returns that accrue from any venture regardless of the field of endeavor. He is probably saying that all aspects of the undertaking may not be clear. Nonetheless enter into those projects where significant results are expected. He further recommends that one not invest in only one project. Its collapse will result in total failure. The adage, "Don't put all your eggs in one basket", expresses the same sentiment.

In spite of the fact that these things are totally out of human control (v. 3), if one were to wait until success could be guaranteed nothing would be accomplished. The mystery that surrounds the beginnings of life and human inability to pierce its veil have not prevented women and men from perpetuating the human race. Caution before embarking on a venture is laudable, but procrastination and inertia are condemned.

ENJOY LIFE
Qoheleth 11:7-10

> [7]Light is sweet, and it is pleasant for
> the eyes to behold the sun.
>
> [8]For if a man lives many years, let him rejoice in them all; but let him remember that the days of darkness will be many. All that comes is vanity.
>
> [9]Rejoice, O young man, in your youth, and let your heart cheer you in the days of your youth; walk in the

ways of your heart and the sight of your eyes. But know that for all these things God will bring you into judgment.

[10]Remove vexation from your mind, and put away pain from you body; for youth and the dawn of life are vanity.

Qoheleth gives every appearance of having been swept up in the majesty of his own praise of life. He extols its sweetness and delight and proclaims that one should rejoice in each year that comes from the hand of God. Employing the 'light/life versus darkness/death' motif, he proves to be committed to the art of living. Gone is the dour voice of caution. In its place is a song of exaltation. Despite the mention of the final days of darkness, Qoheleth does not intend to lessen the enthusiasm for life that he is advocating. Finality merely serves to highlight the fleeting character of life and the urgency of savoring all of the pleasures it offers. Youth has always been celebrated as that time of life most suited for enjoyment because then one has full use of human powers. Age has not yet weakened the impulses nor lessened the energies. This is not a glorification of youth but an admonition to seize the opportunities of the moment before they are lost.

Verse 9c has been credited to a pious editor because it is the only place in the book where Qoheleth mentions judgment. Twice he speaks of "vanity" (vv. 8 and 10). In the first case it is the future that is vain. Understanding this statement within the context of the entire book, one could say that preoccupation with the future is pointless, as is looking to some future time to begin enjoying life. Verse 10 urges peace of mind and wishes good health. One should take advantage of youth for it is not lasting and slips away like a passing vapor. Qoheleth's message is clear. God has given men and women the capacity for profound enjoyment. In addition to this, life offers countless pleasures to be enjoyed. The truly wise person will lay hold of every occasion for happiness that is offered and will delight in it to the full for this has been ordained by God.

ALLEGORY ON OLD AGE
Qoheleth 12:1-8

> **12** Remember also your Creator in the days of your youth, before the evil days come, and the years draw nigh, when you will say, "I have no pleasure in them"; [2]before the sun and the light and the moon and the stars are darkened and the clouds return after the rain; [3]in the day when the keepers of the house tremble, and the strong men are bent, and the grinders cease because they are few, and those that look through the windows are dimmed, [4]and the doors on the street are shut; when the sound of the grinding is low, and one rises up at the voice of a bird, and all the daughters of a song are brought low; [5]they are afraid also of what is high, and terrors are in the way; the almond tree blossoms, the grasshopper drags itself along and desire fails; because man goes to his eternal home, and the mourners go about the streets; [6]before the silver cord is snapped, or the golden bowl is broken, or the pitcher is broken at the fountain, or the wheel broken at the cistern, [7]and the dust returns to the earth as it was, and the spirit returns to God who gave it. [8]Vanity of vanities, says the Preacher; all is vanity.

Throughout the centuries of biblical interpretation, both Jewish and Christian believers have viewed this passage as one of the most impressive poetic descriptions of aging. Although there is agreement as to the overall theme, there still remains great diversity in understanding the meaning of the individual images. Some hold that they refer to the debility of various parts of the body. Others prefer the description of an approaching storm, which symbolizes death, and the fear and powerlessness experienced by those threatened by this advancing menace. Still others see a comparison of the waning of physical powers with the gradual decay of a wealthy estate. There is no need to choose one interpretation over another since the different imagery is interwoven and, consequently, difficult to separate. Besides, the biblical authors often employed metaphor upon metaphor to make a point.

Three very different interpretations have been offered for the Hebrew word that is here translated *creator*. Because Qoheleth never refers to God in this way throughout the entire book and because the word is in plural form, some translators prefer *pit* or *grave,* a word that is very similar in form and sound to the one found in the text. Those who hold this view believe that this is closer to the meaning of the section. At the end of the previous chapter, the author urged the reader to remember death (cf. 11:8) especially during the time of youth. This same exhortation appears in chapter 12.

A second alternative translation is *source* (sometimes used as a reference to wife); a word that in Hebrew is also similar in form and sound. However, nowhere else does Qoheleth speak of a wife in this way, nor does this translation contribute to the sense of the passage. The renowned ancient Jewish sage Akiba resolved the problem with an ingenious interpretation. "Know whence you came (your source), whither you are going (your grave), and before whom you must give an accounting (your creator)." In spite of the arguments in favor of alternate translations, *creator* appears to be the best rendering.

After singing the praises of life and enjoining delight in its pleasures, Qoheleth reminds the youth of the inevitability of old age and the necessity of establishing the right relationship with God while they are in full control of their human powers. This exhortation takes on significance when one remembers that earlier Qoheleth had implied that those who ignore the happiness of the moment can rightfully be called sinners (cf. p. 241). To be in the right relationship, then, includes accepting and enjoying the life that God gives. One must act thus while enjoyment is possible.

The description of the heavenly bodies losing their light (v. 2) has been applied to the features of the face. As one advances in years the light often leaves the countenance, the eyes cloud, and a kind of darkness sets in. This decline takes place in the emotions as well as in the body. The limbs become weak and tremble (v. 3a), the teeth cannot chew as they did earlier (v. 3b), and the eyes are dimmed (v. 3c). Social life is curtailed and isolation becomes a serious problem (v. 4a). Elderly people often sleep fitfully and sometimes there is a change in the quality of the voice (v. 4b). Knowing that they are unsteady they become fearful of falling and are vulnerable in the street (v. 5a). Their hair turns snow white, they find that they lag, and often feel like they are dragging themselves around. Even their sexual desire fails them (v. 5b).

If one prefers the storm imagery, it cannot be used comfortably after verse 4a. The darkness mentioned in verse 2 occurs outside of the individual rather than within. It is the world that grows dark. As a result of this, all of the work of the household slows down and gradually stops (vv. 3-4a) and the doors are secured against the storm. The remaining imagery is obviously intended to describe the characteristics of aging. The third interpretation of this passage is limited to verses 3 and 4. The estate falls into disrepair because the servants of the household are too feeble and too few for the upkeep.

The meaning of verses 5c-7 is quite clear. The author is speaking of death, the ultimate end of each human being. The Hebrew word for *man* is *adam,* the general term that includes both woman and man and which is found within the creation narratives. The theme in verse 5c is also found in verse 7 which reflects the creation theme of Genesis 2:7. The mention of *dust* highlights the mortality of humankind. The dust of the earth is not substantial and, without the spirit of God that has invigorated the creature, cannot sustain human life. This may be a poetic understanding of the perishability of humanknd, but the very choice of words leads one to these conclusions. Within the context of Qoheleth's reflections on the transitoriness of everything in life, there are few terms more appropriate than *dust.* Another very important point is Qoheleth's reluctance to use arguments from morality. He does not insist that death is the punishment for sin. In fact, he argues in quite a different direction. Experience shows that both the wise/righteous and the foolish/sinner die. Death cannot be the direct result of sin if the good as well as the evil must face it. This allows one to say, then, that death is more a consequence of the basic perishability of humankind than of its moral failure.

Both the preciousness and the fragility of life are depicted in verse 6. The greatest treasure, life itself, is fragile and at the mercy of forces beyond its control. Because of this, Qoheleth will warn against any foolish striving for what is out of one's reach. He ends his reflections as he began them. "Vanity of vanities." It is all pointless.

EPILOGUE
Qoheleth 12:9-14

> [9]Besides being wise, the Preacher also taught the people knowledge, weighing and studying and arranging proverbs with great care. [10]The Preacher sought to find pleasing words, and uprightly he wrote words of truth.
> [11]The sayings of the wise are like goads, and like nails firmly fixed are the collected sayings which are given by one Shepherd. [12]My son, beware of anything beyond these. Of making many books there is no end, and much study is a weariness of the flesh.
> [13]The end of the matter; all has been heard. Fear God, and keep his commandments; for this is the whole duty of man. [14]For God will bring every deed into judgment, with every secret thing, whether good or evil.

It is not difficult to see that this passage came from another hand. Qoheleth had referred to himself in the first person while the pronouns in the Epilogue are third person. Scholars have concluded that a disciple of the sage is responsible for collecting his teaching and completing this work. He probably also inserted the phrase "Says the Preacher" that appears in 1:2; 7:27; and 12:8. His description of Qoheleth indicates that he held the man and his teaching in high regard, although he may not have agreed with every point of the instruction.

Qoheleth is given the highest compliment accorded a teacher. He is called wise. This would also imply that he was a respected member of the upper-class school of wisdom. But in addition to this social standing he taught the people of the other social strata. He was not content to learn the conventional teaching, but he critiqued and continued to study the tradition. He is given credit for his literary skill as well as for his trustworthiness. As has been seen earlier, all of this was implied in the term 'wise'. Verse 10 is an approbation of the teaching found within the book. Although he probed and challenged the customary viewpoint, Qoheleth was not ostracized from the company of the wise nor was his teaching repudiated.

If "the sayings of the wise are like goads", then Qoheleth qualifies for that distinction. He does not merely offer rules of conduct, but urges one to confront life and to come face to face with its mysteries.

The form of the address in verse 12 is in classical wisdom style. The relationship between teacher and pupil was compared to that of father and son, hence the designation. Several commentaries regard verses 12-14 as a second epilogue because of the rather critical view of books such as Qoheleth's and because of the traditional expression of retribution. If this unit comes from yet another hand the fact that a book containing teaching that the final editor felt obliged to temper was even allowed to survive this critique shows that it or its basic doctrine had already gained acceptance within the Jewish community. Were this not the case, it probably would never have been preserved and recognized as authoritative.

The advice given the student is rather curious. What teacher would dissuade study? It could well be that it was speculation of the kind found within Qoheleth that was to be curtailed.

Qoheleth would probably never conclude his work on the note on which the book does end. The admonition to "fear

God and keep his commandments," would most likely receive no opposition. Throughout his reflections he concluded that it was God's will that women and men live fully the life that was granted them. That indeed was their duty. It is the last verse that might be challenged. If God will execute judgment, when will this take place? Qoheleth's observation of life has led him to believe that it has not yet happened, and he has expressed no hope in an afterlife. Perhaps the pious editor who put the finishing touches on the book felt that this expression of orthodoxy was necessary to bring the teaching to an harmonious conclusion. To this Qoheleth would no doubt reply, "And this too is vanity."

IMPLICATIONS FOR TODAY

One might be tempted to ask how a book like Qoheleth could have ever been considered acceptable theology. Unlike Job, who at the end acquiesced to the wisdom and power of God, Qoheleth does not advance one bit from the position that he took at the beginning of the book. This is not an account of a journey in faith but is more like some jottings of a spectator in the reviewing stand. Job's dilemma achieved a religious resolution, while Qoheleth offers no apparent spiritual advice. Many interpreters believe that it is only because of its attribution to Solomon that the book made its way into the collection of sacred tradition, for there is, they contend, little if any religious value to this secular work.

Contrary to this negative judgment, Qoheleth rightfully deserves its place within the biblical tradition. The world of thought that it represents is consistent with a later development within the wisdom movement and the skepticism that it expresses is not unlike that found in Job. The charge of heterodoxy is a harsh one and fails to recognize the underlying faith in divine concern that Qoheleth professes. Qoheleth may have been a skeptic but he was not an atheist. He professed that God was responsible for the universe and its operations. What he rejected was any thought of its intelligibility. He did not share Job's struggle with theodicy, i.e., God's defense against the accusation of injustice. The errors to which he spoke were human not divine and so the advice he offered sought to reform human misconception. He was not wasting his time with some obscure speculation nor with peripheral concerns but focused on the fundamental goals and primary endeavors of life. Several interwoven yet individually distinct points can be discerned in his teaching.

Qoheleth would probably be unrelenting in his criticism of many of the attitudes found within contemporary society. He had witnessed the instability of prosperity and its inability to assure happiness even when it was at one's disposal. To the effort and contention that often accompany the struggle for wealth is added the frustration that attends the realization of its fleeting nature, thereby making this endeavor doubly oppressive. Society is so complex today, and the economic situation is such, that very few projects promise the success they may have in the past. Those intent upon amassing goods could very well benefit from Qoheleth's advice. This is true about individuals as well as nations. Much of the injustice in society today stems from greed and an avaricious devouring of the wealth of the world.

Closely related to this issue is a second consideration. Qoheleth would never disparage industry and ingenuity. His disdain was directed toward judging the worth of human endeavor in terms of the amount of output rather than the quality of input. There is a very thin line between training all of one's energies toward the accomplishment of a worthy goal and sacrificing everything for the sake of success. Qoheleth wholeheartedly endorsed the former and condemned the latter. He would criticize any attitude or system that placed more value on the product than on the producer. Business practices, whether local, national or international, would come under Qoheleth's scrutiny in this regard.

What has been said about wealth can be applied to any other human undertaking be it climbing the ladder of prominence and power, gaining acceptability in prestigious social circles, or acquiring the reputation for wisdom or exceptional intelligence.

When men and women do not or cannot find simple enjoyment and contentment in life activities, something is amiss either in their own priorities or in the societies of which they are members. Qoheleth was not blind to the disappointments and tragedies of life, but neither was he a prophet advocating social change. There are many things that are beyond one's power to alter. He is not speaking of these situations but of those which result from one's preferences and decisions. The situations that are inevitable must be accepted as part of life.

A third consideration that plays a significant role in Qoheleth's thought is the inscrutability of the future. It cannot be manipulated by human decision nor determined by human behavior. The future is in the hand of God, and God is not bound by the theories of women and men. This incomprehensibility can produce two decidely different tendencies: indecisions and an appreciation of *joie de vivre*. If one's primary goal is success then it is of the utmost importance that one make only those decisions that will accomplish the end. However, life is often a labyrinth of circumstances and options that could intimidate even the most daring. Men and women have frequently regretted lost opportunities that might have been seized but for a lack of courage. When security has been the ideal, what might otherwise be considered reasonable risks are avoided because of the uncertainty involved. This attitude demonstrates, in Qoheleth's view, a lack of trust in God as well as adherence to the wrong priorities.

On the other hand, life is primarily for living and every endeavor must be seen against this setting. All work, all progress, all organization have but one purpose and that is the promotion and enhancement of life. Any other objective is at best secondary or even totally inappropriate. This is the message that Qoheleth advances. It is in fact a religious theme for he acknowledges that the creator has placed the capacity for happiness within each human heart, has made living an exciting enterprise, and wills that every person be afforded the opportunity to find pleasure in it. Qoheleth would roundly condemn any materialistic motivation that might minimize or deny this basic reality. He was a champion of the greatest of God's gifts — life itself!

ADDITIONAL READING

BOOKS

Fuerst, Wesley. *The Books of Ruth, Esther, Ecclesiastes, The Song of Songs, Lamentations,* Cambridge Bible Commentary. London: Cambridge, 1975.

Gordis, Robert. *Koheleth — The Man and His World.* (3rd Ed.), New York: Schocken, 1968.

Kidner, Derek. *A Time To Mourn, and A Time To Dance.* Downers Grove, Illinois; Leicester, England: Intervarsity Press, 1976.

Scott, R.B.Y. *Proverbs and Ecclesiastes.* Anchor Bible. Garden City: Doubleday, 1965.

Articles

Crenshaw, James L. "The Eternal Gospel," *Essays in Old Testament Ethics.* Crenshaw, James L. & Willis, John T. eds.   New York: KTAV, 1974, 23-55.

Gordis, Robert. "The Wisdom of Koheleth," *Poets, Prophets and Sages.* Bloomington: Indiana University Press, 1971, 325-350.

Johnston, Robert K. "Confessions of a Workaholic," *Catholic Biblical Quarterly,* 38 (1976), 14-28.

Williams, James G. "What Does It Profit a Man?" *Studies in Ancient Israelite Wisdom,* selected by Crenshaw, James L. New York: KTAV, 1976, 375-389.

Wright, Addison G. "The Riddle of the Sphinx," *Catholic Biblical Quarterly,* 30 (1968), 313-334.

———. "The Riddle of the Sphinx Revisited," *Catholic Biblical Quarterly,* 42 (1980), 38-51.